WHAT IS CREATION SCIENCE?

By

Henry M. Morris

and

Gary E. Parker

WHAT IS CREATION SCIENCE?

Copyright © 1982
Revision Copyright © 1987

Master Books
P.O. Box 1606
El Cajon, CA 92021

Library of Congress Catalog Card Number 82-70114

ISBN 0-89051-081-4

Cataloging in Publication Data

Morris, Henry Madison, 1918-
    What is creation science?   /   By Henry M. Morris and
Gary E. Parker

    1. Science. 2. Life — Origin. 3. Creation. 4. Evolution. I. Title.
II. Parker, Gary E. 1940-   , jt. auth.
                            501   82-70114

ISBN 0-89051-081-4

Cover by Marvin Ross

Printed in the United States of America

Foreword

The creation-evolution controversy is entering a critical, perhaps even climactic stage. Not only does this vital subject have great public visibility due to extensive media coverage of the various trials, hearings, and debates on the subject, but more and more professional scientists holding evolutionary views are beginning to take the creationists' scientific challenge seriously for the first time. The eventual result may well be a major change in the way the subject of origins is taught in our schools and universities. However, there continues to be widespread misunderstanding in the scientific community concerning just what "creation science" is. Many have considered it to be simply religion in disguise and have chosen to shun it altogether, even to the point of refusing to examine any scientific creationist writings. This situation is regrettable and exhibits a degree of closemindedness quite alien to the spirit of true scientific inquiry.

My own initiation into creationist scientific writing came in 1976 with the geological sections of Whitcomb and Morris' *The Genesis Flood,* and somewhat later, A. E. Wilder-Smith's *The Creation of Life: A Cybernetic Approach to Evolution.* It soon became apparent to me that the creationist challenge to evolutionism was indeed a formidable one, and I no longer believe that the arguments in *Biochemical Predestination* (Kenyon and Steinman, McGraw-Hill, 1969) and in similar books by other authors, add up to an adequate defense of the view that life arose spontaneously on this planet from nonliving matter. Over the last number of years I have extensively reviewed the scientific case for creation and now believe that all students of the sciences (at any level) should be taught the major arguments of both the creation and evolutionary views.

For professional scientists, teachers and students, and for laymen (including those in the news media) seeking to gain an understanding of the scientific creationist view of origins, I know of no better book than *What is Creation Science?* The authors have lucidly set forth the major arguments in favor of the creation model and the major arguments for and against the evolutionary model. As an empiricist I am especially impressed with the authors' superb ability to avoid undisciplined speculation and to keep their reasoning in close conformity with the actual data of nature.

Although the book is not written at the level or in the style of a formal scientific treatise aimed only at the professional scientist, it nevertheless conveys the essence of the creationist model vividly, cogently, and with compelling intellectual force. In fact, for those of my colleagues with sufficiently open minds, who are willing to lay aside possible objections to writing style, and the occasional temptation to dispute minor points, this book is sure to be intellectually tantalizing. Especially helpful are the authors' discussions of created order versus the order that arises from the inherent properties of matter operated on by time and chance, multivariate analysis of fossils, the punctuated equilibria theory, the concept of the "geologic column," and the vexing problem of evolution and Second Law of Thermodynamics.

If after reading this book carefully and reflecting on its arguments one still prefers the evolutionary view, or still contends that the creationist view is religion and the evolutionary view is pure science, he should ask himself whether something other than the facts of nature is influencing his thinking about origins.

Dean H. Kenyon
Professor of Biology
San Francisco State University

Dean H. Kenyon, Ph.D., is Professor of Biology and Coordinator of the General Biology Program at San Francisco State University. He has taught courses on evolution and the origin of life for many years and is co-author of Biochemical Predestination, *a standard work on the origin of life. His published research, some of which was carried out at NASA-Ames Research Center, has been primarily on the chemical origins of life.*

Henry M. Morris, Ph.D.

Henry M. Morris is President of the Institute for Creation Research and author of many books on scientific creationism. In addition, he has written a number of books in his own scientific fields. He has the B.S. from Rice University and the M.S. and Ph.D. from the University of Minnesota, the latter with a major in hydraulics and hydrology, minors in geology and mathematics. He is a full member of Sigma Xi and Phi Beta Kappa, as well as a Fellow of the American Association for Advancement of Science. He has published many research papers in refereed scientific journals and spent 28 years on the faculties of five important universities before founding ICR in 1970, 18 of those years as chairman of major academic departments. He has given creation science lectures on at least 250 college and university campuses, including at least 40 formal creation/evolution debates.

Gary E. Parker, Ed.D.

Gary Parker earned his doctorate in biology, with a cognate in geology (paleontology). He is the author of several technical articles and four programmed textbooks in biology. He has earned several academic awards, including election to the national university scholastic honorary society, Phi Beta Kappa, and a Science Faculty Fellowship from the National Science Foundation. His research in amphibian endocrinology earned his election to the American Society of Zoologists.

With ten year's college teaching experience (part of it as an evolutionist), Dr. Parker came in 1976 to the Institute for Creation Research and Christian Heritage College, where he is now Professor and Chairman of the Biology Department.

There he and other scientists are engaged in speaking, writing, and research in the creation sciences.

Introduction

"Just what *is* this creation science the newspapers keep writing about?" Questions like this come frequently these days, as the creation/evolution conflict is receiving more and more attention around the nation at school board meetings and legislative assemblies, as well as in packed auditoriums for debates on university campuses. No longer is the topic of the creation of the world a subject only for occasional mention; it is on the agenda at scientific conventions and political gatherings and has been the subject of feature articles (usually negative and critical articles) in almost every journal and newspaper in the country. It is now receiving similar attention in many other nations as well.

"But is it really possible that there is scientific evidence for creation, as the creationists claim?" "Isn't creation just a religious belief, as the evolutionists claim?"

This book has been written to answer such questions as these and to show that the concept of creation is every bit as scientific as the concept of an ongoing naturalistic evolutionary process. We have tried to discuss some of the key scientific evidences that bear on the question, and to do it in a way that (we hope) will be sufficiently nontechnical for everyone to understand and to get the point.

The creation/evolution question is, after all, not merely a trivial issue that concerns only biologists on the one hand or religious people on the other. The issue permeates in one way or another every field of academic study and every aspect of national life. It deals with two opposing basic world views—two philosophies of origins and destinies, of life and meaning. Consequently, it is (or should be) of special concern to everyone.

One of these two world views—evolution—assumes that the universe is self-contained, and that the origin and development of all its complex systems (the universe, living organisms, man, etc.) can be explained solely by time, chance, and continuing natural processes, innate in the very structure of matter and energy.

The second world view—creation—maintains that the universe is *not* self-contained, but that it must have been created by processes which are not continuing as natural processes in the present.

One or the other of these two philosophies (or "models," as they are frequently called) must be true, since there are only these two possibilities. That is, all things either can—or cannot—be explained in terms of a self-contained universe by ongoing natural processes. If they can, then evolution is true. If they cannot, then they must be explained, at least in part, by completed extranatural processes in a universe which itself was created.

The Evolution Model, by its very nature, is an atheistic model (even though not all evolutionists are atheists) since it purports to explain everything without God. The Creation Model, by *its* nature, is a theistic model (even though not all creationists believe in a personal God) since it requires a creator able to create the whole cosmos. The Creation Model is at least as scientific as the Evolution Model, and evolutionism is at least as religious as creationism. Theism and atheism are mutually exclusive philosophies and are therefore in the same category. It is not more nonreligious for a view to be atheistic than to be theistic.

Many evolutionists say that, since creation requires a creator, whose work of creation cannot be observed or tested in a scientific laboratory, that very fact removes it from the domain of science. "Even though it may be true," they will say, "it is not scientific, and thus should not be taught in school science courses."

But who ever defined "science" as "naturalism"? The word *science*, comes from the Latin *scientia,* meaning "knowledge." To assume that knowledge can be acquired solely on the assumption of naturalism is to beg the question altogether. Scientists are supposed to "search for truth," wherever that search leads. It is at least possible that creation could be the true explanation of origins, and it is thus both premature and bigoted for certain scientists to exclude it from the domain of science by mere definition.

Science is based on observation of facts and is directed at finding patterns of order in the observed data. There is nothing about *true science* that excludes the study of created objects and order.

Furthermore, evolution cannot be observed or tested in a scientific laboratory any more than creation. Evolution in the "vertical" sense—that is, "macroevolution," transmutation of one type of organism into a more complex type of organism—cannot be observed even if it is true, since it presumably requires immense spans of time. No instance of such macroevolution has ever been observed, in all recorded history, by any human being. Thus if creation is excluded from science because it cannot be observed in action, so must evolution be excluded on the same basis. Both the Creation Model and the Evolution Model are, at least potentially, *true* explanations of the scientific data related to origins, and so should be continually compared and evaluated in scientific studies related to origins

"Creation Science," therefore, is a perfectly valid area of scientific study. The Creation Model is as legitimate a scientific model as the Evolution Model. In fact, we believe we can show it to be a *better* scientific model, but readers can make their own judgments on that score, after they have read the book. We do hope they will read it with open minds, evaluating the evidences without prejudice. Each reader should always remember that it is at least possible that creation is true.

We should also mention that "scientific creationism"

and "creation science" are synonymous terms. Some creationists prefer the former since neither evolution nor creation can be a "science" in the sense of laboratory demonstration. Some prefer the latter, since they feel the term "creationism" sounds too religious. Neither term is ideal, for it is not possible to use any one simple term to identify such a complex and comprehensive subject.

In any case, if the term "creationism" is used, then "evolutionism" should be used correspondingly. "Scientific creationism" can be discussed quite independently of "religious creationism," just as "scientific evolutionism" can be discussed independently of "religious evolutionism" (e.g., atheism, humanism, pantheism, liberal theology).

Creationists believe that both scientific creationism and scientific evolutionism should be taught in public schools, but not religious creationism or the humanistic and pantheistic implications of evolutionism. There is no more reason for excluding creation science on the ground that it may lead students to become religious than there is for excluding evolution science on the ground that it leads students to become atheists or communists.

Nevertheless, evolutionism has been taught almost exclusively in the public schools for decades. This obviously unfair situation has been defended by saying that evolution is science. The fact is, however, that the Creation Model fits the real facts of science at least as well as the Evolution Model, as we have tried to show in this book. At the very least, the two should be considered as equally valid scientific alternatives. The evidences and arguments on each side, pro and con, should all be presented in the schools, letting the students then make their own choice as to which model they believe best fits the available data. If evolution is *really* as scientific as evolutionists maintain, they would surely have nothing to fear from such a two-model approach. *Creationists are perfectly willing to let the issue be decided on the basis of the scientific evidence alone, so why aren't the evolutionists?*

In this book, we have tried to present in summary form some of the main scientific evidences supporting the Creation Model. We have not used theological literature or arguments—only science. Since the natural sciences are commonly divided into the life sciences and the physical sciences, the book has likewise been divided into these two categories, with three chapters on each. The chapters on the life sciences have been written by Dr. Parker, those on the physical sciences by Dr. Morris. Several others on the ICR staff have also contributed by reading the manuscript and making helpful suggestions.

Our aim has been to make the book easily understood, even by nonscientists, since everyone is vitally affected by the creation/evolution question. At the same time, we believe the book is soundly scientific on all the individual phenomena with which it deals. Extensive use has been made of the writings of evolutionists and, wherever such a source is used, full documentation is given. We would strongly encourage the reader to look up all these references, if possible, and to read the whole context in each case. We have found that one of the most effective ways to win people to creationism is to get them to read what evolutionists actually believe and the basis they give for such beliefs, as stated in their own words! Such a careful reading of sources cited will also disprove the common assertion that creationists quote evolutionists out of context.

Because of the broad scope of the subject and the limited size of this book, many significant topics related to the question of origins are treated very briefly or not at all. This is necessarily intended as only a survey of the field, although we believe the evidences and arguments cited herein should be more than sufficient to convince open-minded readers of the validity and importance of the Creation Model of origins. We hope also that many readers will be encouraged to study the more extensive and diversified treatments of different aspects of creationism in the many books and articles now available on the subject.

Finally, in Appendix A are given answers to the main questions and criticisms that have been raised concerning creation science. An index of names and subjects is also included.

We believe this book will be suitable for use in formal classes or group discussions, as well as individual study. Scientists and school officials, religious leaders and news reporters, parents and teachers, all need to learn more about creation science, as taught by creation scientists, and we trust this book will help meet that need. Polls have shown that an overwhelming majority of the American people want creation to be restored to our public school curricula. Furthermore, there are now thousands of scientists, all thoroughly familiar with the evidences and arguments on both sides, who have become convinced creationists. Consequently, this is an issue that will not be going away, and sooner or later *everyone* will need to know these evidences and arguments, in order to make his or her own decision. It will be an important decision—perhaps the most important they will ever make.

Contents

List of Illustrations

List of Tables

Part I

Evolution: Science or Faith?

By Henry M. Morris

Chapter I

The Vanishing Case for Evoluion

One of the "buzz-words" of recent years is *oxymoron* (meaning, essentially, a contradiction in terms), and evolutionists are fond of applying this patronizing term to "creation science," alleging that the concept of creation is religious, not scientific. The fact is, however, that the term could better be applied to "evolution science." The essence of real science (i.e., *knowledge*) is observation and experimentation, but no one has *ever*, in all human history, observed true evolution taking place anywhere. Furthermore, all the facts of science which we *can* observe seem to contradict the very idea of evolution. As the evolutionist, George Marsden, has admitted (1973): "Evolution...strains popular common sense. It is simply difficult to believe that the amazing order of life on Earth arose spontaneously out of the original disorder of the universe."

Therefore, before attempting a detailed case for "creation science," we want to give a summary of the evidence against "evolution science." If one wishes to *believe* in evolution, it is a free country, but he must believe it strictly as a matter of faith; there is no scientific evidence for evolution that cannot be explained at least as well, and usually better, by creation.

Evolutionists allege that evolution is a proved scientific fact, based on a multitude of scientific proofs, but they are unable to document even one of these supposed proofs! This curious situation is illustrated below in quotations from several leading evolutionary scientists.

The Altogether Missing Evidence

No Evolution at Present. The lack of a case for evolution is most clearly recognized by the fact that no one has ever seen it happen.

> "Evolution, at least in the sense that Darwin speaks of it, cannot be detected within the lifetime of a single observer (David Kitts, 1974a).

"Horizontal variations" (e.g., the different varieties of dogs) are not real evolution, of course, nor are "mutations," which are always either neutral or harmful, as far as all known mutations are concerned. A process which has never been observed to occur, in all human history, should not be called scientific.

No New Species. Charles Darwin is popularly supposed to have solved the problem of "the origin of species," in his famous 1859 book of that title. However, as the eminent Harvard biologist, Ernst Mayr, one of the nation's top evolutionists, has observed:

> "Darwin never really did discuss the origin of species in his *On the Origin of Species*" (Niles Eldredge, 1985a).

Not only could Darwin not cite a single example of a new species originating, but neither has anyone else, in all the subsequent century of evolutionary study.

> "No one has ever produced a species by mechanisms of natural selection. No one has gotten near it..." (Colin Patterson, 1982).

No Known Mechanism of Evolution. It is also a very curious fact that no one understands how evolution works. Evolutionists commonly protest that they know evolution is true, but they can't seem to determine its mechanism.

"Evolution is...troubled from within by the troubling complexities of genetic and developmental mechanisms and new questions about the central mystery—speciation itself" (Keith S. Thomson, 1982).

One would think that in the 125 years following Darwin, with thousands of trained biologists studying the problem and using millions of dollars worth of complex lab equipment, they would have worked it out by now, but the mechanism which originates new species is still "the central mystery."

No Fossil Evidence. It used to be claimed that the best evidence for evolution was the fossil record, but the fact is that the billions of known fossils have not yet yielded a single unequivocal transitional form with transitional structures in the process of evolving.

"The known fossil record fails to document a single example of phyletic evolution accomplishing a major morphologic transition..." (Steven M. Stanley, 1979a).

This ubiquitous absence of intermediate forms is true not only for "major morphologic transitions," but even for most species.

"As is now well known, most fossil species appear instantaneously in the fossil record, persist for some millions of years virtually unchanged, only to disappear abruptly..." (Tom Kemp, 1985a).

As a result, many modern evolutionists agree with the following assessment:

"In any case, no real evolutionist...uses the fossil record as evidence in favor of the theory

of evolution as opposed to special creation..."
(Mark Ridley, 1981).

No Order in the Fossils. Not only are there no true
transitional forms in the fossils; there is not even any *general*
evidence of evolutionary progression in the actual fossil
sequences.

> "The fossil record of evolution is amenable
> to a wide variety of models ranging from
> completely deterministic to completely
> stochastic" (David Raup, 1977).

> "I regard the failure to find a clear 'vector
> of progress' in life's history as the most puzzling
> fact of the fossil record.... we have sought to
> impose a pattern that we hoped to find on a
> world that does not really display it" (Stephen
> J. Gould, 1984).

The superficial appearance of an evolutionary pattern
in the fossil record has actually been imposed on it by
the fact that the rocks containing the fossils have themselves
been "dated" by their fossils.

> "And this poses something of a problem: If
> we date the rocks by their fossils, how can we
> then turn around and talk about patterns of
> evolutionary change through time in the fossil
> record?" (Niles Eldredge, 1985b).

> "A circular argument arises: Interpret the fossil
> record in the terms of a particular theory of
> evolution, inspect the interpretation, and note
> that it confirms the theory. Well, it would,
> wouldn't it?" (Tom Kemp, 1985b).

No Evidence that Evolution is Possible. The basic reason
why there is no scientific evidence of evolution in either
the present or the past is that the law of increasing entropy,

or the second law of thermodynamics, contradicts the very premise of evolution. The evolutionist assumes that the whole universe has evolved upward from a single primeval particle to human beings, but the second law (one of the best-proved laws of science) says that the whole universe is running down into complete disorder.

"How can the forces of biological development and the forces of physical degeneration be operating at cross purposes? It would take, of course, a far greater mind than mine even to attempt to penetrate this riddle. I can only pose the question...." (Sydney Harris, 1984).

Evolutionists commonly attempt to sidestep this question by asserting that the second law applies only to isolated systems. But this is wrong!

"...the quantity of entropy generated locally cannot be negative irrespective of whether the system is isolated or not" (Arnold Sommerfeld, 1956).

"Ordinarily the second law is stated for isolated systems, but the second law applies equally well to open systems" (John Ross, 1980).

Entropy can be *forced* to decrease in an open system, if enough organizing energy and information are applied to it from outside the system. This externally introduced complexity would have to be adequate to overcome the normal internal increase in entropy when raw energy is added from the outside. However, no such external source of organized and energized information is available to the supposed evolutionary process. Raw solar energy is *not* organized information!

No Evidence from Similarities. The existence of similarities between organisms—whether in external morphology or internal biochemistry—is easily explained as the Creator's design of similar systems for similar functions, but such similarities are *not* explicable by common evolutionary descent.

"It is now clear that the pride with which it was assumed that the inheritance of homologous structures from a common ancestor explained homology was misplaced" (Gavin de Beer, 1971).

"The really significant finding that comes to light from comparing the proteins' amino acid sequences is that it is impossible to arrange them in any sort of an evolutionary series" (Michael Denton, 1985a).

No Recapitulation or Vestigial Organs. The old arguments for evolution based on the recapitulation theory (the idea that embryonic development in the womb recapitulates the evolution of the species) and vestigial organs ("useless" organs believed to have been useful in an earlier stage of evolution) have long been discredited.

"...the theory of recapitulation...should be defunct today" (Stephen J. Gould, 1980).

"An analysis of the difficulties in unambiguously identifying functionless structures...leads to the conclusion that 'vestigial organs' provide no evidence for evolutionary theory" (S. R. Scadding, 1981).

The Residual Case for Evolution

In spite of these admissions, all the scientists quoted above continue to believe in evolution. Although I have not tried to give the full context of each quotation, each point noted is fully warranted in context, and will be more extensively documented later.

What, then, remains of the case for evolution? Stephen Gould falls back on what he believes are "imperfections" in nature.

> "If there were no imperfections, there would
> be no evidence to favor evolution by natural
> selection over creation" (Jeremy Cherfas, 1984).

But this is essentially the same as the old discredited argument from vestigial organs, and merely assumes that our present ignorance is real knowledge. Even if there *are* imperfections in nature (as well as harmful mutations, vestigial organs, extinctions, etc.), such trends are *opposite* to any imaginary evolutionary progress, so can hardly prove evolution.

There is one final argument, however: Gould's fellow atheist and Marxist at Harvard, geneticist Richard Lewontin, says,

> "No one has ever found an organism that is
> known not to have parents, or a parent. This
> is the strongest evidence on behalf of evolution"
> (Tom Bethell, 1985).

That is, if one denies a Creator, the existence of life proves evolution!

But apart from its necessity as a support for atheism or pantheism, there is clearly no scientific evidence for evolution.

The absence of evidence for evolution does not, by itself, prove creation, of course; nevertheless, special creation is clearly the only alternative to evolution.

> "Creation and evolution, between them,
> exhaust the possible explanations for the origin
> of living things. Organisms either appeared on
> the earth fully developed or they did not. If they
> did not, they must have developed from pre-
> existing species by some process of modification.
> If they did appear in a fully developed state,
> they must have been created by some omnipotent
> intelligence" (D. J. Futuyma, 1983).

While we admittedly cannot *prove* creation, it is

important to note that all the above facts offered as evidence against evolution (gaps between kinds, no evolutionary mechanism, increasing entropy, etc.) are actual *predictions* from the creation "model!"

Creationists prefer the reasonable faith of creationism, which is supported by all the real scientific evidence, to the credulous faith of evolutionism, which is supported by no real scientific evidence. The question remains unanswered (scientifically, at least) as to why evolutionists prefer to believe in evolution.

The Evolution Model versus the Creation Model

As noted in the Introduction, it is not possible to prove, in the experimental sense, either evolution or creation, since we can neither observe past history directly nor reproduce it in the laboratory. Nevertheless, we can compare and contrast the respective abilities of the evolution and creation models to explain—and even to predict—those scientific data which can be directly observed. Scientists who are creationists maintain that the creation model is far more effective than the evolution model in doing this.

There is certainly *no* undisputable scientific evidence for evolution and no *real* scientific evidence even for an old earth. Furthermore, thousands of fully qualified scientists today agree with these statements. Most of these, like Dr. Parker and myself, were evolutionists during their student days and then later, after seriously studying the evidence on both sides, became creationists.

In this section, I want to survey this evidence a little more fully, though still in only an introductory fashion. If those who read the book do not have time to study the more detailed discussions in Parts II and III (evidences from the biological sciences and the physical sciences, respectively), this section should at least give them a broad, general understanding of the basic scientific case against evolution and for creation.

The Nature of True Science

Science means "knowledge," not speculative philosophy or naturalism. The essence of the scientific method is measurement, observation, repeatability. The great philosopher of science, Karl Popper, stresses that "falsifiability" is the necessary criterion of genuine science. That is, a hypothesis must—at least in principle—be testable and capable of being refuted, if it is truly scientific.

Clearly, neither model of origins—creation or evolution—is scientific in this sense. Neither one can be tested, for the simple reason that we cannot repeat history. The origin of the universe, the origin of life, the origin of man, and all such events took place in the past and cannot now be studied in the laboratory. They are entirely beyond the reach of the scientific method in the proper sense.

That does not mean, however, that their *results* cannot be observed and tested. That is, we can define two "models" of origins, and then make comparative predictions as to what our observations should find if evolution is true, and conversely, what we should find if creation is true. The model that enables us to do the best job of predicting things which we then find to be true on observation is the model most likely to be true, even though we cannot prove it to be true by actual scientific repetition.

According to the evolution model, the origin and development of all things can be explained in terms of continuing natural laws and processes operating in a self-contained universe. The basis of the creation model is that at least some things must be attributed to completed supernatural processes in an open universe. These are really the only two possibilities.

In this form the creation model is quite independent of the Biblical record, and can be evaluated solely in terms of the scientific data. This is the only form proposed for public school curricula.

Complex Array of Living Systems. In the creation model we would expect to see a great array of complex functioning organisms, each with its own system of structures optimally designed to accomplish its purpose in creation. Different organisms would exhibit an array of similarities and differences—similar structures for similar functions, different structures for different functions.

This, of course, is exactly what we do see. Everything in the world of living organisms correlates, naturally and easily, with a creation origin. Every creature is a marvel of creative design, and the endless variety and beauty of things, even at the submicroscopic level, is a continual testimony to the handiwork of their Creator.

The evolution model, on the other hand, could never "predict" even the simplest living thing, since there is no known natural process that can generate organized complexity. All *real* processes tend to go in the opposite direction, from organization to disorganization, from complexity to simplicity, from life to death. To believe that chance processes could somehow produce life from nonlife requires a high degree of credulity. Leading British scientist Sir Fred Hoyle said (1981), "The notion that... the operating programme of a living cell could be arrived at by chance in a primordial organic soup here on the Earth is evidently nonsense of a high order."

Stability of the Basic Types of Organisms. An obvious implication of the creation model is that organisms will reproduce only their own types. The creationist expects to see many "horizontal changes," at the same level of complexity, within each type, but no "vertical changes," from one type to a higher type. Evolution, of course, requires belief in the transmutation even of basic types.

This prediction from the creation model is explicitly confirmed in nature. New varieties are easily developed. The peppered moth changes color, insect populations become resistant to DDT, and fruit flies experience many mutations. But the moth is still the same species of moth, and so are the fruit flies. No one has ever documented the development of a more complex *species*, let alone a new *genus or family!* Harvard's top evolutionist, Stephen Jay Gould, has admitted (1977):

> "Most species exhibit no directional change during their tenure on earth. They appear in the fossil record looking much the same as when they disappear; morphological change is usually limited and directionless."

Science involves observation—what we *see* and *know!* No one in all recorded history has ever seen an instance of real evolution, from one type into a more complex type. What we *see* is always horizontal change within the types and unbridged gaps between the types, exactly as predicted from the creation model.

No Transitional Fossils. Not only does the creation model "predict" clearcut gaps between basic types in the living world; it also predicts the same in the fossil world. Evolutionists should expect to see transitional forms in the fossil record, which supposedly records the history of life during the geological ages of the past. In fact, if evolution really was taking place during all those ages, it would seem that *all* forms ought to be transitional forms.

The fact is, however, that the same kinds of gaps exist in the fossil record as in the living world. All of the great phyla (the basic structural plans) of the animal kingdom seem to have existed unchanged since the earliest of the supposed geological ages, including even the vertebrates. There are no true transitional forms (that is, in the sense of forms containing incipient, developing or transitional structures—such as half-scales/half-feathers, or half-legs/half-wings) anywhere among all the billions of known fossil forms. Listen to evolutionary paleontologist Steven Stanley:

> "Established species are evolving so slowly that major transitions between genera and higher taxa must be occurring within small rapidly evolving

populations that leave no legible fossil record"
(1982).

David Kitts says:

"Evolution requires intermediate forms
between species and paleontology does not
provide them" (1974b).

Thus, within the fossil record there are no evolutionary
transitional forms between species, and none between
genera or higher categories, according to these top
evolutionist authorities. This is another striking
confirmation of an important prediction from the creation
model.

However, evolutionists infer that the lack of transitional
forms is because of "rapidly evolving populations that leave
no legible fossil record." They are effectively saying that
no one sees evolution take place today because evolution
proceeds too slowly, and no one sees evolution in the record
of the past because it went too fast. In reality, no one
can really *see* any evidence of evolution anywhere! What
we actually *see* is exactly what creationists predict from
the creation model. Therefore, in terms of either past or
present systems and processes, creation is more scientific
than evolution.

The Law of Decay. Evolution and creation are the only
two comprehensive worldviews, defining diametrically
opposing concepts concerning the origin and development
of all things. If evolution is true, there must be a universal
principle operating in nature that brings organization to
random systems and adds information to simple systems.
Over the ages, if evolution is true, primeval particles have
evolved into molecules and galaxies, inorganic chemicals
have developed into living cells, and protozoans have
evolved into human beings, so there must be some grand
principle of increasing organization and complexity
functioning in nature.

On the other hand, creationism implies two universal

principles, one of conservation of quantity, the other one of decaying quality. That is, horizontal changes (e.g., one form of energy into another, one state of matter into another, one variety of plant or animal into another) are predicted as a conservational device, enabling the total entity to be conserved even though environmental effects cause it to change in form. Vertical changes, however, are predicted to have a net downward impact (e.g., energy degraded into nonusable heat energy, materials wearing out, useful organs becoming atrophied, species becoming extinct). Any apparent vertically upward change requires an excessive input of ordering energy, matter, or information into the system, and can be maintained only temporarily, and at the cost of decay of the overall system outside.

Now these predictions from the creation model have been precisely and universally confirmed. The two most universal laws of science are the laws of conservation and decay, exactly as predicted. In the physical realm they are called the first and second laws of thermodynamics, but they have their analogues in *every* realm.

The evolution model not only cannot "predict" the decay law; it seems to exclude it.

> "One problem biologists have faced is the apparent contradiction by evolution of the second law of thermodynamics. Systems should decay through time, giving less, not more order" (Roger Lewin, 1982).

Now Lewin and others may talk vacuously about "open systems," hoping somehow to enable the "universal laws" of evolution and decay to coexist thereby, but such arguments are purely metaphysical and are never seen working in real life (therefore, they are not real science).

> "But an answer can readily be given to the question 'Has the second law of thermodynamics been circumvented?' Not yet" (Frank Greco, 1982).

Apparently the reason *present processes* do not show evolution in action, and the reason the fossil record of the *past processes* shows no evidence of evolution in former times, is that the fundamental laws of science governing *all possible processes* effectively preclude it at all! Furthermore, all of this is specifically predicted from the creation model and is specifically "contra-predicted" by the evolution model. Why, therefore, should creation not be recognized as a much better scientific model than evolution?

No Evidence of Great Age. Furthermore, there is no real scientific proof, or any unequivocal evidence, that the earth is older than several thousand years. Significantly, all real history (in the form of written records, whether Biblical or extrabiblical) goes back only a few thousand years. Archaeologist/anthropologist Colin Renfrew says:

> "The Egyptian king lists go back to the First Dynasty of Egypt, a little before 3000 B.C. Before that, there were no written records anywhere" (1973).

Prior to written history, of course, chronologists are forced to rely on various changing physical systems (e.g., decaying radioactive minerals, eroding continents, buildup of chemicals in oceans) for time estimates. Such calculations must always be based on the various assumptions of uniformitarianism (e.g., system isolated, rate of change constant, initial composition known), none of which assumptions are provable, testable, or even reasonable. The radiocarbon method, for example, is now known to be so unreliable that many archaeologists have abandoned it altogether.

> "The troubles of the radiocarbon dating method are undeniably deep and serious.... It should be no surprise, then, that fully half of the dates are rejected. The wonder is, surely, that the remaining half come to be *accepted*" (Robert E. Lee, 1981).

The assumption of uniformitarianism is also truly unscientific.

"The idea that the rates or intensities of geological processes have been constant is so obviously contrary to the evidence that one can only wonder at its persistence.... Modern uniformitarianism...asserts nothing about the age of Earth or about anything else" (James H. Shea, 1982).

As far as methods for guessing the age of the earth are concerned, the evaluation of evolutionist William Stansfield is noteworthy:

"It is obvious that radiometric techniques may not be the absolute dating methods that they are claimed to be. Age estimates on a given geological stratum by different radiometric methods are often quite different (sometimes by hundreds of millions of years). There is no absolutely reliable long-term radiological 'clock'" (1977a).

Recent Origin of Civilization. All communities, metallurgy, ceramics, construction, written language, and so on—appeared at essentially the same time, only several thousand years ago, probably in the Middle East. There is an abundance of archaeological evidence to this effect. It is anomalous that evolutionists believe man's physical body evolved more than a million years ago, and yet also believe that man began to evolve culturally only a few thousand years ago.

Furthermore, human populations also conform to a recent origin. If the world's initial population was only one man and one woman, and the population then began to increase geometrically (which was Charles Darwin's approach to population studies) at a rate of only 2 percent per year (which is the present worldwide rate), it would take only about 1,100 years to attain the present world population. If man has been on the earth a million years or more, untold trillions of men and women must have lived and died on the earth. Where are their bones?

Physical Evidences of Recent Creation. There are also scores of physical evidences that the earth is young. Some of these include the decay of the earth's magnetic field, the buildup of atmospheric radiocarbon, the efflux of helium into the atmosphere, the influx of uranium, nickel, and other chemical elements and ions into the ocean, the breakup of comets, the influx of cosmic dust, and many others, all indicating (even with the standard uniformitarian assumptions) that the earth could be only a few thousand years old. All these evidences are well-documented in creationist literature.

Another implication of recent creation is that the great Geological Column, the assemblage of fossil-bearing sedimentary rocks around the world, was not formed over many long ages of earth history, but at essentially one epoch, during a worldwide hydraulic cataclysm and its geophysical aftereffects. This is a very big and complex subject, but there is, indeed, good evidence that the column is a unit, formed continuously and contemporaneously. Rocks of all types, minerals and metals of all types, coal and oil, structures of all types, are found indiscriminately in rocks of all "ages." Even fossil assemblages from the various "ages" are frequently found out of order—in fact, in any order—in the column, and many examples are known of fossils from different "ages" found in the same formation. Furthermore, there are no worldwide "unconformities" in the column (that is, time breaks, or periods of erosion rather than deposition), so that the entire column from bottom to top reflects unbroken continuity of the depositional process.

Now when this fact is combined with the fact that every unit of the column was formed rapidly (see R. H. Dott, 1982; Derek Ager, 1981, etc.), we naturally conclude that the earth's sedimentary rocks were all formed recently, essentially at the time of a great flood described in the records of most ancient nations of the world.

Thus the facts of science not only support the general creation model but recent creation. All of these evidences are discussed much more fully in later chapters of this book.

Evolution as Religion

It is an amazing thing that the modern establishments in science, education and the news media continually portray creationism as religious and evolutionism as scientific. While the purpose of this book is to discuss only the scientific aspects of the two models, it is important also that readers at least be aware that evolutionism is much more "religious" in essence than creationism. Not only does the creation model explain the scientific data better than the evolution model, but evolution serves as the basic philosophy for many more religions of the world, past and present, than does special creation.

Evolutionary religions. The following is a partial listing of those religions that are structured around an evolutionary philosophy.

Buddhism	Animism	Liberal Judaism
Hinduism	Spiritism	Liberal Islam
Confucianism	Occultism	Liberal Christianity
Taoism	Satanism	Unitarianism
Shintoism	Theosophy	Religious Science
Sikhism	Bahaism	Unity
Jainism	Mysticism	Humanism

Many of the above, of course, could be broken down into various religious sub-groups, all believing in evolution.

I am not claiming that all of these are based on modern Darwinism, for most of them antedate Charles Darwin. Nevertheless, they are all anti-creationist evolutionary religions, and have generally adapted easily to modern "evolution science."

The basic criterion of evolutionism is the rejection of

a personal transcendent Creator who supernaturally called the space-time universe into existence out of nothing but His own omnipotence. All of the above religions regard the universe itself as eternal, constituting the only ultimate reality. Processes innate to the eternal space-time cosmos have developed the universe and its inhabitants into their present forms. These natural processes may, in many cases, be personified as various gods and goddesses, but they are really just the natural processes innate to the universe itself. In some cases, the cosmos itself may be regarded as living and intelligent, giving rise not only to animals and people but also to "spirits" who inhabit it. All of these concepts are evolutionary concepts, since none of the components or inhabitants of the universe are accepted as the products of fiat creation by an eternal Creator. The very existence of such a Creator is either denied or incorporated into the cosmos itself.

The religions listed above are all extant religions, but the same discussion could apply to all the ancient pagan religions as well, all of which were essentially various forms of pantheism, and none of which were based on creation. Many of them (Epicurianism, Atomism, Stoicism, Gnosticism, pre-Confucian Chinese religions and many others) had cosmogonies quite similar to modern "scientific" evolutionary cosmogonies. Most of them incorporated astrology, spiritism and idolatry into their systems as well.

Thus, evolution is surely a religion, in every sense of the word. It is a world view, a philosophy of life and meaning, an attempt to explain the origin and development of everything, from elements to galaxies to people, without the necessity of an omnipotent, personal, transendent Creator. It is the basic philosophy of almost all religions (except the few monotheistic religions), both ancient and modern. It is absurd for evolutionists to insist, as they often do, that evolution is science and creation is religious.

What they really mean is that evolution is *naturalistic*, and they arbitrarily define science as "naturalism," instead of retaining its traditional meaning as "knowledge" or "truth." However, to insist arbitrarily that the origin and development of everything must be explained naturalistically begs the whole question and amounts to nothing but atheism. Not all evolutionists are atheists, of course, but evolutionism itself is atheism, essentially by definition, since it purports to explain *everything* in the universe without God.

Atheism, of course, is also religious in essence. It must be accepted solely on faith, for it would be completely impossible to prove. Isaac Asimov admits as much:

> "Emotionally, I am an atheist. I don't have the evidence to prove that God doesn't exist, but I so strongly suspect he doesn't that I don't want to waste my time" (Asimov, 1982).

Now Asimov has an enormous knowledge of the scientific data in every field, and is probably the most prolific science writer of all time. If *he* doesn't have the evidence to prove atheism, then no one does! He *believes* it; it is his religion, and the same is true of most of the *leaders* of evolutionary thought today. The American Humanist Association, of which he is current president, defines humanism as "a non-theistic religion," and the first two Tenets of the famous Humanist Manifesto state that humanism is based on the naturalistic origin of the universe, and of man, respectively.

Not only are the religions of atheism and humanism firmly grounded in evolutionary philosophy, but so also are a host of social, economic and psychological systems which have had profound effect on human moral behavior and thus also are fundamentally religious. This includes such politico-economic systems as Marxism, Fascism and Nazism, and such psychological systems as Freudianism, behaviorism and existentialism. It would include racism, imperialism and laissez-faire capitalism on the one hand, and socialism, communism and anarchism on the other. The list could go on and on, every item illustrating and reinforcing the fact that evolution is basically a religious concept, not a scientific theory. It is "evolution science," not "creation science," that is the oxymoron!

Creationist Religions. There are essentially only three modern creationist religions, in contrast to the dozens of evolutionary religions and religious philosophies. These are the *monotheistic* faiths—orthodox Judaism, orthodox Islam, and orthodox Christianity. These are all founded upon belief in one self-existent eternal Creator, who called the universe itself into existence in the beginning, as well as all its basic laws and systems.

Belief in this primeval special, completed, supernatural creation is consistent with all genuine facts of science, which is sufficient warrant for identifying this belief as "scientific creationism" or "creation science." This is further strengthened by the historical fact that most of the great scientists of the past who founded and developed the key disciplines of science were creationists. Note the following sampling:

Physics (Newton, Faraday, Maxwell, Kelvin)
Chemistry (Boyle, Dalton, Pascal, Ramsay)
Biology (Ray, Linnaeus, Mendel, Pasteur)
Geology (Steno, Woodward, Brewster, Agassiz)
Astronomy (Kepler, Galileo, Herschel, Maunder)

These men, as well as scores of others who could be mentioned, were all creationists, not evolutionists, and their names are practically synonymous with the rise of modern science. To them, the scientific enterprise was a high calling, one dedicated to "thinking God's thoughts after Him," as it were, certainly not something dedicated to destroying creationism.

It is also noteworthy that the various evolutionary religions of the world, discussed in the preceding section, are probably decadent forms of a primeval worldwide monotheism. Ethnologists, archaeologists and cultural anthropologists have frequently noted evidence, in the traditions and artifacts of peoples all over the world, of dim recollections of a "high God," recognized originally as the Creator of all things in the earliest forms of their faith, but long since having deteriorated into an evolutionary pantheism, polytheism and animism. In the modern world, these have still further deteriorated into atheistic materialism, often now mis-labeled "evolution science." See Samuel Zwemer (1945) and Don Richardson (1981) for further discussion of the worldwide primeval belief in creation and an omnipotent Creator.

Still more recently, however, the barren materialism of modern evolutionism is provoking a return to evolutionary pantheism, now being arrayed in the more sophisticated terminology of modern technological scientism.

The New-Age Movement. A strange religion has been coming into prominence in recent years. Sometimes mis-called the "New Age Movement," this phenomenon is in reality a complex of modern science and ancient paganism, featuring systems theory, computer science, and mathematical physics along with astrology, occultism, religious mysticism and nature worship. Ostensibly offered as a reaction against the sterile materialism of Western thought, this influential system appeals both to man's religious nature and his intellectual pride. Its goal is to become the world's one religion.

Although New-Agers have a form of religion, their "god" is still Evolution, not the true God of creation. Many of them regard the controversial priest, Teilhard de Chardin, as their spiritual father. His famous statement of faith was as follows:

"(Evolution) is a general postulate to which all theories, all hypotheses, all systems must henceforward bow and which they must satisfy in order to be thinkable and true. Evolution is a light which illuminates all facts, a trajectory which all lines of thought must follow" (1977).

The ethnic religions of the East (Hinduism, Taoism, Buddhism, Confucianism, etc.), which in large measure continue the polytheistic pantheism of the ancient pagan religions, have long espoused evolutionary views of the universe and its living things, and so merge naturally and easily into the evolutionary framework of the New Age philosophy. It is surprising, however, to find that Julian Huxley and Theodosius Dobzhansky, the two most prominent of the western scientific neo-Darwinians, were really early proponents of this modern evolutionary religion. In a eulogy following Dobzhansky's death, geneticist Francisco Ayala said:

> "Dobzhansky was a religious man, although he apparently rejected fundamental beliefs of traditional religion, such as the existence of a personal God.... Dobzhansky held that in man, biological evolution has transcended itself into the realm of self-awareness and culture. He believed that mankind would eventually evolve into higher levels of harmony and creativity. He was a metaphysical optimist" (1977).

Dobzhansky himself penned the following typical New Age sentiment:

> "In giving rise to man, the evolutionary process has, apparently for the first and only time in the history of the Cosmos, become conscious of itself" (1967).

More recently, the socialist Jeremy Rifkin, expressed this concept in picturesque language, as follows:

> "Evolution is no longer viewed as a mindless affair, quite the opposite. It is mind enlarging its domain up the chain of species" (1983a).

> "In this way one eventually ends up with the idea of the universe as a mind that oversees, orchestrates, and gives order and structure to all things" (1983b).

Lest anyone misunderstand, this universal mind is not intended to represent the God of the Bible at all. Harvard University's Nobel prize-winning biologist, George Wald, who used to state that he didn't even like to use the word "God" in a sentence, has come to realize that the complex organization of the universe cannot be due to chance, and so has become an advocate of this modernized form of pantheism. He says:

> "There are two major problems rooted in science, but unassimilable as science, consciousness and cosmology.... The universe wants to be known. Did the universe come about to play its role to empty benches?" (1983).

Modern physicists have played a key role in the recent popularization of evolutionary pantheism, with what they have called the "anthropic principle."

> "At the least the anthropic principle suggests connections between the existence of man and aspects of physics that one might have thought would have little bearing on biology. In its strongest form the principle might reveal that the universe we live in is the only conceivable universe in which intelligent life could exist" (George Gale, 1981).

This remarkable compatibility of the universe to its human occupants is not accepted as a testimony to divine design, however, but as a deterministic outcome of the cosmic mind. The anthropic principle is emphasized in a quasi-official "New Age" publication, as follows:

> "Given the facts, our existence seems quite improbable—more miraculous, perhaps, than the seven-day wonder of Genesis. As physicist Freeman Dyson of the Institute for Advanced Study in Princeton, New Jersey, once remarked, 'The universe in some sense must have known we were coming'" (Judith Hooper, 1985).

Prior to these modern developments, Sir Julian Huxley,

arguably the leading architect of the neo-Darwinian system, had written an influential book called *Religion without Revelation*, and had become, with John Dewey, a chief founder of the American Humanist Association. As first Director-General of UNESCO, he formulated the principles of what he hoped would soon become the official religion of the world.

> "Thus the general philosophy of UNESCO should, it seems, be a scientific world humanism, global in extent and evolutionary in background" (1979).

> "The unifying of traditions into a single common pool of experience, awareness and purpose is the necessary prerequisite for further major progress in human evolution. Accordingly, although political unification in some sort of world government will be required for the definitive attainment of this state, unification in the things of the mind is not only necessary also, but it can pave the way for other types of unification" (*ibid.*).

The neo-Darwinian religionists (Huxley, Dobzhansky, Dewey, etc.) thought that evolutionary gradualism would become the basis for the coming world humanistic religion. Evolutionists of the new generation, on the other hand, have increasingly turned to punctuationism—or revolutionary evolutionism—as the favored rationale, largely because of the scientific fallacies in gradualism increasingly exposed by creationists. This development has facilitated the amalgamation of Western scientism with Eastern mysticism.

> "The new systems biology shows that fluctuations are crucial in the dynamics of self-organization. They are the basis of order in the living world: ordered structures arise from rhythmic patterns.... The idea of fluctuations as the basis of order...is one of the major themes

in all Taoist texts. The mutual interdependence of all aspects of reality and the nonlinear nature of its interconnections are emphasized throughout Eastern mysticism" (Fritjof Capra, 1982).

The author quoted, Dr. Fritjof Capra, at the University of California (Berkeley), is one of the New Age Movement's main scientific theoreticians, particularly in the application of modern computerized networking and systems analysis to the study of past and future evolution, also appropriating the unscientific idea of "order through chaos," an ancient pagan notion reintroduced to modern thought by Ilya Prigogine.

The incorporation of Eastern religious evolutionism into Western evolutionary thought was greatly facilitated also by the "Aquarian Age" emphasis of the student revolution of the sixties. Not all of the scientific "New-Agers" accept the astrological and occult aspects of this movement, but even these features are becoming more prominent and intellectually acceptable with the growth of its pantheistic dimensions. John Allegro makes the following ominous prediction:

> "It may be that, despite our rightly prized rationality, religion still offers man his best chance of survival,... If so, it must be a faith that offers something more than a formal assent to highly speculative dogma about the nature of a god and his divine purpose in creation; it must promise its adherents a living relationship that answers man's individual needs within a formal structure of communal worship.... Historically, the cult of the Earth Mother, the ancient religion of the witches, has probably come nearest to fulfilling this role, and being sexually oriented has been especially concerned with this most disturbing and potentially disruptive element in man's biological constitution" (1986).

"Gaia," the religion of the Earth Mother—Mother Nature—is essentially ancient pantheis-. It is now returning, even in "Christian lands," in all its demonic power. When combined with the pervasive controls made possible by modern computerized systems technology, the global goals of evolutionary humanism seem very imminent indeed. Jeremy Rifkin considers them to be inevitable.

> "We no longer feel ourselves to be guests in someone else's home and therefore obliged to make our behavior conform with a set of pre-existing cosmic rules. It is our creation now. We make the rules. We establish the parameters of reality. We create the world, and because we do, we no longer feel beholden to outside forces. We no longer have to justify our behavior, for we are now the architects of the universe. We are responsible to nothing outside ourselves, for we are the kingdom, the power, and the glory forever and ever" (1983c).

Rifkin, though certain this is the world's future, is despondent. He closes his book with these words of despair:

> "Our future is secured. The cosmos wails" (1983d).

New Age evolutionism is not so new, after all. Scientifically speaking, however, New Age evolutionism, with its absurd ideas of order through chaos and quantum speciations, is even less defensible than Darwinian gradualism.

Conclusion

In this chapter, I have tried to stress two vitally important facts, both widely misunderstood as a result of evolutionist propaganda in the schools and news media.

(1) "Evolution science" is not nearly as effective

in explaining, correlating and predicting real scientific data as is "creation science." The scientific arguments briefly outlined in this introductory chapter will be much more fully discussed and documented in the subsequent chapters of this book.

(2) Evolution is much more "religious" than creation, as is evident not only from the fact that it is purely a belief system, unsupported by true science, but also by virtue of the numerous religions which are based on it.

Consequently, there is more than ample reason for any serious-minded person to consider the strong scientific case that can be made for "creation science." This is the purpose of the later chapters of this book. In Part II (Chapters 2-4), Dr. Gary Parker discusses the evidence from the life sciences, and in Part III (Chapters 5-7), I discuss the evidence from the physical sciences.

There are still other types of evidence for creation, of course (Biblical, theological, sociological, etc.), but these are beyond the scope of this book. As any fair-minded reader can see, creationism is strongly supported by true science, and can surely compete successfully in the scientific marketplace of ideas, if only it is given a reasonably fair hearing.

Part II

The
Life
Sciences

By Gary E. Parker

Chapter 2

Evidence of Creation in Living Systems

Introduction

The Canadian Broadcasting Corporation (CBC) produced a program involving the creation/evolution question. Tom Kelly, its producer, invited me, along with scientists from Canada, to be filmed as a part of the program. The result was one of the fairest, most enlightening, and well produced programs ever done by the public media on the subject of origins (Kelly, 1981).

Most encouraging was the letter I received from Tom, especially this section:

> "For the record, I went into the program as an evolutionist, without knowing why or quite what that meant. But by the time I had done the research, of one thing I was sure—that if evolution is true, the chance-and-time processes just don't work."

In those few sentences, Tom sums up the situation for a lot of us. Like Tom, and like many of you, I believed evolution "without knowing why or quite what that meant." Evolution was all I ever heard from grammar school to graduate school, and the "experts" all seemed to believe it. So when it came to my turn to teach university biology, I taught evolution and taught it with enthusiasm, most simply because it was the "in thing"—the "educated thing"—to do.

As I learned, by teaching, more about the "chance-and-time processes" that underlie evolution, like Tom I began to have second thoughts. But what alternative could there be? "Creation?" Wasn't that just the simple, ignorant belief of religious fanatics? Could plan and design ever be an intelligent, scientific alternative to time and chance?

The thoughts circled through my mind that must have gone through Tom's and perhaps yours. Sure I believe in evolution—I think. Everyone believes it, at least all the "experts"—don't they? The only alternative is creation, and that's just for uneducated religious types—isn't it?

In this section, I'd like to work though some of those questions with you. I want you to understand what evolution is and what it means, so, as a biologist who teaches evolution at the university level, I'll try to explain, fairly and clearly, the standard text book evidence used to support evolution. But I also want you to hear a logical, rational, intelligent alternative to evolution, one with a great deal of scientific support.

Take your time. Be critical. Think it through. It took me three years of re-examining the evidence before I reluctantly gave up my deep-seated belief in evolution and concluded, like thousands of other scientists in recent times, that creation is really a more logical inference from our scientific observations. Leaving any decision completely up to you, of course, I'd like to share with you now a small part of the large body of scientific evidence that favors the creation idea.

Tools for Inquiry:
Observation and Inference

What do I mean by "evidence of creation?" Isn't creation something you either believe or don't believe? How can we talk about *scientific* evidence of creation?

For many people, that question is a major stumbling block. Some even use it as an excuse to throw creation out of the courtroom or classroom without even hearing the evidence. But nothing is really easier for scientists and just "ordinary people" than finding and recognizing evidence of creation.

To illustrate, let me borrow your imagination for a moment. Imagine that you are walking along a creek on a lazy summer afternoon, idly kicking at the pebbles along the bank. Occasionally you reach down to pick up a pebble that has an unusual shape. One pebble reminds you of a cowboy boot (Fig. 1).

As you roll the pebble around in your hand, you notice that the softer parts of the rock are more worn away than the harder parts, and that lines of wear follow lines of weakness in the rock. Despite some appearance of design, the boot shape of the tumbled pebble is clearly the result of time, chance, and the processes of weathering and erosion.

But then your eye spots an arrowhead lying among the pebbles (Fig. 1). Immediately it stands out as different. In the arrowhead, chip marks cut through the hard and soft parts of the rock equally, and the chip line goes both with and across lines of weakness in the rock. In the arrowhead, we see matter shaped and molded according to a design that gives the rocky material a purpose.

You have just done what many people dismiss as impossible. In comparing the pebble and arrowhead, you were easily able to recognize evidence of creation. I am speaking here only of human creation, of course. The arrowhead might have been carved by one of my ancestors (a Cherokee), for example. But the same approach can be used even when we don't know who or what the creative agent might have been.

What does it take to recognize evidence of creation? Just the ordinary tools of science: logic and observation.

Using your knowledge of erosional processes and your observations of hard and soft rock, you were able to distinguish a result of time and chance (the tumbled pebble) from an object created with plan and purpose (the arrowhead). If we had found such objects as arrowheads on Mars, all scientists would have recognized them immediately as the products of creation, even though in that case we would have no idea who made them or how. Carl Sagan, the evolutionist of *Cosmos* television fame, wants the government to listen for signals from outer space, because he knows full well that we can tell the difference between wave patterns produced by time and chance from those sent with design and purpose (Parker, 1977c).

Note: You don't have to see the creator, and you don't have to see the creative act, to recognize evidence of creation. Even when we don't know who or what the creative agent is, then, there are cases where "creation" is simply the most logical inference from our scientific observations.

Although the pebble and the arrowhead are made of the same substance, they reflect two radically different kinds of order. The tumbled pebble has the kind of order that results from time and chance operating through weathering and erosion on the inherent properties of matter. Those same factors will eventually destroy the arrowhead, which has the kind of order clearly brought into being by design and creation.

In a way, the tumbled pebble represents the idea of *evolution*. As I once believed and taught, evolutionists believe that life itself is the result, like the tumbled pebble, of *time, chance, and the inherent properties of matter*. The arrowhead represents the *creation* idea, that living systems have *irreducible properties of organization* that were produced, like the arrowhead, by *design and creation*.

In our daily experience, all of us can distinguish two kinds of order. On the basis of logic and observation, for example, we recognize that wind-worn rock formations are the products of time, chance, and the inherent properties of matter. But those same techniques (logical inference from scientific observations) convince us that pottery fragments and rock carvings must be the products of acts of creation giving matter irreducible properties of organization.

Now, let's apply these ordinary scientific techniques to the study of living systems. When it comes to the origin of life, which is the most logical inference from our observations: time, chance, and the evolution of matter . . . or design and creation?

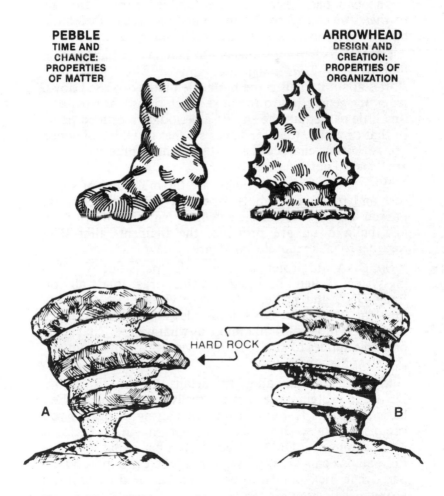

Figure 1. Try your hand at recognizing scientific evidence of creation. Both rock formations above resemble a man's head, but examine the relationship between hard and soft rock in each. Which (A or B) is most likely the result, like the tumbled pebble, of *time and chance* acting on the properties of hard and soft rock? Which is most likely the result, like the arrowhead, of *design and creation?* Can you recognize evidence of creation without seeing either the creator or the creative act?

The Origin of Life: DNA and Protein

The two basic parts of the tumbled pebble and arrowhead we considered are hard and soft rock. Two basic parts of every living system are DNA and protein.

DNA is the famous molecule of heredity. It has been on the cover of *Time* magazine, and we often hear news stories about it. This is the molecule that gets passed down from one generation to the next. Each of us starts off as a tiny little ball about the size of a period on a printed page. In that tiny ball, there are over six feet of DNA all coiled up. All of our characteristics (brown hair, blue eyes, etc.) are "spelled out" in the DNA.

What are proteins? Proteins are the molecules of structure and function. Hair is mostly protein; skin cells are packed full of proteins; the enzymes that break down food and build it up are proteins; the filaments that slide together to make muscles work are proteins.

So, DNA and protein are two basic "parts" of every living system. When you get down to a virus, that's all you find—DNA and protein. (In some viruses, RNA substitutes for DNA.) The DNA molecules we code for produce the protein molecules that make us what we are. That same principle applies to all life forms—viruses, plants, animals, as well as human beings.

My students study all of the details (Parker, 1977a) but DNA and protein molecules are really quite simple in their basic structure. If you can picture a string of pearls, you can picture DNA—it is a chain of repeating units. Fig. 2-A is a diagram of a DNA molecule. The parts that look like railroad box cars are sugars and phosphate groups, and the parts that stick out from each box car in the chain are groups called *bases*.

Proteins are built in about the same way. Proteins are also chains of repeated units. As shown in Fig. 2-B, the links in protein chains are called *amino acids*. In all living things, inherited chains of DNA bases are used to line up chains of amino acids. These amino acid chains are the

Figure 2-A. *DNA* is built like a string of pearls, whose links (specifically the *bases* G, C, A, and T) act like alphabet letters that "spell out" hereditary instructions.

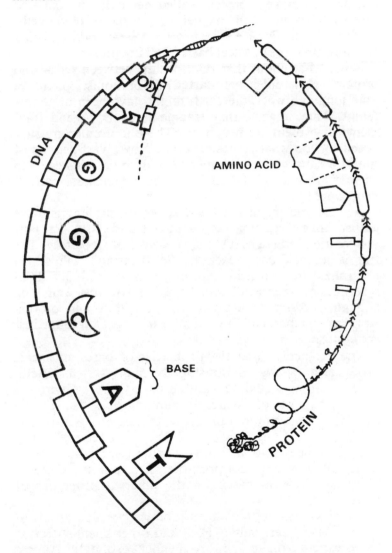

Figure 2-B. *Proteins* are chains of *amino acids*. Each chain coils into a special shape that has some special function—muscle contraction, digestion, oxygen transport, holding skin together, etc., etc.

protein molecules responsible for structure and function. For example, chains of several hundred DNA bases tell the cell how to make a protein called hemoglobin, and that protein functions as the oxygen carrier in red blood cells. In short form, *DNA* ⟶ *protein* ⟶ *trait,* and that relationship is the physical basis of all life on earth.

Now, what about that relationship between DNA and protein? How did it get started? Evolutionists picture a time long ago when the earth might have been quite different. They imagine that fragments of DNA and fragments of protein are produced. These molecules are supposed to "do what comes naturally" over vast periods of time. What's going to happen? Will time, chance, and chemical reactions between DNA and protein automatically produce life?

At first you might think so. After all, nothing is more natural than a reaction between acids and bases. Perhaps you've used soda (a base) to clean acid from a battery. The fizz is an acid-base reaction. So is using "Tums" to neutralize stomach acid. Nothing is more common than reactions between acids and bases. If you just wait long enough, acid-base reactions will get DNA and protein working together, and life will appear—right? Wrong! Just the opposite.

The problem is that the properties of bases and acids produce the *wrong* relationship for living systems. Acid-base reactions would "scramble up" DNA and protein units in all sorts of "deadly" combinations. These reactions would prevent, not promote, the use of DNA to code protein production. Since use of DNA to code protein production is the basis of all life on earth, these acid-base reactions would prevent, not promote, the evolution of life by chemical processes based on the inherent properties of matter.

These wrong reactions have produced serious problems for Stanley Miller, Sidney Fox, and other scientists trying to do experiments to support chemical evolution. Almost all biology books have a picture of Miller's famous spark chamber (Fig. 3). In it, Miller used simple raw materials and electric sparks to produce amino acids and other sim-

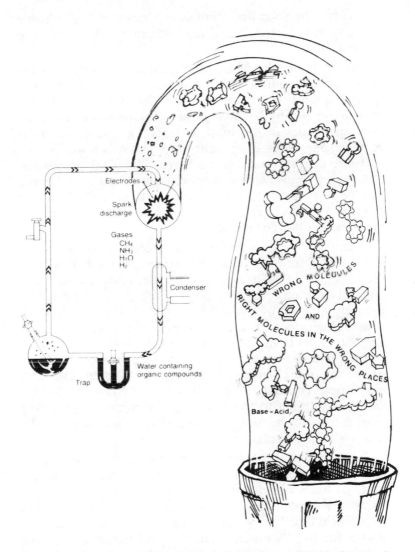

Labels in figure:

Electrodes

Spark discharge

Gases
CH₄
NH₃
H₂O
H₂

Condenser

Water containing organic compounds

Trap

WRONG MOLECULES AND RIGHT MOLECULES IN THE WRONG PLACES

Base – Acid

Figure 3. Left to time, chance, and their chemical properties, the bases and amino acids of DNA and proteins would react in ways that would prevent, not promote, the evolution of life. In the same way, reactions among molecules in Miller's famous "spark chamber" would destroy any hope of producing life. Living systems must constantly repair the chemical damage done to them, and when biological order loses out to inherent chemical processes, death results—even though a dead body has all the right molecules in the right places in the right amounts at the right times (almost!).

ple acids—the so-called "building blocks of life." Some newspapers reported that Miller had practically made "life in a test tube."

But the molecules Miller made did not include only the amino acids required in living systems; they included even greater quantities of amino acids that would be highly destructive to any "evolving" life. Furthermore, even the right molecules in his spark chamber would react in far more wrong ways than right ways. In other words, left to time, chance, and their inherent chemical properties, Miller's molecules would react in ways that would destroy any hope of producing life. (See Parker, 1970; Bliss and Parker, 1984; Wilder-Smith, 1981; and Thaxton, Bradley and Olsen, 1984, for details.)

Chemistry, then, is not our ancestor; it's our problem. When cells lose their biological order and their molecules start reacting in chemical ways, we die. A dead body contains all the molecules necessary for life and approximately the right amount of each. What's lost at death are balance and biological order that otherwise use food to put us together faster than chemistry tears us apart!

Time and chance are no help to the evolutionist either, since time and chance can only act on inherent chemical properties. Trying to throw "life" on a roll of molecular dice is like trying to throw a "13" on a pair of gambling dice. It just won't work. The possibility is not there, so the probability is just plain *zero*.

The relationship between DNA and protein required for life is one that no chemist would ever suspect. It's using a series of bases (actually taken three at a time) to line up a series of R-groups (Fig. 4). R-groups are the parts of each amino acid that "stick out" along the protein chain. "R" stands for the "variable *r*adical," and variable it is! An R-group can be acid; it can be a base; it can be a single hydrogen atom, a short chain, a long chain, a single ring, a double ring, fat-soluble, or water soluble!

The point is this: there is no inherent chemical tendency for a series of bases to line up a series of R-groups in the orderly way required for life. The base-R group relation-

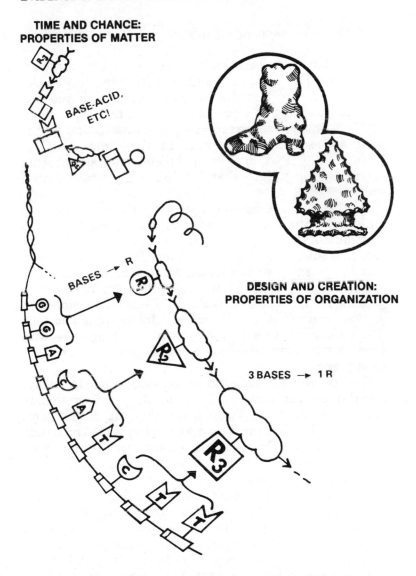

TIME AND CHANCE: PROPERTIES OF MATTER

BASE-ACID, ETC!

BASES → R

DESIGN AND CREATION: PROPERTIES OF ORGANIZATION

3 BASES → 1 R

Figure 4. All living cells use groups of three DNA bases as code names for amino acid R groups. But all known chemical reactions between these molecules (e.g., base-acid) would prevent, not promote, development of this relationship. Is the hereditary code, then, the logical result of time, chance, and the inherent properties of matter (like the water-worn pebble); or does it have the irreducible properties of organization (like the arrowhead) that scientists ordinarily associate with design and creation?

ship has to be *imposed on* matter; it has *no basis within* matter.

The relationship between hard and soft rock in the arrowhead in Fig. 1 had to be imposed from the outside. All of us could recognize that matter had been shaped and molded according to a design that could not be produced by time, chance, and weathering processes acting on the hard and soft rock involved. In the same way, our knowledge of DNA, protein, and their chemical properties should lead us to infer that *life also is the result of creation*.

Let me use a simpler example of the same kind of reasoning. Suppose I asked you this question: "Can aluminum fly?" Think a moment. Can aluminum fly? I'm sure that sounds like a trick question. By itself, of course, aluminum can't fly. Aluminum ore in rock just sits there. A volcano may throw it, but it doesn't fly. If you pour gasoline on it, does that make it fly? Pour a little rubber on it; that doesn't make it fly either. But suppose you take that aluminum, stretch it out in a nice long tube with wings, a tail, and a few other parts. *Then* it flies; we call it an airplane.

Did you ever wonder what makes an airplane fly? Try a few thought experiments. Take the wings off and study them; they don't fly. Take the engines off, study them; they don't fly. Take the little man out of the cockpit, study him; he doesn't fly. Don't dwell on this the next time you're on an airplane, but an airplane is a collection of non-flying parts! Not a single part of it flies!

What does it take to make an airplane fly? The answer is something every scientist can understand and appreciate, something every scientist can work with and use to frame hypotheses and conduct experiments. What does it take to make an airplane fly? *Creative design and organization*.

Take a look at the features of a living cell diagrammed in Fig. 5. Don't worry; I am not going to say much about this diagram. Just notice the DNA molecule in the upper left circle and the protein in the lower right. What are all the rest of those strange looking things diagrammed in the cell? Those represent just a few of the molecules that a cell

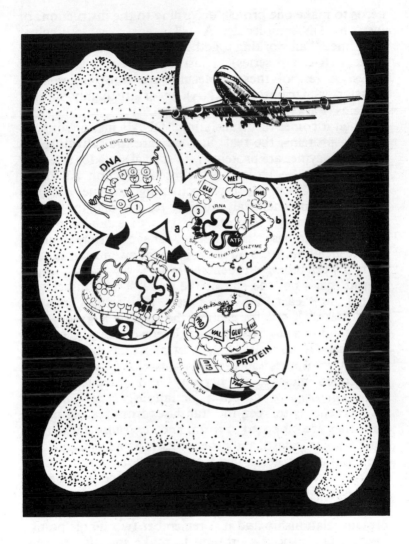

Figure 5. Living cells use over 75 special kinds of protein and RNA molecules to make one protein following DNA's instructions. What we know about airplanes convinces us that their flight is the result of creation and design. What scientists know about the way living cells make protein suggests, just as clearly, that life also is the result of creation. (Drawing after Bliss and Parker. 1979. *Origin of Life*. CLP Pubs., San Diego.)

needs to make one protein according to the instructions of just one DNA molecule. A cell needs over 75 "helper molecules," all working together *in harmony,* to make one protein (R-group series) as instructed by one DNA base series. A few of these molecules are RNA (messenger, transfer, and ribosomal RNA); most are highly specific proteins (Parker, 1977a).

When it comes to "translating" DNA's instructions for making proteins, the real "heroes" are the activating enzymes. Enzymes are proteins with special slots for selecting and holding other molecules for speedy reaction. As shown in Fig. 5 (Circle 3), each activating enzyme has *five* slots—two for chemical coupling *(c, d),* one for energy (ATP), and, most importantly, two to establish a non-chemical three-base "code name" for each different amino acid R group *(a, b).* You may find that awe-inspiring, and so do my cell biology students!

And that's not the end of the story. The living cell requires at least 20 of these activating enzymes ("translases"), one for each of the specific R-group/code name (amino acid/tRNA) pairs. Even so, the whole set of translases (100 specific active sites) would be *worthless* without ribosomes (50 proteins plus rRNA) to break the base-coded message of heredity into three-letter code names; *destructive* without a continuously renewed supply of ATP energy to keep the translases from tearing up the pairs they are supposed to form; and *vanishing* if it weren't for having translases and other specific proteins to re-make the translase proteins that are continuously and rapidly wearing out because of the destructive effects of time and chance on protein structure!

But let's forget about all the complexity of the DNA-protein relationship and just remember two simple points. First, it takes specific proteins to make specific proteins. That may remind you of the chicken-and-egg problem—how can you get one without the other? (See Lagerkvist, 1980.) That problem is solved, if the molecules needed for "DNA-protein translation" are produced by creation.

Second, among all the molecules that translate DNA into protein, there's not one molecule that is alive. There's not a single molecule in your body that's alive. There's not a single molecule in the living cell that's alive. A living cell is a collection of nonliving molecules.

What does it take to make a living cell alive? The answer is something every scientists recognizes and uses in a laboratory, something every scientist can logically infer from his observations of DNA and protein. What does it take to make a living cell alive? *Creation.*

Only creation could organize matter into the first living cells. *But once all the parts are in place, there is nothing "magical" or "mysterious" in the way cells make proteins.* *If* they are continually supplied with the right kind of energy and raw material— and *if* all 75-plus of the RNA and protein molecules required for DNA-protein "translation" are present in the *right* places at the *right* times in the *right* amounts with the *right* structure—*then* cells make proteins by using DNA's base series (quite indirectly!) to line up amino acids at the rate of about two per second. *In ways scientists understand rather well,* it takes a living cell only about four minutes to "crank out" an average protein (500 amino acids) according to DNA specifications.

Scientists also understand how airplanes fly. For that very reason, no scientist believes that airplanes are the result of time, chance, and the properties of aluminum and other materials that make up the airplane. Flying is a property of organization, not substance. A Boeing 747, for example, is a collection of 4½ million nonflying parts, but thanks to design and creation (and a continuous supply of energy and of repair services!), it flies.

Similarly, "life" is a property of organization, not of substance. A living cell is a collection of several billion nonliving molecules, and death results when a shortage of energy or a flaw in the operational or repair mechanisms allows inherent chemical processes to destroy its biological order.

It's what we *do know* and *can explain* about aluminum and the laws of physics that would convince us that airplanes are the products of creation, even if we never saw the acts of creation. In the same way, it's what we *do know* and *can explain* about DNA and protein and the laws of chemistry which suggest that life itself is the result of creation.

My point is not based on design *per se,* but on the *kind of design* we observe. As creationists point out, some kinds of design, such as snowflakes and wind-worn rock formations, *do* result from time and chance—*given* the properties of the materials involved. Even complex relationships, such as the oxygen-carbon dioxide balance in a sealed aquarium, can result from organisms "doing what comes naturally," *given* the properties of living things. But just as clearly, other kinds of design, e.g. arrowheads and airplanes, are the direct result of creative design and organization giving matter properties it doesn't have and can't develop on its own. What we know about the DNA-protein relationship suggests that living cells have the *created kind* of design.

In the well known *Scientific American* issue made into a book, *Evolution,* Dickerson (1978) seems to support my point (without meaning to, I'm sure). After describing the problems in producing the right kinds of molecules for living systems, he says that those droplets that by "sheer chance" contained the right molecules survived longer. He continues, "This is not life, but it is getting close to it. The missing ingredient is . . . . "

What will he say here? The "missing ingredient" is . . . one more protein? . . . a little more DNA? . . . an energy supply? . . . the right acid-base balance? No, he says: "The missing ingredient is an orderly mechanism . . . ." An *orderly mechanism!* That's what's missing—but that's what life is all about. As I stated before, life is not a property of substance; it's a property of organization. The same kind of reasoning applies to the pyramids in Egypt, for example. The pyramids are made of stone, but studying the stone does not even begin to explain how the pyramids were built. Similarly, until evolutionists begin to explain the origin of the "orderly mechanism," they have not even begun to talk about the origin of life.

When it comes to the evolutionary origin of that orderly mechanism, Dickerson adds, we have "no laboratory models: hence one can speculate endlessly, unfettered by inconvenient facts." With "no laboratory models" to provide data, the case for the *evolution* of life must be based on *imagination*. But, as Dickerson admits, "We [evolutionists] can only imagine what probably existed, and our imagination so far has not been very helpful."

The case for *creation,* however, is not based on imagination. Creation is based instead on *logical inference* from our *scientific observations,* and on simple acknowledgment that everyone, scientists and laymen alike, recognize that certain kinds of design imply creation.

Creation stands between the classic extremes of mechanism and vitalism. Mechanists, including evolutionists, believe that both the *operation* and *origin* of living things are the results of the laws of chemistry which reflect the inherent properties of matter. Vitalists believe that both the operation and origin of living systems depend on mysterious forces that lie beyond scientific description. According to creation, living things *operate* in understandable ways that can be described in terms of scientific laws —but, these observations include properties of organization that logically imply a created origin for life.

The creationist, then, recognizes the orderliness that the vitalist doesn't see. But he doesn't limit himself only to those kinds of order that result from time, chance, and the properties of matter as the evolutionist does. Creation introduces levels of order and organization that greatly enrich the range of explorable hypotheses and turn the study of life into a scientist's dream.

If the evidence for the creation of life is as clear as I say it is, then other scientists, even those who are evolutionists, ought to see it—and they do.

Francis Crick (1981), who shared a Nobel prize for the discovery of DNA's structure, in now convinced that life could not and did not evolve on earth. In a new book, he argues instead for "directed panspermia," his belief that life reached earth in a rocket fired by intelligent life on some other planet. Crick admits that his view only moves the creation/evolution question back to another time and place, but he argues that different conditions might give life a chance to evolve that it did not have on earth.

Creationists are pleased that Crick recognizes the same fatal flaws in chemical evolution that they have cited for years, but creationists also point out that the differences between "chemical chemistry" and "biological chemistry" are wrapped up with the fundamental nature of matter and energy and would apply on other planets as well as on earth (Parker, 1970).

That opinion seems to be shared in part by the famous evolutionary astronomer, Fred Hoyle (1981), who made the news recently under the heading: "There *must* be a God." Hoyle and his colleague, Chandra Wickramasinghe, independently reached that conclusion after their mathematical analyses showed that believing life could result from time, chance, and properties of matter was like believing that " . . . a tornado sweeping through a junkyard might assemble a Boeing 747 from the materials therein." (Remember what it takes to make an airplane fly?)

Drawing the logical inference from our scientific knowledge, both scientists concluded that "it becomes sensible to think that the favourable properties of physics on which life depends are in every respect *deliberate.*" (Emphasis Hoyle's.) But both were surprised by their results. Hoyle called himself an agnostic, and, in the same article, Wickramasinghe said he was an atheistic Buddhist who " . . . was very strongly brainwashed to believe that science cannot be consistent with any kind of deliberate creation."

My purpose in quoting these scientists (and others later on) is not, of course, to suggest that they are creationists who would endorse all my views. Rather, it is simply to show that experts in the field, even when they have no preference for creationist thinking, at least agree with the creationists on the facts. And when people with different viewpoints agree, we can be pretty sure what the facts are. I also want to show that scientists who are not creationists are able to see that creation is a legitimate scientific concept whose merits deserve to be compared with those of evolution.

In that light, I'd like to call your attention to a fascinating and revolutionary book, *Evolution: A Theory in Crisis,* by a prominent molecular biologist, Dr. Michael Denton (1985b). In a television program we did together, and in our extensive personal conversations, Dr. Denton describes himself as a child of the secular age who desires naturalistic explanations—when he can find them. But when it comes to the origin of life, Dr. Denton explains with authority and stark clarity that evolutionists are nowhere near a naturalistic explanation at present. After comparing the genetic programs in living things to a library of a thousand volumes encoding a billion bits of information and all the mathematically intricate algorithms for coordinating them, Dr. Denton refers to the chemical evolution scenario as "simply an affront to reason," i.e., an insult to the intelligence! (p. 351).

He openly and frankly states that the thesis of his book is "anti-evolutionary" (p. 353), but it seems to me that he is cautiously taking a step even further. The first chapter of his book is titled "Genesis Rejected," and he would react very strongly against being called a creationist, but in his honest analysis of the creation-evolution controversy through history, Dr. Denton freely admits that many of the scientific views of the early creationists have been vindicated by modern discoveries in science.

Take William Paley's classic old argument that design in living things implies a Designer just as clearly as design in a watch implies a watchmaker. Denton states, "Paley was not only *right* in asserting an analogy between life and a machine, but also *remarkably prophetic* in guessing that the technological ingenuity realized in living systems is vastly in excess of anything yet accomplished by man." (Emphasis added). Then Denton goes on to summarize his thinking on life's origin (p. 34):

> "The almost irresistible force of the analogy has completely undermined the complacent assumption, prevalent in biological circles over most of the past century, that one design hypothesis can be excluded on the grounds that the notion is fundamentally a metaphysical *a priori* (sic) concept and therefore scientifically

unsound. *On the contrary, the inference to design is a purely posteriori (sic) induction based on a ruthlessly consistent application of the logic of analogy.* The conclusion may have religious implications, but it does not depend on religious presuppositions" (Emphasis added).

Now that's quite a mouthful! Even though he would strenuously deny any leaning toward a Christian concept of creation, this leading molecular biologist sees quite plainly that a scientific concept of creation can be constructed, just as I've said, using the ordinary tools of science, logic and observation. (In fact, Denton intimates that creation scientists have shown more respect than evolutionists for empirical evidence and a "ruthlessly consistent" application of logic!)

It's also time, as Denton concludes, that creation may have religious implications—but that should not prevent our evaluating its scientific merits on the basis of logic and observation alone. Notice, I am *not* suggesting at this point that I've somehow "proved evolution is false and creation is true." Rather, I'm simply suggesting that the creation-evolution controversy, far from being a dead issue, is a live and lively question that demands serious scientific consideration.

Even that "simple" suggestion may prove too much for some. In what seems to me a real fear of discussing the scientific weakness of evolution and the scientific strengths of creation, it has become fashionable among anti-creationists to accuse creation scientists of mis-quoting authorities. After spending a fabulous four-hour evening with Dr. & Mrs. Denton, I then quoted him extensively in a conference (April, 1987) in Sydney, Australia, which he attended—and at which he spoke briefly after my presentations. Whatever others might say, at least Michael Denton doesn't believe I mis-quoted him!

But again my point: I am *not* quoting Dr. Denton as if he agreed with all my thinking; on the contrary, my point is that a fellow scientist who shares *neither* my basic assumptions *nor* conclusions regarding world-and-life view, nevertheless recognizes that the concept of creation can be explained scientifically, and that the concept has at least some scientific merit.

Dr. Denton is, of course, not alone in that stand. In a short but thought-provoking article, British physicist H. S. Lipson (1980) first expresses his interest in life's origin, and his feeling—quite apart from any preference for creation—thus:

> In fact, evolution became in a sense a scientific religion; almost all scientists have accepted it and many are prepared to "bend" their observations to fit with it.

After wondering how well evolution has stood up to scientific testing, Lipson continues:

> To my mind, the theory [evolution] does not stand up at all.

(As a physicist, he cites particularly the thermodynamic problems discussed by Dr. Morris in Chapter 5). Then he comes to the heart of the matter:

> If living matter is not, then, caused by the interplay of atoms, natural forces, and radiation, how has it come into being?

After dismissing a sort of directed evolution, Lipson concludes:

> I think, however, that we must go further than this and admit that the only acceptable explanation is *creation*. [Emphasis his.]

Like Hoyle and Wickramasinghe, Lipson is a bit surprised and unhappy with his own conclusion. He writes, "I know that this [creation] is anathema to physicists, as indeed it is to me, ... " But his sense of honesty and scientific integrity force him to conclude his sentence:

> . . . but we must not reject a theory that we do not like if the experimental evidence supports it.

That's the spirit I'd like to encourage in this book: a willingness to look openly at all sides of an issue, to draw the most logical inference from the weight of evidence, and to follow "truth" wherever it might lead, regardless of personal preference and preconceptions.

By the way, let me assure you that not all who see the evidence of creation are unhappy about it! Witness Dr. Dean Kenyon. Dr. Kenyon is a molecular biologist whose area of research interest is specifically the origin of life. His book on life's origin, *Biochemical Predestination,* opened with laudatory phrases for Darwinian evolution, and he has taught an evolution class at San Francisco State University for many years.

A couple of students in Dr. Kenyon's class once asked him to read a book on creation science. He didn't want to, but, thanks to their polite persistence, he resolved to read it and refute it. But, as he told me in person, he read it and couldn't refute it. Instead, Dr. Kenyon got interested in creation science and began a reevaluation of the scientific evidence that finally led him to the happy conclusion that life, including his, is here as a result of creation. He still presents the evidence cited in favor of evolution in his classes, but he also allows his students to weigh that against the evidence that favors creation.

Like mine, Dr. Kenyon's change from evolution to creation took a long time and involved reexamination of much more than just the evidence from molecular relationships within living cells. Let's take a look now at some evidence of creation from other areas of biology.

Comparing Similarities: Homology

Look at your arm for a moment and try to picture the bones inside. There's one bone attached to the body, two bones in the forearm, and a little group of wrist bones, and bones that radiate out into the fingers. As it turns out, there are many other living things that have a similar pattern—the foreleg of a horse or dog, the wing of a bat, and the flipper of a penguin, for example, as shown in Fig. 6. Biologists use the term "homology" for such similarities in basic structure.

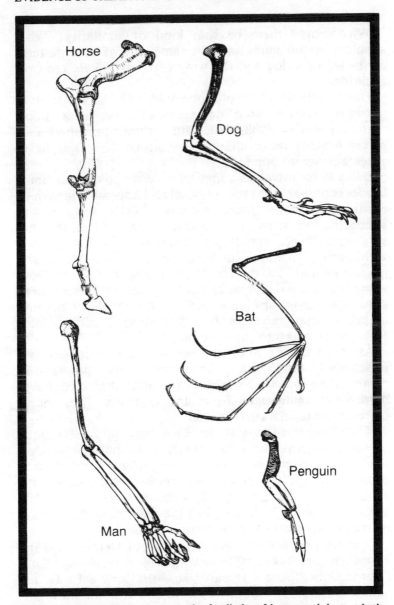

Figure 6. Bones in the human arm, the forelimbs of horses and dogs, a bat's wing, and a penguin's flipper all share a similarity in basic structural pattern called *homology*. What does this similarity (homology) mean: descent from a *common ancestor* (evolution), or creation according to a *common design* (creation)?

Why should there be that kind of similarity? Why should a person's arm have the same kind of bone pattern as the leg of a dog and the wing of a bat? There are two basic ideas.

One of these is the evolutionary idea of *descent from a common ancestor*. That idea seems to make sense, since that's the way we explain such similarities as brothers and sisters looking more alike than cousins do. They have parents closer in common.

Using descent from a common ancestor to explain similarities is probably the most logical and appealing idea that evolutionists have. Isaac Asimov (1981), well known science fiction writer, is so pleased with the idea that he says our ability to classify plants and animals on a groups-within-groups hierarchical basis virtually forces scientists to treat evolution as a "fact." In his enthusiasm, Asimov apparently forgot that we can classify kitchen utensils on a groups-within-groups basis, but that hardly forces anyone to believe that knives evolved into spoons, spoons into forks, or saucers into cups and plates.

After all there's another reason in our common experience why things look alike. It's *creation according to a common design*. That's why Fords and Chevrolets have more in common than Fords and sailboats. They share more design features in common.

What's the most logical inference from our observation of bone patterns and other examples of homology—descent from a common ancestor, or creation according to a common design? In many cases, either explanation will work, and we can't really tell which is more reasonable. But there seem to be times when the only thing that works is creation according to a common design.

I get support for my claim again from Denton (1985), in his chapter titled "The Failure of Homology." Dr. Denton is not only a research scientist with a Ph.D. in molecular biology but also an M.D. with an intimate knowledge of comparative anatomy and embryology. As a self-diagnosed "child of the secular age," he admits his desire to find naturalistic explanations for patterns of similarity among organisms (homology), but he also admits the failure of evolutionary explanations.

Like every other scientist, Denton recognizes the striking similarity in bone pattern evident in a comparision of vertebrate fore- and hindlimbs. "Yet no evolutionist," he says, "claims that the hindlimb evolved from the forelimb, or that hindlimbs and forelimbs evolved from a common source."

I was once taught to refer to corresponding parts of the male and female reproductive systems as "sexual homology." But homology in that case could not possibly be explained by descent from a common ancestor; we can't even imagine that males evolved from females, or visa versa, or that human beings evolved from some animal that had only one sex.

Worse yet for evolution, structures that appear homologous often develop under the control of genes that are not homologous. In such cases, the thesis that similar structures developed from genes modified during evolutionary descent is precisely falsified.

Our observation of similarity or homology is real enough, but that's true, Denton points out, "whether the causal mechanism was Darwinian, Lamarckian, vitalistic *or even creationist*" (Emphasis added). Although the evidence is not as spectacular and compelling as the biomolecular data, I would say the weight of our present knowledge of homology favors Denton's final alternative: creation according to a common design.

The nonbranching nature of trait distribution produces practical problems for the biologist. One of the students I taught, for example, had a passion for lizard ear bones. He came in late in the evening and early in the morning—always dissecting lizard ear bones, sectioning them, and so on. That got him interested in lizards in general. But he noted that in attempts to classify lizards, one fellow would go on the field characteristics and he'd come up with one system. Another fellow would go by the bone patterns and he'd come up with another system. Internal organs suggested a third, and so on. The pattern is not a branching one suggesting evolutionary descent from a common ancestor; rather, it is a mosaic or modular pattern (which

I'll discuss further in the next chapter) suggesting creation.

Perhaps the clearest anatomical evidence of creation is "convergence." The classic example is the similarity between the eyes of humans and vertebrates and the eyes of squids and octopuses. Evolutionists recognize the similarity between the eyes easily enough, but they've never been able to find or even imagine a common ancestor with traits that would explain these similarities. So instead of calling these eyes homologous organs, they call them examples of "convergent evolution." That really means that we have another example of similarity in structure that cannot be explained as evolutionary descent from a common ancestor.

"Convergence," in the sense of similar structures designed to meet similar needs, would be expected, of course, on the basis of creation according to a common design. And as we'll see later, both the octopus eye and the vertebrate eye are complete, complex, and totally distinct from one another right from their first appearance in the fossil sequence. Michael Land (1979), biologist at Sussex University, sounds like a creationist when he mentions in passing that the vertebrate eye "shares design features but not evolution with the eye of the cephalopod molluscs such as the octopus."

The real focus of Land's article, however, is "divergence," the occurrence of quite distinct structures in plants and animals that are otherwise supposed to be close evolutionary relatives. Certain shrimp-like animals that live in deep ocean darkness, he says, have compound eyes with lenses all arranged to focus light at a common point (rather than forming multiple images, as most compound eyes do). But, he continues, some members of the group have "lens cylinders" that smoothly bend the incoming light (because of smoothly varied refractive indices), whereas others have square facets with a "mirror system" for focus (utilizing even a double corner bounce). Ingenious use of physics and geometry should be evidence enough of creation it seems to me—but there's more.

Comparing the mirrors with the lens cylinder system, Land says: "Both are successful and very sophisticated image-forming devices, but I cannot imagine an intermediate form [or common ancestral type] that would work at all." The kind of design in these eyes, he says, seems impossible to explain as a result of evolutionary relationship. So Land goes on to suggest that the shrimp-like animals with different systems should not be classified as evolutionary relatives, even though they are otherwise quite similar.

Even more interesting is Land's statement about how he felt when he was trying to figure out the mirror system. He said he was "trying not to come to the conclusion that these eyes had been put there by God to confuse scientists." May I suggest instead that these eyes were put there by creation to *inform* scientists. As such cases show, a mind open to examples of created order can hasten and enrich the scientific search for understanding.

Some evolutionists admit they have failed to find good evidence of evolution in comparing large structures, so they are looking instead for homology among molecules. In a timeless book basically decribing the three-dimensional structures then known for proteins, Dickerson and Geis (1969) make the statement: "One fact . . . has emerged in the last 15 years from the perfection of protein sequence and structure analysis . . . we can pin down with great precision the relationships between the species and how the proteins evolved." Then, with every example they give, they proceed to *disprove* that evolutionary prediction.

Consider hemoglobin, for example, the protein that carries oxygen in red blood cells. Dickerson says that hemoglobins pose " . . . a puzzling problem. Hemoglobins occur sporadically among the invertebrate phyla [the animals without backbones], in no obvious pattern." That is, they don't occur in an evolutionary *branching* pattern. I would suggest that they do occur in a creationist *mosaic* or *modular* pattern, like bits of blue-colored stone in an artist's mosaic. We find hemoglobin in nearly all vertebrates, but we also find it in some annelids (the earthworm group), some echinoderms (the starfish group), some mollusks (the clam group), some arthropods (the insect group), and even in some bacteria! In all these cases, we find the same kind of molecule—complete and fully functional. As Dickerson observes, "It is hard to see a common line of descent snaking in so unsystematic a way through so many different phyla . . . . "

If evolution were true, we ought to be able to trace how hemoglobin evolved. But we can't. Could it be repeated evolution, the spontaneous appearance of hemoglobin in all these different groups independently, asks Dickerson? He answers that repeated evolution seemed plausible only as long as hemoglobin was just considered red stuff that held oxygen. It does not seem possible, he says, that the entire eight-helix folded pattern appeared repeatedly by time and chance. As far as creationists are concerned, hemoglobin occurs, complete and fully functional, wherever it is appropriate in creation, somewhat like a blue-colored tile in an artist's mosaic.

The same seems to be true for a fascinating protein called lysozyme. Lysozyme is the enzyme in tears that "bites holes" in the cell walls of bacteria so that they explode. (Listen for the "pop" on a quiet evening!) Egg whites are rich in the same enzyme, and that's what keeps eyes and egg whites from easily getting infected.

By comparing lysozyme and lactalbumin, Dickerson was hoping to "pin down with great precision" where human beings branched off the mammal line. The results are surprising. In this test, it turned out that humans are more closely related to the *chicken* than to any living mammal tested! Every evolutionist knows that can't be true, but how can he get around the objective evidence? In his concluding diagram, Dickerson slips in a wiggly line for rapid evolution, and that brings the whole thing back in line again with his evolutionary assumptions. But notice that his protein data, the facts that he observed, did not help him at all with his evolutionary idea.

In fact, when it comes to many of the similarities among molecules, the theory of evolution is not only weak, it has been *falsified*. That conclusion was expressed by Colin Patterson (1981) of the British Museum in an address to leading evolutionists he gave at the American Museum of Natural History.

Patterson first lamented that his topic, creation and evolution, had been forced on him, and then he acknowledged that he has recently been entertaining nonevolutionary or even antievolutionary ideas. Why? Because, he said, after twenty years of research in evolution, he asked himself to name just one thing about evolution he knew for sure—and he couldn't come up with anything. When he asked other leading evolutionists, the only thing anyone could come up with was that "convergence is everywhere." (Remember convergence and creation discussed earlier?) Finally, Patterson said with dismay, he was forced to conclude that evolution is an "anti-theory" that generates "anti-knowledge"—a concept full of explanatory vocabulary that actually explains nothing and that even generates a false impression of what the facts are.

Evolutionists have been leveling these same accusations against creation for decades, Patterson said, but now we have to admit that they apply to evolution as well. His chief example? Molecular taxonomy, using similarities among molecules to try to establish evolutionary lines of descent.

Evolutionists "know," for example, that organisms which are closely related (more recently descended from a common ancestor) have more traits in common than those which are more distantly related. But this knowledge turns out to be "anti-knowledge" and the theory of evolution that sugested it is falsified by the data in hand.

Patterson multiplies examples. When it comes to comparing similarities among amino acids in alpha hemoglobin sequences, crocodiles have much more in common with chickens (17.5%) than with vipers (5.6%), their fellow reptiles. Myoglobin sequences do show one reptile/reptile pair (lizard/crocodile) with greater similarity (10.5% to 8.5%) than the reptile/bird (crocodile/chicken) pair, but it also puts the lizard as close to the chicken (10.5%) as to its fellow reptile. Averaging all the data for three various reptiles, three kinds of crocodiles and three kinds of birds shows—completely contrary to the predictions of evolutionary descent from a common ancestor—that the greatest similarity is between the crocodiles and chickens, although there is little difference between any two groups.

Patterson said that he finally awoke, after having been duped into taking evolutionism as revealed truth all his life, to find that evolutionary theory makes bad systematics (the science of classification). He then proceeded to examine the data as a creationist would, in simple recognition that creationists produce testable hypotheses and that he can understand and explain what inferences creationists would draw from the data, without either agreeing or disagreeing with them. What a superb example of healthy scientific skepticism! Patterson is able to see the data regarding homology in their wholeness, to experience the unbridled freedom to wonder not only *how* but *whether* evolution occurred.

Michael Denton (1985) independently reached the same kind of conclusion regarding homology and the so-called "molecular clock." After documenting the misfit of molecular data with both of two competing evolutionary views, he writes this summary (p. 306):

> "The difficulties associated with attempting to explain how a family of homologous proteins could have evolved at constant rates has created chaos in evolutionary thought. *The evolutionary community has divided into two camps*—those still adhering to the *selectionist* position, and those rejecting it in favor of the *neutralist*. The devastating aspect of this controversy is that neither side can adequately account for the constancy of the rate of molecular evolution; yet *each side fatally weakens the other*. The selectionists wound the neutralists' position by pointing to the disparity in the rates of mutation per unit time, while the neutralists destroy the selectionists' position by showing how ludicrous it is to believe that selection would have caused equal rates of divergence in 'junk' proteins or along phylogenetic lines so dissimilar as those

of man and carp. Both sides win valid points, but in the process the credibility of the molecular clock hypothesis is severely strained and with it *the whole paradigm of evolution itself is endangered*" (Emphasis added).

But Denton doesn't stop with these devastating anti-evolutionary comments (and a comparision of belief in molecular clocks with belief in medieval astrology!). He also describes data from molecular homology as a "biochemical echo of typology," where typology is the pre-evolutionary view of classification developed by scientists on the basis of creationist thinking.

Embryonic Development

Another marvelous reflection of creation is the astonishing process of embryonic development, including the way a human being develops in his or her mother's womb.

But right at this point, evolutionists come on with one of their strongest arguments. They say, in effect, "Look, if you're talking about creation, then surely the creator must not be very good at it, or else there wouldn't be all those mistakes in human embryonic development."

Fig. 7 shows an early stage in human development. Consider it your first "baby picture." You start off as a little, round ball of unformed substance. Then gradually arms, legs, eyes, and all your other parts appear. At one month, you're not quite as charming as you're going to be, and here's where the evolutionist says, "There's no evidence of creation in the human embryo. Otherwise, why would a human being have a yolk sac like a chicken does and a tail like a lizard does? Why would a human being have gill slits like a fish does? An intelligent creator should have known that human beings don't need those things."

Well, there they are, "yolk sac, gill slits, and a tail." Why are they there? What's a creationist going to say? The evolutionist believes these structures are there only as useless leftovers or "vestiges," of our evolutionary

ancestry—remainders of the times when our ancestors
were only fish and reptiles.

The concept of vestigial organs even resulted in cases of
"evolutionary medical malpractice." Young children once
had their healthy (and helpful, disease-fighting) tonsils
removed because of the widespread belief that they were
only useless vestiges. That idea actually slowed down scientific research for many years. If you believe something is a
useless, nonfunctional leftover of evolution, then you
don't bother to find out what it does.

Fortunately, other scientists didn't take that view. Sure
enough, studies have shown that essentially all 180 organs
once listed as evolutionary vestiges have quite important

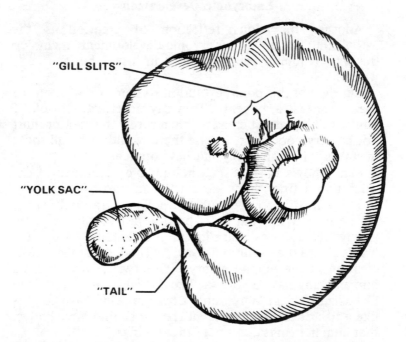

Figure 7. The marvelous development of the human embryo should make everyone a creationist, it seems to me—but evolutionists say that the so-called "gill
slits, yolk sac, and tail" are useless evolutionary leftovers (vestiges) that virtually
"prove" we evolved from fish and reptiles. How does the creationist respond?

functions in human beings.

Take the yolk sac, for instance. In chickens, the yolk contains much of the food that the chick depends on for growth. But we, on the other hand, grow attached to our mothers and they nourish us. Does that mean the yolk sac can be cut off from the human embryo because it isn't needed? Not at all. The so-called "yolk sac" is the source of the human embryo's first blood cells, and death would result without it.

Now here's an engineering problem for you. In the adult, you want to have the blood cells formed inside the bone marrow. That makes good sense, because the blood cells are very sensitive to radiation damage and bone would offer them some protection. But you need blood in order to form the bone marrow that later on is going to form blood. So, where do you get the blood first? Why not use a structure similar to the yolk sac in chickens? The DNA and protein for making it are "common stock" building materials. And, since it lies conveniently outside the embryo, it can easily be discarded after it has served its temporary—but vital—function.

Notice, this is exactly what we would expect as evidence of good creative design and engineering practice. Suppose you were in the bridge-building business, and you were interviewing a couple of engineers to determine whom you wanted to hire. One fellow says, "Each bridge I build will be entirely different from all others." Proudly he tells you "Each bridge will be made using different materials and different processes so that no one will ever be able to see any similarity between the bridges I build." How does that sound?

Now the next fellow comes in and says, "Well, out back in your yard I saw a supply of I-beams and various sizes of heavy bolts and cables. We can use those to span either a river or the San Francisco Bay. I can adapt the same parts and processes to meet a wide variety of needs. You'll be able to see a theme and a variation in my bridge building, and others can see the stamp of authorship in our work." Which fellow would you hire?

As A. E. Wilder-Smith points out (1980), we normally

recognize in human engineers the principles of creative economy and variations on a theme. That's what we see in human embryonic development. The same kind of structure that can provide food and blood cells to a chicken embryo can be used to supply blood cells (all that's needed) for a human embryo. Rather than reflecting time and chance, adapting similar structures to a variety of needs seems to reflect creation.

The same is true of the so-called "gill slits." In the human embryo at one month, there are wrinkles in the skin where the "throat pouches" grow out. Once in a while, one of these pouches will break through, and a child will be born with a small hole in the neck. That's when we find out for sure that these structures are *not* gill slits. If the opening were really part of a gill, if it really were a "throwback to the fish stage," then there would be blood vessels all around it, as if it were going to absorb oxygen from water as a gill does. But there is no such structure. We simply don't have the DNA instructions for forming gills.

Unfortunately, some babies are born with three eyes or one eye. That doesn't mean, of course, that we evolved from something with one eye or three eyes. It's simply a mistake in the normal program for human development, and it emphasizes how perfect our design features and operation must be for life to continue.

The throat (or pharyngeal) grooves and pouches, falsely called "gill slits," are *not* mistakes in human development. They develop into absolutely essential parts of human anatomy. The middle ear canals come from the second pouches, and the parathyroid and thymus glands come from the third and fourth. Without a thymus, we would lose half our immune systems. Without the parathyroids, we would be unable to regulate calcium balance and could not even survive. Another pouch, thought to be vestigial by evolutionists until just recently, becomes a gland that assists in calcium balance. Far from being useless evolutionary vestiges, then, these so-called "gill slits" are quite essential for distinctively human development.

As with yolk sacs, "gill slit" formation represents an ingenious and adaptable solution to a difficult engineering problem. How can a small, round egg cell be turned into an animal or human being with a digestive tube and various organs inside a body cavity? The answer is to have the little ball (or flat sheet in some organisms) "swallow itself," forming a tube which then "buds off" other tubes and pouches. The anterior pituitary, lungs, urinary bladder, and parts of the liver and pancreas develop in this way. In fish, gills develop from such processes, and in human beings, the ear canals, parathyroid, and thymus glands develop. Following DNA instructions in their respective egg cells, fish and human beings each use a similar process to develop their distinctive features. (See Fig. 8.)

What about the "tail"? Some of you have heard that man has a "tail bone" (also called a coccyx), and that the only reason we have it is to remind us that our ancestors had tails. You can test this idea yourself, although I don't recommend it. If you think the coccyx is useless, fall down the stairs and land on it. (Some of you may have actually done that—unintentionally, I'm sure!) What happens? You can't stand up; you can't sit down; you can't lie down; you can't roll over. You can hardly move without pain. In one sense, the coccyx is one of the most important bones in the whole body. It's an important point of muscle attachment required for our distinctive upright posture (and also for defecation, but I'll say no more about that).

So again, far from being a useless evolutionary leftover, the coccyx is quite important in human development. True, the end of the spine sticks out noticeably in a one-month embryo, but that's because muscles and limbs don't develop until stimulated by the spine (see Fig. 8). As the legs develop, they surround and envelop the coccyx, and it winds up inside the body.

Once in a great while a child will be born with a "tail." But, is it really a tail? No, it's not even the coccyx. It doesn't have any bones in it; it doesn't have any nerve cord either. The nervous system starts stretched out open on the back. During development, it rises up in ridges and rolls shut. It starts to "zipper" shut in the middle first, then it zippers toward either end. Once in a while it doesn't go far

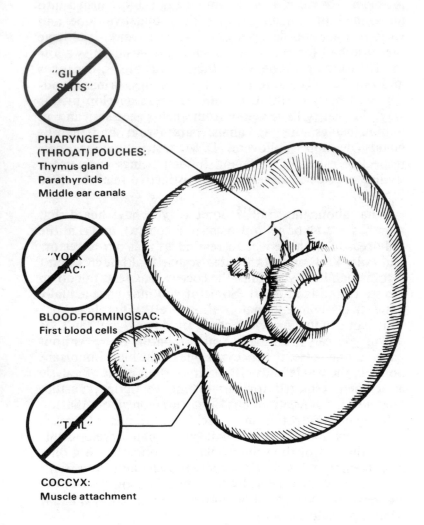

Figure 8. Far from being "useless evolutionary leftovers," the mis-named structures above are absolutely essential for normal human development. Similar structures are used for different functions in other embryos—and we normally consider variation on a theme and multiple uses for a part as evidence of good creative design.

enough, and that produces a serious defect called spina bifida. Sometimes it rolls a little too far. Then the baby will be born—*not* with a tail, but with a fatty tumor. It's just skin and a little fatty tissue, so the doctor can just cut it off. It's not at all like the tail of a cat that has muscle, bones, and nerve, so cutting it off is not complicated. (So far as I know, no one claims that proves we evolved from an animal with a fatty tumor at the end of its spine.) The details of human development are truly amazing. We really ought to stop, take a good look at each other, and congratulate each other that we turned out as well as we did!

Evolutionists used to say that human embryonic development retraced stages in our supposed evolutionary history. That idea, the now defunct "biogenetic law," was summarized in the pithy phrase, "ontogeny recapitulates phylogeny." (Want to sound educated? Just memorize that phrase!) The phrase means that the development of the embryo is supposed to retrace the evolution of its group. As leading anti-creationist Stephen Gould (1980) points out, "the theory of recapitulation . . . should be defunct today," but Dr. Down named a syndrome "Mongoloid idiocy" because he thought it represented a "throwback" to the "Mongolian stage" in human evolution. It was even once believed that the fertilized egg, for example, would represent our one-celled ancestors, sort of the "amoeba stage."

Sure enough, we start as small, round structures looking somewhat like single cells. But notice how superficial that argument is. The evolutionists were just looking at the outside appearance of the egg cell. If we look just on the outside appearance, then maybe we're related to a marble, a beebee, or a ball bearing—they're small, round things! An evolutionist (or anyone else) would respond, of course, "That's crazy. Those things are totally different on the inside from a human egg cell."

But, that's exactly the point. If you take a look on the inside, the "dot" we each start from is totally different from the first cell of every other kind of life. A mouse, an elephant, and a human being are identical in size and shape at the moment of conception. Yet in terms of DNA and protein, right at conception each of these types of life is as totally different chemically as each will ever be structurally. Even by mistake, a human being can't produce a yolk or gills or a tail, because we just don't have, and never had, those DNA instructions.

The human egg cell, furthermore, is not just human, but also a special individual. Eye color, general body size, and perhaps even temperament are already present in DNA, ready to come to visible expression. Embryonic development is not even analogous to evolution, which is meant to indicate a progressive increase in potential. The right Greek word instead would be *entelechy,* which means an unfolding of potential present right from the beginning. That's the kind of development that so clearly requires creative design.

In reviewing the decline and fall of orthodox Darwinism, John Davy (1981) points out that even evolutionists see the need for "theories *of another kind"* (emphasis his) to explain both the origin and development of distinctive "building plans" among organisms. "Instead of seeing animals as collections of devices for survival, we may have to look at them as more like works of art." *Works of art*—that's the way creationists have viewed living beings all along!

Adaptation and Ecology:
The Marvelous Fit of Organisms to Their Environment

We've looked now at molecules, bone patterns, and embryonic development, but the clearest and simplest evidence of creation is "the marvelous fit of organisms to their environment." In the *Scientific American* book, *Evolution,* Harvard evolutionist, Richard Lewontin (1978), says that " . . . the marvelous fit of organisms to their environment . . . was [and I say *is*] the chief evidence of a Supreme Designer." In fact, Lewontin says that organisms "appear to have been carefully and artfully designed." Seeing it himself only as a tough case to be solved in evolutionary theory, Lewontin nevertheless seems to see that our observations of careful and artful design could logically imply creation.

There are literally thousands of examples of the special adaptations that suit each type of organism for its special role in the web of life (Fig. 9). The fantastic features of structure, function, and behavior that make the honeybee so special, for example, are familiar to almost anyone. But then there's the shock-absorbing skull and wrap-around tongue of the flicker woodpecker; the explosive chemical defense system of the bombardier beetle; the navigational skills of migrating reptiles, birds, fish, and mammals; etc., etc. But let me single out one example for now.

There are many large fish with sharp teeth that roam the oceans. But as they feed on smaller fish and shrimp, their mouths begin to accumulate food debris and parasites. Lacking recourse to a toothbrush, how is such a fish going to clean its teeth?

For several kinds of fish, the answer is a visit to the local cleaning station. These are special areas usually marked by the presence of certain shrimp and small, brightly colored fish, such as wrasses and gobis. Often fresh from chasing and eating other small fish and shrimp, a predatory fish may swim over to take its place in line (literally!) at the nearest cleaning station. When its turn comes, it opens its mouth wide, baring the vicious-looking teeth.

You might suspect, of course, that such a sight would frighten off the little cleaner fish and shrimp. But no, into the jaws of death swim the little cleaners. Now even a friendly dog will sometimes snap at you if you try to pick off a tick, and it probably irritates the big fish to have a shrimp crawling around on its tongue and little fish picking off parasites in the soft tissues of the mouth. (Try to imagine shrimp crawling around on *your* tongue!) But the big fish just hovers there, allowing the cleaners to do their work. It even holds its gill chamber open so that the shrimp can crawl around on the gill filaments picking off parasites!

At the end of all this cleaning, the second "miracle" occurs. You might think the fish would respond, "Ah, a clean set of teeth; SNAP, a free meal!" But, no. When the cleaning is done, the big fish lets the little cleaner fish and

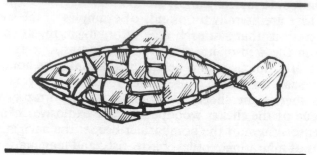

Figure 9. As evolutionist Lewontin acknowledges, living things "appear to have been carefully and artfullly designed." Each type possesses various features complete and well fitted into the whole, like the tiles in an artist's mosaic. Although other animals share such adaptations with the platypus as milk glands, a leathery egg, and echo-location ability, it seems to me that these could be put together into a single fascinating, functioning whole only by creation.

shrimp back out. Then the big fish swims off—and begins hunting again for little fish and shrimp to eat!

The fantastic relationship just described is called *cleaning symbiosis*. Perhaps you have seen cleaner fish in a major public aquarium, or seen pictures of their behavior in television footage or nature magazines. Cleaning symbiosis is a well-known example of mutualism, an intimate relationship of benefit to both types of species involved, in this case, the "cleaner and the cleanee."

Obviously, cleaning symbiosis has survival value for both types of species involved. But does survival value explain the *origin* of this special relationship? Of course not. It makes sense to talk about survival value only *after* a trait or relationship is already in existence.

Question: Did the survival value of this cleaning relationship result from time and chance or from design and creation?

Evolutionists believe that all adaptations begin with time and chance, that is, with random changes in DNA and hereditary traits called mutations. In evolutionary theory, those chance mutations that suit an organism better to its environment are preserved by the process called natural selection. But natural selection can't act until the favored traits arise by mutation, i.e., by time and chance.

Well, what about mutations? Mutations certainly do occur, and they are responsible for perhaps 1500-2000 hereditary defects in human beings alone. But could mutations produce the coordinated set of behavioral adaptations necessary to originate cleaning symbiosis? Here's what two well-known evolutionary biologists have to say about it:

Nobel prize winner Albert Szent-Gyorgyi (1977) writes the following about a relationship much simpler than cleaning symbiosis. He is only talking about how a young herring gull pecks at a red spot on the beak to get the adult to spit up some food (if you'll pardon the example).

He says, "All this may sound very simple, but it involves a whole series of most complicated chain reactions with a horribly complex underlying nervous mechanism . . . . " (It's the same for cleaning symbiosis; the whole behavior pattern of several species of large and small fish and shrimp has to be affected.)

"All this had to be developed simultaneously," he says. It's the same thing for cleaning symbiosis; it's no good if the little fish gets the idea to go into the big fish's mouth before the big fish inherits the final random mutational change to let it back out again! What are the odds of getting all the random mutations required for an advantageous behavioral response at the same time? Szent-Gyorgyi says that as a random mutation, it has the probability of . . . .

What will he say here? The probability of one, that is, a certainty, given natural processes like selection and vast amounts of time? Some low figure like $10^{-3,000,000}$ (odds Huxley gave against the evolution of the horse)? Szent-Gyorgyi says that a coordinated behavioral adaptation, such as cleaning symbiosis, as "random mutation, has the probability of zero." Just zero. Nothing. Its survival value, he says, just can't come about by time and chance and the process of mutation.

Then Szent-Gyorgyi goes on to say, "I am unable to approach this problem without supposing an innate 'drive' in living matter to perfect itself." That innate drive he calls "syntropy," the opposite of "entropy" (the universal law of disorder). In other words, here's a brilliant scientist, and an evolutionist, whose observations of the living world force him to postulate at least an *impersonal creative force.* Here's a scientist who recognizes that creation can be logically inferred from observations of certain kinds of order, even when we don't know who or what the creative agent is.

Garrett Hardin, a noted biologist and textbook author, seems to go even further than this in an old, but timeless, *Scientific American* book on adaptations and ecology, *39 Steps to Biology.* The first section, titled "Fearfully and Wonderfully Made," describes several marvels of adaptation often used as evidence of creation. In the second section, "Nature's Challenges to Evolutionary Theory," Hardin discusses cleaning symbiosis and other remarkable relationships which, he says, " . . . are only a few of the unsolved puzzles facing biologists who are committed to the Darwinian [evolutionary] theory." Then he openly wonders, "Is the [evolutionary] framework wrong?" That is, do our observations of the living world force us, at least for the present, to rule out evolution as an explanation for origins? (See Fig. 10.)

But Hardin doesn't stop there. He goes on to ask, "Was Paley right?" If you're like me, you never heard of William Paley. But Hardin explains. Paley was a thinker in the 18th century who argued that the kind of design we see in the living world points clearly to a designer. Then, the evolutionists came along in the 19th century and argued that they could explain design on the basis of time, chance, and properties of matter that did not require a designer. Now, says Hardin in the 20th century, "Was Paley right" after all? Do the kinds of design features we see in living things point to a designer? And Paley was not thinking of an "impersonal creative force" like Szent-Gyorgyi; he was thinking instead of a personal creator.

Hardin's conclusion? "Think about it!"

Think About It!

"Think about it!" What a sane and yet sensational idea. What a rallying point for both creationists and evolutionists.

The Scopes trial showed it was foolish to teach only creation; is it any wiser to teach only evolution? A detailed doctoral study by Richard Bliss (1978) showed that students using a two-model (creation/evolution) approach to origins showed more improvement in inquiry skills than those using the traditional evolution-only approach. (And, by the way, the two-model students learned evolution concepts better than those taught evolution only.) Furthermore, a two-model approach cannot be accused of indoctrination; can evolution only? Surely the only way students can "think about it" is when they have access to *all* the relevant data and the true academic freedom to explore *both* models of origin.

As Garrett Hardin so perceptively observes, the challenge to evolution does not come simply from a few

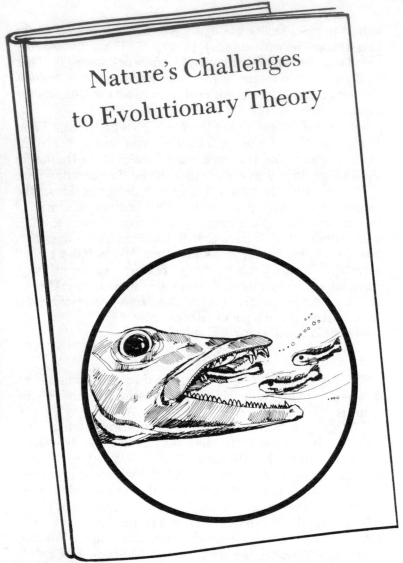

Figure 10. Cleaner fish are described under the heading "Nature's Challenges to Evolutionary Theory" in a *Scientific American* book edited by Garrett Hardin. Even though he's an evolutionist, Hardin asks, "Is the [evolutionary] framework wrong?" Then he goes on to ask, "Was Paley right?" when he said the kind of design we see in the living world requires a designer. Then, in an expression of open-ended fairness everyone can appreciate, Hardin concludes, "Think about it!" *Think about it.*

fanatics. The challenge to evolution comes from the study of nature itself. "Nature's Challenges to Evolutionary Theory," he calls it. Even if various pressure groups (ironically operating under the guise of "academic freedom") succeed in suppressing all views except evolution, the case for creation will still be presented.

The case for creation will be evident in certain special ecological relationships like cleaning symbiosis; in sets of adaptations working together, such as we see in the chemical system of the bombardier beetle (next chapter); and in the fantastic molecular integration within cells, such as the relationship between DNA and protein. Because of the way things have been made, the case for creation will always be present in the subject matter of science itself, especially in lab and field work.

We can distinguish the stone implements produced by human creative effort from those shaped by time, chance, and erosion. Similarly, we can distinguish created relationships among living things, such as those between the cleaner and the one cleaned.

One other special feature of creation is so obvious we often fail to notice it: its beauty. I once took my invertebrate zoology class to hear a lecture on marine life by a scientist who had just returned from a collecting trip to the Philippines. Toward the end of his lecture he described the brightly colored fish he had observed below the 190-foot level. But then he said that at that depth in those waters all wavelengths of light were absorbed except for some blue. In their natural habitat, the fish could not even see their own bright colors, so what possible survival value could the genetic investment in this color have? Then he challenged the students to pose that question to their biology professors.

When my students asked me, I said something like this: We normally expect to find aspects of beauty as well as usefulness in the artifacts of human creation; perhaps we should expect to find beauty in the creation of life as well.

Remember, though, that I'm not trying to convince you of all these things in one short book. I used to teach evolution in university biology classes, and it took me three years to change my thinking from evolution to creation. And let's face it, there is a lot to be said for evolution. In fact, I still present the case for evolution to my classes, then let them hammer me with questions which I answer as an evolutionist. That certainly surprises some of my students, but it stimulates all of them to "think about it."

And that's my purpose in this book—to stimulate your thinking. The case is not all one-sided in favor of creation, but it's certainly not one-sided in favor of evolution, either. When it comes to origins, we can't appeal to direct observation, nor can we run experiments on the past. We're stuck with *circumstantial evidence,* i.e., evidence subject to more than one interpretation. Our goal must be to weigh *all* the relevant evidence, asking ourselves what is the most logical inference from the weight, on balance, of our scientific observations.

The case for creation I've presented so far is based on what we *do know* and *can explain* in the areas of molecular biology, homology, embryology, and certain relationships in ecology. But, what about Darwinian natural selection and the fossil evidence? Well, let's dig in. All you need is an inquiring mind, a sharp eye, and a willing heart. "Think about it." What's the most logical inference from our scientific observations of genetics and the fossil evidence—time, chance, and the evolution of matter, or design and the creation of irreducible properties of organization?

Chapter 3

Darwin and the Nature of Biologic Change

To the intellectual giants who founded the experimental sciences in the 17th and 18th centuries, the evidence of creation seemed clear and convincing. But in 1859 came the publication of Charles Darwin's *Origin of Species*. After biologist Michael Denton identified himself on television (Kelly, 1981) as a sceptic regarding both creation and evolution, the interviewer asked him what he thought the chief impact of Darwin's book had been. After a pause, Denton replied that its chief impact had been to make atheism possible, or at least respectable. The much admired historian and philosopher, Will Durant (1980), said that we are now coming out of a pagan era that began in 1859 with Darwin's *Origin*.

Design Without Creation?

Many people have called Darwin's book second only to the Bible in its influence on man's thinking (and some would put it *first).* In fact, the past 100 years have been called "Darwin's Century." Darwin himself was a cautious scientist, painstaking in his work. But others, especially T. H. Huxley and Herbert Spencer, grabbed Darwin's idea and used it to argue that we could explain design without creation. Darwin's book changed the whole course of history.

Natural Selection

In spite of its revolutionary philosophic impact, Darwin's concept is quite easy to understand. The concept, called natural selection, was based on observations of artificial selection, the results of selective breeding by farmers and animal fanciers. Darwin, for example, referred to all the different breeds of pigeons that had been produced by artificial selection. The ordinary one in Fig. 11 is the wild rock pigeon, the one you often find around city statues and country barns. But all the other birds pictured are just pigeons, too—the fan tail, the one with the neck pouch, etc. All these birds can be bred from the wild rock pigeon, and crossing among the different varieties can lead right back to the wild rock pigeon. Everyone knows, of course, about the results of selective breeding with dogs, cats, cattle, roses, and so on.

"So," Darwin said in effect, "we see what artificial selection by man can do. I believe selection can also happen in nature. After all, there is a constant *'struggle for survival'* because of population growth and limited resources, and certainly each kind can produce many varieties. Therefore, there will be *'survival of the fittest,'* or *natural selection,* of those varieties that fit best into their environment. Given enough generations [time] and the right trait combinations [chance], organisms that seem designed for their environment will simply result from natural selection [natural processes]." Apparent design in nature was not the result of creation, Darwin was saying, but of time, chance, and the properties of matter.

Darwin's argument certainly seems logical. Is there any evidence that Darwin was right? Can nature select as well as man? Answer: There is considerable evidence that Darwin was indeed correct about natural selection.

Perhaps the best example of Darwinian selection is the one that's in all the biology textbooks: the peppered moths. Take a look first at Fig. 12-A, which represents a camera close-up of a tree with some moths on it. How many moths do you see? One is easy to see, and most people see two. (Some claim to see three, but I've never found the third!) At least we can agree that one moth stands out and one is camouflaged.

Presumably that's the way birds saw it, too, back in the 1850's. The darker moth stood out, but the lighter one was camouflaged against the mottled gray lichen that encrusted

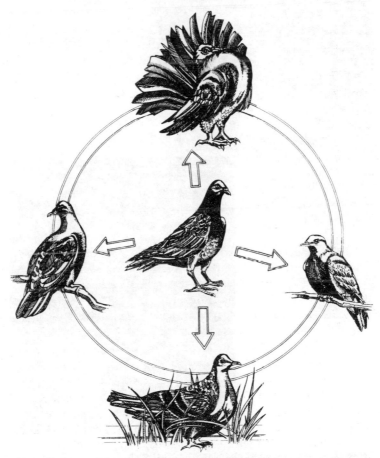

Figure 11. By artificial selection, all the "fancy" varieties of pigeons above have been bred from the common wild rock pigeon, and they can be bred back to the wild rock pigeon (just as special varieties of dogs and cats can be bred from and to the "mongrel" types). Darwin used *artificial selection*, selective breeding by man, as a model for *natural selection*, survival of the fittest selected by nature in the struggle for life. But does natural selection lead to evolution, or point back to creation?

Figure 12. "Evolution going on today" . . . that's what many people say about the peppered moth. Because of a change in the color of their background, the light forms so common in 1850 (well-camouflaged in the top photo) lost out in the struggle for life to the more "fit" variety (camouflaged by the dark background in the bottom photo). By 1950, most of the moths were the dark (melanic) variety. Can you accept that as "proof of evolution," or do you wonder if there are boundary conditions that limit the amount of change natural selection can produce?

the trees back then. As a result, birds ate mostly dark moths and light moths made up over 98% of the population.

But then pollution killed the lichen on the trees, revealing the dark color of the bark. As a result, the dark moths were more camouflaged than the light ones. The moths themselves didn't change; there were always dark moths and always light moths from the earliest observations. But the environment changed, so that the dark ones were better camouflaged. Thus, the dark ones had a better chance of surviving and leaving more offspring that grew into dark moths in succeeding generations. Sure enough, just as Darwin would have predicted, the population shifted. The "dark environment" just naturally selected the dark moths as more likely to survive and reproduce. By the 1950's the population was over 98% dark colored—proof positive of "evolution going on today." At least that's the way it's stated in many biology books, and that's what I used to tell my biology students.

When I was an evolutionist, sometimes an unsuspecting student would approach me and say, "Look, if evolution is true, why don't we see it going on today?" And I would say, "Evolution going on today? Glad you brought that up! It just so happens that we have a perfect example of evolution in action." Then I would launch into the peppered moth story. Those moths are *the* showcase for evolution. Over twenty years after they first became famous, they were chosen, for example, as the frontispiece for Lewontin's article on adaptation in the 1978 *Scientific American* book, *Evolution*.

Well, the peppered moths *do* seem to provide strong evidence of natural selection. But is that evidence of evolution? Notice I've changed the question. That's a key point. First I asked if there was any evidence that Darwin was correct about natural selection. The answer quite simply is, "Yes, there is." But now I'm asking a radically different question, "Is there any evidence for evolution?" Many people say, "Isn't that the same question? Aren't natural selection and evolution the same thing?" Answer: NO, absolutely not.

When someone asks if I believe in evolution, I'll often say, "Why yes, no, no, yes, no." The answer really depends on what the person means by evolution. In one sense, evolution means "change." Do I believe in change? Yes, indeed—I've got some in my pocket.

But change isn't the real question, of course. Change is just as much a part of the creation model as the evolution model. The question is, what kind of change do we see: change only within type (creation) or change also from one type to others (evolution)?

Take a look again at the peppered moth example (Fig. 12). What did we start with? Dark and light varieties of the peppered moth, species *Biston betularia*. After 100 years of natural selection, what did we end up with? Dark and light varieties of the peppered moth, species *Biston betularia*. All that changed was the percentage of moths in the two categories—that is, just variation within type. According to creationists, natural selection is just one of the processes that operate in our present world to insure that the created types can indeed spread throughout the earth in all its ecologic and geographic variety.

As a matter of fact, 24 years before Darwin's publication, a scientist named Edward Blyth published the concept of natural selection in the context of creation. He saw it as a process that adapted varieties of the created types to changing environments. A book reviewer once asked, rather naively, if creationists could accept the concept of natural selection. The answer is, "Of course. *We* thought of it first" (See Leslie, 1984).

But if natural selection is such a profound idea, and Blyth published it before Darwin, then why isn't Blyth's name a household word? Perhaps because he was a creationist. It was not principally the scientific applications of natural selection that attracted attention in 1859; it was its presumed philosophic and religious implications.

Evolutionists were not content to treat natural selection as simply an observable ecological process. They (T. H. Huxley and Herbert Spencer much more than Darwin) insisted on making natural selection the touchstone of a new philosophy, a "religion without revelation," as Julian Huxley later called it. For them, as for many others, the real significance of the Darwinian revolution was religious and philosophic, not scientific. These early evolutionists were basically anti-creationists who wanted to explain design without creation.

But in spite of what might be claimed, natural selection has been observed to produce only variation within type— merely shifts in populations, for example, to ones with greater percentages of darker moths, flies resistant to DDT, or bacteria resistant to antibiotics. Evolution means more than change from moth to moth, fly to fly, or bacterium to bacterium. Real evolution, "mega- or macro-" evolution, means change from one type to another—"Fish to Philosopher," as the title of Homer Smith's book puts it, or "Molecules to Man," the subtitle of the government-funded BSCS "blue version" high school biology textbook.

But I must admit that there is a potential connection between observed natural selection within types and hypothetical evolution from one type to another. That connection is called "extrapolation," following a trend to its conclusion. Scientists extrapolate from population records, for example, to predict changes in the world population. If world population growth continues at the rate observed in the '60's, statisticians say, then the world population by 2000 A.D. would be over 6 billion. Similarly, if natural selection continues over very long periods of time, evolutionists say, the same process that changes moths from mostly light to mostly dark forms will gradually change fish to philosophers or molecules to men.

Now there's nothing wrong with extrapolation in principle. But there are things to watch for in practice. For example, simple extrapolation would suggest a population of a quadrillion by 3000 A.D. But, of course, there will come a point when the earth is simply not big enough to support any more people. In other words, there are limits, or boundary conditions, to logical extrapolation.

Consider my jogging (or should I say "slogging") times. Starting at an embarrassing 12 minutes per mile, I knocked a minute off each week—a mile in 11 minutes, then 9, 8, 7, 6, 5, 4, 3, 2, 1. Wait a minute! As you well know, I reached my limit long before the one-minute mile! (Just where, I'll keep secret!) This is an embarrassing example, but it makes an important point: no scientist would consider extrapolation without also considering the logical limits or boundary conditions of that extrapolation.

Evolutionists are aware of the problem. In their textbook, *Evolution,* the late Theodosius Dobzhansky (1977) and three other famous evolutionists distinguish between *SUBspeciation* and *TRANSspeciation.* ("Sub" is essentially variation within species, and "trans" is change from one species to another.) The authors state their belief that one can "extrapolate" from variation within species to evolution between species. But they also admit that some of their fellow evolutionists believe that such extrapolation goes beyond all logical limits, like my running a one-minute mile.

What does the evidence suggest? Can evolution from "molecules to men" be extrapolated from selection among dark and light moths? Or, are there boundary conditions and logical limits to the amount of change time, chance, and natural selection can produce?

The answer seems to be: "Natural selection, yes; evolution, no." As it turns out, there are several factors that sharply limit the amount of change that can be produced by time, chance, and Darwinian natural selection. For exquisite detail on *The Natural Limits to Biological Change*, see Lester and Bohlin, 1984.)

Perhaps the biggest problem for evolutionists is "the marvelous fit of organisms to their environment." As I mentioned in the first chapter, an adaptation often involves a whole group of traits working together, and none of the individual pieces has any survival value ("Darwinian fitness") until the whole set is functioning together.

Take the flicker woodpecker, for example (Bliss, 1985). Here's a bird that makes its living banging its head into trees. Whatever gave it the idea to do that in the first place? Was it frustration from losing the worm to the early bird? How did banging its head into trees increase its likelihood for survival—until *after* it had accumulated (by chance?) a thick skull with shock absorbing tissues, muscles, etc.! And what would be the survival value of all these features (and how could they build up in the population) until *after* the bird started banging its head into trees?

And what about the beetle under the bark? The beetle is surely aware of all the woodpecker's pounding. So, while the woodpecker is pounding, the beetle is crawling further down its hole or digging another hole. So, *before* any of the drilling adaptations can have any fitness, the woodpecker must have a long, sticky tongue to reach what it somehow knows is good food under that tough tree bark.

But if you have a long, sticky tongue and you're a bird, where do you put the long tongue? For the woodpecker, the answer is to wrap its tongue under the skin and bring it clear around the head and insert it in the right nostril! Now, if you start as an ordinary bird with a short tongue and no tongue sheath, what would you do in the intermediate states—perhaps, for example, with a tongue too long for the bill but too short to catch the beetles you've just been beating your head into trees to catch?

The example may seem humorous, but the point is serious: How can Darwinian fitness be used to explain traits with many interdependent parts when none of the separate parts has any survival value? Remember the cleaner fish from the first chapter? There's certainly no survival value in a small fish swimming into a large fish's mouth on the hope that the big fish has somehow evolved the desire to let it back out! The situation is even more dangerous for the famous "bombardier beetle."

The bombardier is an ordinary-looking beetle, but it has an ingenious chemical defense mechanism. Imagine: Here comes a mean ol' beetle eater, a toad, creeping up behind the seemingly unsuspecting beetle. Just as he gets ready to flash out that long, sticky tongue, the beetle swings its cannons around, and "boom!" It blasts the toad in the face with hot noxious gases at 100 °C (212 °F), the boiling point of water. Now, that doesn't actually kill the toad, but it sure kills his taste for beetles! In the next scene, the toad is dragging his tongue across the sand trying to get that stuff off his tongue. (There are pictures of this process, diagrammed in Fig. 13, in the Museum at the Institute for Creation Research in San Diego.)

Successful firing of the bombardier beetle's cannons requires two chemicals (hydrogen peroxide and hydroquinones), two enzymes and enzyme blockers, pressure tanks, and a whole series of nerve and muscle attachments for aim and control. Try to imagine all those parts accumulating by time, chance, and natural selection? One crucial mistake, of course, and "boom!" the bombardier beetle blows *itself* up, and there's surely no evolutionary future in that!

The functioning cannons have survival value, of course, but explaining their origin by natural selection requires that each step in the process has some survival value. Otherwise, the genes for those parts cannot build up in the population.

Creationists and evolutionists agree that adaptations such as the woodpecker's skull, cleaning symbiosis, and the bombardier beetle's cannon all have survival value. The question, then, is not one of survival value or fitness, but rather, how did these adaptations originate: by time and chance or by design and creation? When it comes to adaptations that require several traits all depending on one another, the more logical inference from the evidence seems to be creation.

Darwin himself was acutely aware of this evidence of creation and the problem it posed for his theory. In a chapter of *Origin of Species* called "Difficulties With the Theory," he included traits that depend on separately meaningless parts. Consider the human eye with the different features required to focus at different distances, to accommodate different amounts of light, and to correct for the "rainbow effect." Regarding the origin of the eye, Darwin wrote these words:

> To suppose that the eye, [with so many parts all working together] . . . could have been

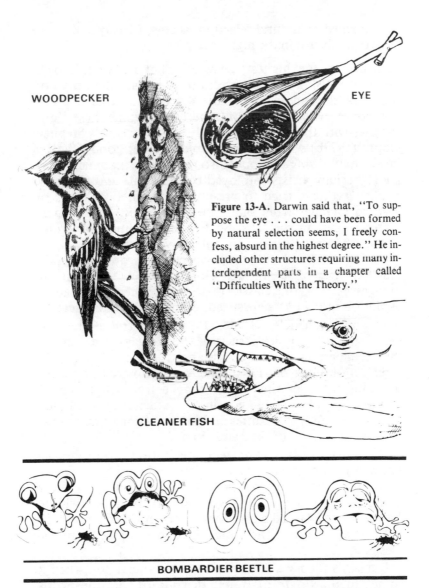

WOODPECKER

EYE

Figure 13-A. Darwin said that, "To suppose the eye . . . could have been formed by natural selection seems, I freely confess, absurd in the highest degree." He included other structures requiring many interdependent parts in a chapter called "Difficulties With the Theory."

CLEANER FISH

BOMBARDIER BEETLE

Figure 13-B. Before it can have any survival value, every part of a bombardier beetle's "cannon" must be in place, and the same is true for the woodpecker's set of "drilling tools" and the "nerve wiring" for cleaning fish behavior. Evolutionist Lewontin says such "perfection of structure" *was,* and I say *is,* "the chief evidence of a Supreme Designer."

formed by natural selection, seems, I freely confess, absurd in the highest degree.

"Absurd in the highest degree." That's Darwin's own
opinion of using natural selection to explain the origin of
traits that depend on many parts working together.
Modern evolutionists continue to recognize these "difficulties with the theory" of evolution. Harvard's Stephen
Gould (1977b) writes, for example, "What good is half a
jaw or half a wing?" Gould also recognizes that many people (especially artists employed by museums and textbook
publishers) have tried to present a hypothetical series of
gradual changes from one type to another. So he adds,
"These tales, in the 'Just-So Stories' tradition of evolutionary natural history, do not prove anything . . . concepts salvaged only by facile speculation do not appeal
much to me." Even though Gould is an evolutionist, he
recognizes that the classic textbook concept of gradual
evolution rests on "facile speculation" and not on facts.

In another article, Gould (1979a) points out that the
perfection of complex structures has always been one of
the strongest evidences of creation. After all, he says,
"perfection need not have a history," no trial and error
development over time from chance trait combinations
and selection. So, Gould continues, evidence for evolution
must be sought in "oddities and imperfections" that clearly show the effects of time and chance.

But creationists recognize imperfection, too. We acknowledge that the effects of "time and chance" have indeed distorted creation. Imperfection, then, is not the
issue; perfection is. And evolutionists from Darwin to
Lewontin and Gould admit that "perfection of structure"
has always been "the chief evidence of a Supreme
Designer."

Darwin's theory also points us back to creation when it
comes to the *origin* of traits. In spite of the title of his
book, *Origin of Species,* the one thing Darwin never really
dealt with was the *origin* of species. That is, he never explained the origin of the truly new traits needed to produce
a truly new type of organism, something more than just a

variation of some existing type. There are many other logical limits to extrapolation from natural selection to evolution, but the simplest is this: natural selection can't explain the origin of traits.

Take the famous example of "Darwin's finches" (Fig. 14). On the Galapagos Islands about 600 miles west of Ecuador, Darwin observed a variety of finches, some with small beaks for catching insects, others with large beaks for crushing seeds, and one with the ability to use spines to pry insects from their burrows. How did Darwin explain the "origin" of these various finches? Exactly the same way a creationist would. He saw finches with variation in beak type on the South American mainland and presumed these finches may have reached the islands on a vegetation mat or something similar. The ones with seed-crushing beaks survived where seeds were the major food source, and those with insect-catching beaks out-reproduced others where insects were the major source of food. *Given* finches with a variety of beak types, then, natural selection helps us to explain how and where different varieties survive as they spread throughout the earth. That, of course, is just what a creationist would say.

Natural selection works great—it helps us explain how and where traits survive—**if** you have adapted or adaptable traits to start with. In his article on "Adaptation" in the *Scientific American* book, *Evolution,* Lewontin emphasizes this point over and over again.

> . . . evolution cannot be described as a process of adaptation because all organisms are already adapted . . . .
>
> . . . adaptation leads to natural selection, natural selection does not necessarily lead to greater adaptation.

That is, adaptation has to come *first, before* natural selection can act. Natural selection obviously cannot explain the origin of traits or adaptations if the traits have to be there first.

Lewontin recognizes that this simple (but crucial) point is often overlooked, so he gives an example. As a region

Figure 14. "Darwin's Finches." Darwin explained the location of finches with different beak types on the Galapagos Islands the same way a creationist would—by starting with a population of finches with variation in beak type. In fact, the creationist Edward Blyth published the concept of natural selection 24 years before Darwin did, and he used it to help explain the process by which created types spread throughout the different environments on earth.

becomes drier, he says, plants can respond by developing a deeper root system or a thicker cuticle (waxy coating) on the leaves, but *"only if* their gene pool contains genetic variation for root length or cuticle thickness." (Emphasis added.) Here again, the genes for deep roots and thick waxy coats must be present among the genes of a type *before* natural selection can select them. And if the genes are already there, we are talking only about variation within type—i.e., creation, not evolution. As creationists were saying even before Darwin's time, natural selection does *not* explain the *origin* of species or traits, but only their *preservation.*

Lewontin is an evolutionist and outspoken anti-creationist, but he honestly recognizes the same limitations of natural selection that creation scientists do:

> . . . natural selection operates essentially to enable the organisms to *maintain* their state of adaptation rather than to improve it. [Emphasis added.]

Natural selection does not lead to continual improvement (evolution); it only maintains features organisms already have (creation). Lewontin also notes that extinct species seem to have been every bit as fit to survive as modern ones, so he adds:

> . . . natural selection over the long run does *not* seem to improve a species' chances of survival, but simply enables it to "track," or keep up with, the constantly changing environment. [Emphasis added.]

It seems to me that natural selection works only because each type was created with sufficient variety to migrate over the earth in all its ecologic and geographic variety. Without realizing it at the time, Darwin actually discovered important evidence pointing to *creation.*

Pangenes: Use and Disuse

Darwin called natural selection "the preservation of favored races," and he recognized that selection alone could not explain origin. When it came to the actual origin of new traits, Darwin wrote that it was "from use and disuse, from the direct and indirect actions of the environment" that new traits arose.

About 40 years before Darwin. a famous French evolutionist, Jean Lamarck, argued for this kind of evolution based on the inheritance of traits acquired by use and disuse. Most books on the subject hint that we should laugh at Lamarck—but Darwin believed exactly the same thing.

Consider the supposed origin of the giraffe. According to both Darwin and Lamarck, the story begins back on the African prairies a long time ago. Because of prolonged drought, the prairie dried up. But there were green leaves up in the trees, and some of the animals started stretching their necks to reach them. As a result, their necks got a little longer (Fig. 15). Now that could be partly true. If you really work at it hard enough and long enough, you could add a little bit to your height. People used to do that to get into the army or some special service where you have to be a certain height.

The problem, however, is that the offspring of "stretched" parents start off just as small as all the others. The long neck could not be passed on to the next generation. Darwin didn't know about the mechanism of heredity. He thought that at reproduction each organ produced *"pangenes"* that would collect in the blood and flow to the reproductive organs. So, a bigger neck made more neck pangenes. Some people still believe this sort of concept. You've probably run into people who say, for instance, that people will eventually have bigger heads because we think a lot, and no toes because we wear shoes all the time.

Darwin even believed that pangenes could be transferred from the male's semen into the female's body, where they might affect the traits of later offspring. That's how Darwin explained the offspring of Lord Morton's mare. Faint forequarter striping showed up in the animal produced when the mare was mated with a quagga, but the striping continued to show up when the mare was later mated to a stripeless Arabian. More of the story is told by Stephen Gould (1981a) in an article which, like most of his recent articles, is intended to put creationists in their place. But

Figure 15. For the *origin* of new traits, Darwin (like Lamarck) resorted to "use and disuse" and the inheritance of acquired characteristics. Giraffes got longer necks, for example, because their ancestors stretched for leaves in trees, then passed on more neck "pangenes" to their offspring. This idea of "progress through effort" contributed to the early popularity of evolution, but has since been discarded.

the "flimsy facts" he cites, like pangenesis, are those that reflect evolutionary misconceptions. (He also describes how evolutionists believed for years that a fossil oyster, *Gryphaea,* became extinct by coiling itself shut—until someone finally noticed that it was only a bit of mud wedged between the coil and top shell on the single specimen that had kept its "lid" closed.)

Science has since disproven these "flimsy facts" of early evolutionary thought, but back in Darwin's time, pangenes captured people's imagination probably even more than natural selection did. To some, Darwin's original theory of evolution suggested continual progress. How do you make something happen? By use and disuse. If you want to get smarter, use your brain, and both you and your children will be smarter. If you want to be strong, use your muscles, and not only will you get stronger, but so will your children.

Well, almost unfortunately, that's not the modern theory of evolution. The use-disuse theory doesn't work and had to be discarded. A man named Weismann, for example, cut off the tails of mice for twenty-some generations—only to find that baby mice were still born with tails. Traits acquired by use and disuse just don't affect heredity.

Mutations

The modern evolutionist is called a *neo-Darwinian.* He still accepts Darwin's ideas about natural selection, but something new (neo-) has been added. The modern evolutionist believes that new traits come about by chance—by random changes in genes called "mutations" and *not* by use and disuse.

Almost everyone has heard about mutations from Saturday morning cartoons or horror movies, if nowhere else. In those flicks, some atomic disaster produces people with gnarled skin, one big bulging eye, and other "new traits." In the real world, mutations are responsible for a number of genetic defects, including hemophilia (bleeder's disease), loss of protective color in the skin and eyes, and certain kinds of cancer and brain malfunction.

We have abundant evidence that various kinds of radiations and certain chemicals can indeed produce mutations, and mutations in reproductive cells can be passed on to future generations. Fig. 16 shows some of the changes that have been brought about in fruit fly wings because of mutations: shorter wings, very short wings, curled wings, spread-apart wings, miniature wings, wings without cross-veins. My genetics students at Christian Heritage College work with these fruit flies each year, crossing different ones and working out inheritance patterns.

Then there's the flu virus. Why haven't we ever been able to solve the flu problem? Part of the problem is that this year's vaccine and your own antibodies are only good against last year's flu. (They don't usually tell you that when you get the shot, but it's already out of date.) The smallpox virus has the common decency to stay the same year in and year out, so once you're vaccinated or build up an immunity, that's it. But the flu virus mutates quite easily, so each year its proteins are slightly different from last year's. They are still flu viruses, but they don't quite fit our antibodies, so we have to build up our immunity all over again. When it recombines with animal viruses (on the average of once every ten years), the problem is even worse.

Mutations are certainly real. They have profound effects on our lives. And, according to the neo-Darwinian evolutionists, mutations are the raw material for evolution.

But is that possible? Can mutations produce real evolutionary changes? Don't make any mistakes here. Mutations are real; they're something we observe; they do make changes in traits. But the question remains: do they produce *evolutionary* changes? Do they really produce *new* traits? Do they really help to explain that postulated change from molecules to man, or fish to philosopher?

The answer seems to be: "Mutations, yes; evolution, no." In the last analysis, mutations really don't help evolutionary theory at all, for three major reasons.

(1) *Mathematical challenges.* Problem number one is the mathematical one. I won't dwell on this one, because it's written up in many books and widely acknowledged by evolutionists themselves as a serious problem for their theory.

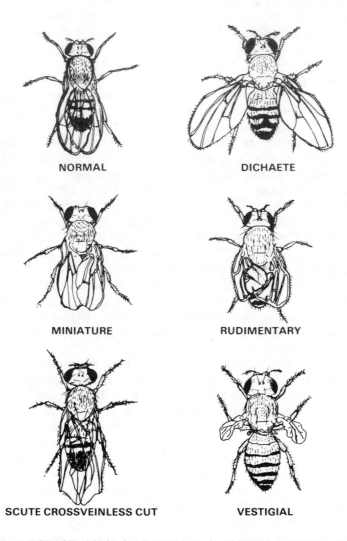

NORMAL

DICHAETE

MINIATURE

RUDIMENTARY

SCUTE CROSSVEINLESS CUT

VESTIGIAL

Figure 16. Mutations are random changes in genes (DNA), usually caused by radiation. The mutations in the wings above were produced by X-raying fruit flies. According to the modern, *neo-Darwinian* view, mutations are the source of new traits for evolution, and selection culls out the fittest combinations that are first produced just by chance. Mutations certainly occur, but are there limits to extrapolating from mutational changes to evolutionary changes (e.g., "fish to philosopher")?

Fortunately, mutations are very rare. They occur on an average of perhaps once in every ten million duplications of a DNA molecule (10^7, a one followed by 7 zeroes). That's fairly rare. On the other hand, it's not *that* rare. Our bodies contain nearly 100 trillion cells (10^{14}). So the odds are quite good that we have a couple of cells with a mutated form of almost any gene. A test tube can hold millions of bacteria, so again, the odds are quite good that there will be mutant forms among them.

The mathematical problem for evolution comes when you want a *series* of *related* mutations. The odds of getting two mutations that are related to one another is the product of the separate probabilities: $10^7 \times 10^7$, or 10^{14}. That's a 1 followed by 14 zeroes, a hundred trillion. Any two mutations might produce no more than a fly with a wavy edge on a bent wing. That's a long way from producing a truly new structure, and certainly a long way from changing a fly into some new kind of organism. You need more mutations for that. So, what are the odds of getting three mutations in a row? That's one in a billion trillion (10^{21}). All of a sudden the ocean isn't big enough to hold enough bacteria to make it likely for you to find a bacterium with three simultaneous or sequential related mutations.

What about trying for four related mutations? 10^{28}. All of a sudden, the earth isn't big enough to hold enough organisms to make that very likely. And we're only talking about four mutations. It would take many more than that to change a fish into a philosopher, or even a fish into a frog. Four mutations don't even make a start toward real evolution. But even at this point some evolutionists have given up the classic idea of evolution, because it just plainly doesn't work.

It was at this level (just four related mutations) that microbiologists gave up on the idea that mutations could explain why some bacteria were resistant to four different antibiotics at the same time. The odds against the mutation explanation were simply too great, so they began to look for another mechanism—and they found it. First of all, using cultures that are routinely kept for long periods of time, they found out that bacteria were resistant to antibiotics, even *before* the antibiotics were "invented." Genetic variability was "built right into" the bacteria. Did the nonresistant varieties get resistant by mutation? No. Resistant forms were already present. Bacteria have little rings of DNA, called plasmids, that they trade around among themselves, and they passed on their resistance to antibiotics in that way. It wasn't mutation at all—just ordinary recombination and variation within type.

Contrary to popular opinion, then, drug resistance in bacteria does *not* demonstrate evolution. It doesn't even demonstrate the production of favorable mutations. It does demonstrate natural selection (or a sort of artificial selection in this case), but only selection among already existing variations within a type. It also demonstrates that when the odds that a particular process will produce a given effect get too low, good scientists normally look for a better explanation.

At this point, evolutionists often say, as George Wald did, that "Time is the hero of the plot." That's what I used to say to my students. "Sure, the odds are low, but there's all that time—nearly 5 billion years!" But 5 billion years is only about 10^{17} seconds, and the whole universe contains fewer than 10^{80} atoms. So even by the wildest "guesstimates," the universe isn't old enough or big enough to reach odds like the 1 in $10^{3,000,000}$ that Huxley, an evolutionist, estimated as the odds against the evolution of the horse.

Back in 1967, a prestigious group of internationally known biologists and mathematicians gathered at the Wistar Institute to consider *Mathematical Challenges to the Neo-Darwinian Interpretation of Evolution*. (See Moorhead and Kaplan, 1967.) All present were evolutionists, and they agreed, as the preface clearly states, that no one would be questioning evolution itself. The only question was, could mutations serve as the basis—with natural selection—as a mechanism for evolutionary change? The answer of the mathematicians: No. Just plain **no**.

Emotions ran high. After a particularly telling paper by Marcel Shutzenberger of the University of Paris, the chairman of the gathering, C. H. Waddington, said, "Your argument is simply that life must have come about by special creation!" The stenographer records, "Schutzenberger: No! Voices: No!" Anything but creation; it wasn't even fair (in spite of the evidence?) to bring up the word.

Dr. Waddington later called himself a "post-neo-Darwinist"—someone who believes in evolution, but who also believes that mutation-selection cannot explain how evolution can occur. Many research evolutionists (but not many textbook writers or teachers) recognize the need for a new generation of evolutionists to forge the "post-neo-Darwinian synthesis" (Felsenstein, 1978, and Gould, 1980a).

Scientists, of course, have considerable respect for mathematics, and the mathematical challenges to mutation-selection are forcing revisions in neo-Darwinian thinking, including discussion of what Gliedman (1982) calls "miracle mutations."

In his chapter "Beyond the Reach of Chance," (Denton (1985) discusses attempts to simulate evolutionary processes on computers. He concludes with these strong words:

> "If complex computer programs cannot be changed by random mechanisms, then surely the same must apply to the genetic programmes (sic) of living organisms. *The fact that systems in every way analogous to living organisms cannot undergo evolution by pure trial and error* [i.e., mutation and selection] and that their functional distribution invariably conforms to an improbable discontinuum *comes, in my opinion, very close to a formal disproof of the whole Darwinian paradigm of nature.* By what strange capacity do living organisms *defy the laws of chance* which are apparently obeyed by all analogous complex systems?" (Emphasis added).

Most gratifyingly, Denton (1985) seems to look beyond the merely negative insufficiency of chance to glimpse a solution to "The Puzzle of Perfection," as he calls it, in the "design hypothesis:"

"It is the sheer universality of perfection, the fact that everywhere we look, we find an elegance and ingenuity of an absolutely transcending quality, which so mitigates against the idea of chance.... In practically every field of fundamental biological research ever-increasing levels of design and complexity are being revealed at an ever-accelerating rate. The credibility of natural selection is weakened, therefore, not only by the perfection we have already glimpsed but by the expectation of further as yet undreamt of depths of ingenuity and complexity" (p. 342).

Unfortunately, we also have evidence that the transcendent ingenuity and design Denton sees deeply has been marred and scarred. In that sense, mathematics isn't even the most serious challenge to using mutations as the basis for evolution.

(2) *Upward or downward?* Even more serious is the fact that mutations are "going the wrong way" as far as evolution is concerned. Almost every mutation we know of is identified by the disease or abnormality that it causes. Creationists use mutations to explain the origin of parasites and disease, the origin of hereditary defects, and the loss of traits. In other words, time, chance, and random changes do just what we normally expect: tear things up and make matters worse. Using mutations to explain the *breakdown* of existing genetic order (creation) is quite the opposite of using mutations to explain the *build up* of genetic order (evolution). Clearly creation is the most direct inference from the effects of mutations that scientists actually observe.

By producing defects or blocking the normal function of certain genes, mutations have introduced numerous genetic abnormalities into the human population. The hemophilia (bleeder's disease) that afflicted the royal houses of Europe may have arisen as a mutant of a clotting factor gene in Queen Victoria, for example, and the dread Tay-Sach's Disease may have arisen in Czechoslavakia in the 1920's as a mutation in the gene for producing an enzyme crucial to brain function.

Some people like to call mutations "the means of creation." But mutations don't create; they corrupt. Both logically and often observationally, as in the examples above, the ordered state must come before mutations can disorder it. Mutations are real, all right, but they point not to creation, but to a corruption of the created order by time and chance.

As a matter of fact, human beings are now subject to over 1500 mutational disorders. Fortunately, we don't show as many defects as we carry. The reason they don't show up is that we each have two sets of genes; one set of genes from our mothers and another set from our fathers. The bad genes we inherit from our mother's side are usually covered up by our father's genes, and vice versa. We can see what is likely to happen when an animal is born with only one set of genes. Fig. 17, based on a description in a genetics textbook, represents a turkey that was hatched from an unfertilized egg, so it had just one set of chromosomes. The poor bird couldn't hold its head up; instead, it bobbed up and down from a neurological disorder. The feathers were missing in patches, and it finally had to be transferred to a germ-free chamber because its resistance to disease was so low.

Now here's the basis for a good Alfred Hitchcock horror movie. Picture a mirror at the end of a dark hall. You claw your way through the spider webs to reach the mirror, and then you press a button. The mirror then splits you in two halves, so you can see what you would look like if you had only your mother's genes or only your father's genes. In the next scene, you're writhing there in agony, your hair turning white as you fall over backward and die of fright!

Unfortunately, that picture exaggerates only slightly what mutations have done to human beings and to the various types of plants and animals, as well. If it weren't for having two sets of genes, few of us would be able to survive.

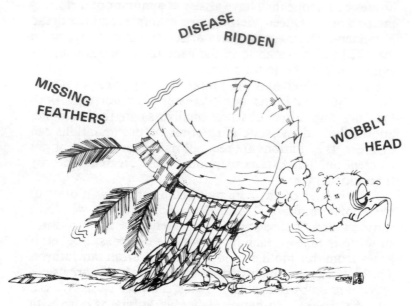

Figure 17. Mutations are mostly harmful, and, as time goes on, they impose an increasingly heavy *"genetic burden"* on a species. The turkey above, lacking a second set of genes to mask its hereditary defects, could scarcely survive. Creationists use mutations to help explain the origin of parasites and disease. Some evolutionists still believe that time, chance, and occasional favorable mutations provide the raw material for "upward-onward" progress, but the "post-neo-Darwinists" are looking for other means to explain evolution.

Evolutionists recognize, of course, the problem of trying to explain "onward and upward" evolution on the basis of mutations that are harmful at least 1,000 times more often than they are helpful. No evolutionist I know believes that standing in front of X-ray machines would eventually improve human beings. No evolutionist argues that destruction of the earth's ozone layer is good because it increases mutation rates and, therefore, speeds up evolution. Evolutionists know that decrease in the ozone layer will increase mutation rates, but they, like everyone else, recognize that this will lead only to increased skin cancer and to other harmful changes. Perhaps a helpful change might occur, but it would be drowned in the sea of harmful changes.

Because harmful mutations so greatly outnumber any helpful ones, it's considered unwise nowadays (and illegal in many states) to marry someone too closely related to you. Why? Because you double the odds, on the average, that bad genes will show up. By the way, you also increase the odds of bringing out really excellent trait combinations. But did you ever hear anybody say, "Don't marry your first cousin or you'll have a genius for a child?" They don't usually say that, because the odds of something bad happening are far, far, far, far, far, greater.

That would not have been a problem, by the way, shortly after creation. Until mutations had a chance to accumulate in the human population, no such risk of bad combinations would exist. Mutations are often carried as "hidden genes" (recessives) that are difficult to eliminate by selection, so they tend to build up to a certain point (mutational equilibrium). The buildup of mutations with time poses a serious problem for plants and animals, as well as human beings.

Geneticists, even evolutionary geneticists, refer to the problem as *"genetic load"* or *"genetic burden."* In their textbook on evolution, Dobzhansky, *et al* (1977) state clearly that the term is meant to imply a burden that "weighs down" a species and lowers its genetic quality. In an article paradoxically titled "The Mechanisms of Evolution," Francisco Ayala (1978) defines a mutation as "an error" in DNA. Then he explains that inbreeding has revealed that mutations in fruit flies have produced "extremely short wings, deformed bristles, blindness, and other serious defects." Does that sound like "the raw material for evolution?"

It's not that beneficial mutations are theoretically impossible. Bacteria that lose the ability to digest certain sugars, for example, can regain that ability by mutation. That's no help to evolution, since the bacterium only gets back to where it started, but at least the mutant is helpful.

Actually, only three evolutionists have ever given me an example of a beneficial mutation. It was the same example all three times: sickle-cell anemia. Sickle-cell anemia is a disease of red blood cells. Why would anyone call that a beneficial mutation? Well, in certain parts of Africa, the

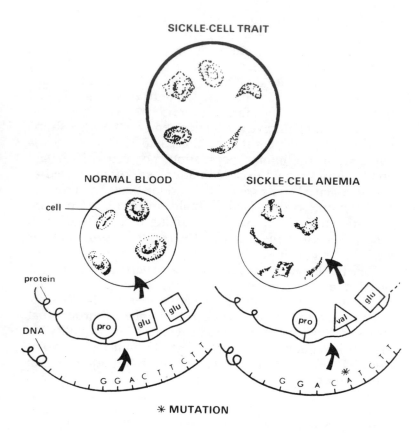

Figure 18. "Sickle-cell anemia" is often given as an example of a favorable mutation, because people carrying sickle-cell hemoglobin in their red blood cells (Ss) are resistant to malaria. But the price for this protection is high—25% of the children of carriers will probably die of the anemia (ss), and another 25% are subject to malaria. The gene will automatically be selected where the death rate from malaria is high, but evolutionists themselves admit that short term advantages—all that natural selection favors—can produce "mischievous results" detrimental to long-term survival. What do you think? Is sickle-cell anemia a "mischievous result," or a good example of evolutionary progress? (Drawing after Parker, Reynolds, and Reynolds. 1977. *Heredity*. 2nd ed. Educational Methods, Inc., Chicago.)

death rate from malaria is over 30%. Malaria is caused by a tiny, one-celled organism that gets inside the red blood cells and eats up the hemoglobin. Now that particular germ doesn't like sickle-cell hemoglobin. Carriers of one sickle-cell gene produce about half normal and half sickle-cell hemoglobin, and the malaria germ leaves them alone, too. So, carriers don't get malaria. But the cost is high: 25% of the children of carriers die of sickle-cell anemia. If you want to call that a good mutation, you're welcome to it. It seems doubtful to me that real improvement of human beings would result from accumulating that kind of "beneficial" mutant, and certainly hemoglobin's ability to carry oxygen was not improved.

The gene for sickle-cell anemia has built up to high levels in certain African populations, not because it is "beneficial" in some abstract sense, but simply because the death rate from anemia in those areas is less than the death rate from malaria. Natural selection is a "blind" process that automatically accumulates genes for short-term survival, even if it reduces the long-term survival of the species. For that reason, evolutionists recognize that natural selection can occasionally lead to "mischievous results" detrimental to genetic quality. That's the effect I think we're seeing with sickle-cell anemia (Fig. 18).

Suppose I told you I had found a way to make cars run uphill without using gasoline. Then, as you watched in eager anticipation, I showed you how applying the brakes would make the car run downhill more slowly. Would you believe I had discovered a means for getting cars to run uphill? Similarly, natural selection can and does slow the rate of genetic decay produced by accumulating mutations (as it does with sickle-cell hemoglobin), but that hardly proves that mutation-selection produces upward and onward progress!

A better example of favorable mutation might be the one possibly involved in the change from teosinte into corn, as described by Beadle in *Scientific American,* January, 1980. But as Beadle points out, the mutation was favorable to people, not to corn. Corn, he says, is a "biological monstrosity" that could not survive on its own, without man's special care. Similarly, Novick (1980) calls bacteria that become resistant to drugs by mutation "evolutionary cripples" because of the harmful side effects of such changes (problems that bacteria trading "resistance genes" don't face).

But once again, let me say that *it's not that good mutations are theoretically impossible. Rather, the price is too high.* To explain evolution by the gradual selection of beneficial mutations, one must also put up with the thousands of harmful mutations that would have to occur along the way. Even though he has been one of the "old guard" defenders of classic neo-Darwinian evolution, Ayala (1978) faces the problem squarely in his article in the *Scientific American* book, *Evolution.* He is talking about variation within species (not type, but species, the smallest possible unit). He says that variation within species is much greater than Darwin postulated. He speaks of such variation as "enormous" and "staggering." Yet when he gets to the actual figures, the variation is less than I, as a creationist, would have expected. (Ayala did say his figures *under*-estimated the real variation.)

For creationists, all this variation poses no problem at all. If living things were created, then great variation within type is simply good design. There would be no price to pay for created variability, since it would result from creation, *not* from time, chance, and mutation. Mutations have introduced further variability since creation, but it's the kind of variability a bull introduces into a china shop!

What problem did Ayala, as an evolutionist, see with all this staggering variability? Just this: For each beneficial mutant a species accumulated, the price would be a thousand or more harmful mutations. When genetic burden gets too great, offspring are so likely to have serious hereditary defects that the ability of the species to survive is threatened. And time only makes this evolutionary problem worse. Thanks to our accumulated genetic burden, serious hereditary defects are present in at least 1% of all human births, and that percentage doubles among the children of

Figure 19. The most logical inference from our scientific observations of mutation, selection, and genetic recombination would seem to be *variation within created types*. There's no "genetic burden" to bear if variety is produced by creation instead of time, chance, and mutation. But could there be enough variation in each created type to produce all the diversity we see today? Creationists now have some promising answers to that question. (Drawing after Bliss. 1978. *Origins: Two Models*. 2nd ed. CLP Pubs., San Diego.)

closely related parents. Most of us have some genetic short comings, and it's really only by common consent that most of us agree to call each other "normal."

(3) *Mutations point back to creation.* After all this talk about mathematics and genetic load, the biggest reason mutations cannot lead to evolution is an extremely simple one. It's so simple, I'm almost afraid to say it. But really, *mutations presuppose creation.* After all, mutations are *only changes in already existing genes.*

Most mutations are caused by radiation. But what do you have to have before you can have a mutation? Obviously, the gene has to be there first, before the radiation can hit it. In one sense, it's as simple as that: The gene has to be there *before* it can mutate. All you get as a result of mutation is just a varied form (allele) of an already existing gene, i.e., variation within type. (See Fig. 19.)

By What Means?

Once in a while an evolutionist will say that any farmer who practices selective breeding is practicing evolution. But as one farmer put it, "Mister, when I cross pigs, I get pigs. I don't get dogs and cats and horses." If the point is that obvious, then other people ought to see it. And they do.

Harvard's Stephen Gould (1977b) quite clearly recognizes the difference between evolution and mutations. Evolution, he says, involves "profound structural transitions," such as a change from fish to philosopher (macroevolution). Mutations, he says, produce only minor variations, like we see in experiments with "flies in bottles," that start as flies and end up as flies. Then Gould chides his fellow evolutionists for illogical extrapolation. He says that "Orthodox neo-Darwinians extrapolate these even and continuous changes to the most profound structural transitions . . . . " For the old line mutation-selection evolutionist, "Macroevolution (major structural transition) is nothing more than microevolution (flies in bottles) extended." But then he asks himself, "How can such processes change a gnat or a rhinoceros into something fundamentally different?" Answering his own question in a later article, Gould (1980a) simply says, "That theory [orthodox neo-Darwinian extrapolationalism], as a general proposition is effectively dead, despite its persistence as textbook orthodoxy."

Gould believes our knowledge of genetics is now sufficient to completely reject the explanation of evolution as the slow, gradual selection of small mutational changes. He prefers to believe instead that evolution occurs in giant steps, radical restructuring of whole DNA sets producing what he himself calls "hopeful monsters." But he admits that no such hopeful monster has ever been observed. His new theory, then, is not any sort of logical inference from observations, but a fantastic faith in the future of a theory that the facts have failed.

And Gould is far from an isolated example. In October of 1980, the world's leading evolutionists met in Chicago for a conference summarized popularly by Adler and Carey in *Newsweek* for Nov. 3, 1980, and professionally by Lewin in *Science* for Nov. 21, 1980. According to the professional summary:

> The central question of the Chicago conference was whether the mechanisms underlying microevolution can be extrapolated to explain the phenomena of macroevolution.

That is, the processes of mutation, selection, and sexual recombination all produce variation within type (microevolution—or creationist adaptation), but can these processes be logically extended (extrapolated) to explain the presumed evolutionary change generally from simpler to more complex types (macroevolution)?

> At the risk of doing violence to the positions of some of the people at the meeting, the answer can be given as a clear, No.

Just plain capital N, No. No, one cannot logically extrapolate from mutation, selection, and sexual recombination to evolution. Creationists pointed out a series of logical and observational limits to that gross over-extrapolation decades ago, and we are pleased, of course, that the world's leading evolutionists now agree with us—without giving us any credit—that the textbook and television picture of minuscule mutations being slowly selected to produce elaborate evolution is just flatly false.

At this point many evolutionists say, in effect, "Well, at least we agree that evolution is a fact, even though we are not certain about the mechanism." Although I used to say that myself, it now sounds almost comically incongruous—both to me and to Colin Patterson (1981), leading palentologist at the British Museum. Evolutionists used to accuse creationists of affirming the fact of diversity without offering any mechanism to explain it, says Patterson, but now, he says, that is what evolutionists are doing. A theory that simply accepts the diversity of life without offering a mechanism to explain how that diversity came into being, adds Patterson, cannot be considered a scientific theory at all.

Evolutionists ultimately believe, to use an example from commercial television, that frogs turn into princes. But if the mechanism turned out to be the kiss of a princess rather than time, chance, and the properties of matter, then the evolutionary explanation for change would be wrong and the theory falsified in this instance. Whether it's the changing of frogs into princes, fish into philosophers, or molecules into men, calling evolution a fact without at least broadly specifying a mechanism is both non-science and non-sense—unless evolutionists are willing to consider the kiss of a princess a potentially valid evolutionary hypothesis!

Creationists don't believe that frogs turn into princes at all, of course, but rather that frogs and people were separately created from the same kinds of molecular "building blocks." Remember the tumbled pebble and the arrowhead (Fig. 1)? Both were shaped from the same substance, one by the means or mechanism of time and chance acting on the inherent properties of matter; the other by the means of mechanism of design and creation, producing irreducible properties of organization. Mechanism—the explanation of how—is, therefore, the heart of the creation/evolution issue. Substance, adaptations, and change are the "givens" or "facts" *shared* by those on *both sides*. The central question is: how—by what means or mechanism—did these patterns of order come into being: by time and chance like the tumbled pebble; or, like the arrowhead, by design and creation?

The large majority of evolutionists at the Chicago conference agreed that the neo-Darwinian mechanism of mutation-selection could no longer be regarded as a scientifically tenable explanation for the origin and diversity of living things. Unfortunately, many of the evolutionists, some quite reluctantly, seemed willing to put their hope instead in the "hopeful monster" mechanism resurrected by Gould and others. A few were willing to fight what *Newsweek* called a "rear guard action" on behalf of otherwise defunct Darwinism. But some scientists are willing to look for truly new hypotheses that have the promise of stimulating more fruitful research.

One such scientist is Pierre Grasse'. He has been called "the dean of French zoologists," yet he rejects mutation-selection as a means of evolutionary change in scathing words: Mutations are "merely hereditary fluctuations around a median position; a swing to the right, a swing to the left, but no final evolutionary effect." He goes on to say that mutations "are not complementary...nor are they cumulative." That is, they don't work together, and they don't add up to anything. "They modify what preexists," says Grasse' (1977a)—which means you can get no more from mutations than variation within type. In fact, you even get *less*, because mutations are mostly harmful, says Grasse', producing "downhill" changes, not "upward-onward" evolution. He strongly condemns attempts to use selection to salvage a few favorable mutations for evolution:

> Directed by all-powerful selection, chance becomes a sort of providence . . . which is secretly worshipped.

Grasse ' is not (yet) a creationist. But he does say that his knowledge of the living world convinces him that there must be some "internal force" involved in the history of life.

That may remind you of Albert Szent-Gyorgyi, the Nobel prize winner, who said that the origin of complex traits by random mutation has the probability of zero. In the first chapter, I mentioned that his observations of living things forced Szent-Gyorgyi, like Grasse ', to postulate at least a creative force.

Maybe you also remember Garrett Hardin from the first chapter. Because of "nature's challenges to evolutionary theory," he asked, "Is the [evolutionary] framework wrong? Was Paley right?" That is, can we infer creation from the kind of design we see among living things? "Think about it."

That's why it is so vital that our students be given every opportunity to explore all aspects of the origins issue, Including the scientific data. (In my experience, by the way, Canadian and Australian students experience much greater academic freedom in this area than students in the "land of the free[?].") After all, it is only students who have access to all the relevant information on a topic who are truly free to "think about it."

Variation Within Created Types

But, "think about it!" doesn't mean "stop here;" it means, "start here."

I have been saying, perhaps too often, that the weight of evidence points to "variation within the created types." Do I really mean that all the tremendous variety we see today was built right into the created types—just a pair as a minimum for most types and perhaps a dozen in one-celled forms with multiple sexes? Could there be enough variation in created human beings, for example, to produce all the variation among human beings we see today?

Answer: "Yes, indeed; no problem!" I get some help here from an unexpected source, evolutionist Francisco Ayala (1978). He says that human beings are "heterozygous" for 6.7% of their genes, on the average. That means that 6 or 7 times in a 100, the pair of genes for a given trait differ like the genes for brown or blue eyes, or for rolling or not rolling the tongue. Now this may not seem like much. But Ayala calculates a single human couple with just "6.7% variety" could produce $10^{2,017}$ children (mathematically, not physically!) before they would have to produce an identical twin. That's 1 followed by 2,017 zeroes! The number of atoms in the known universe is a mere 10^{80}, nothing at all compared with the variety that is present in just two human beings.

Take human skin color, for example. Note first of all that all of us (except albinos) have exactly the *same* skin coloring agent. It's a protein called melanin. We all have the same basic skin color, just different amounts of it. (Not a very big difference, is it?)

How long would it take to get all the variations in the amount of skin color we see among people today? Answer: *one generation!*

Let's see how that works. The amount of skin color we have depends on at least two pairs of genes. Let's call these genes **A** and **B**. People with the darkest skin color have genes **AABB** as their genotype (set of genes for a trait); those with very light skins have **aabb**. People with two "capital letter" genes would be "medium-skinned," and those with 1 or 3 such genes would be a shade lighter or darker.

Now, let's start with two medium-skinned parents, **AaBb**. Fig. 20 is a genetic square that shows the kind of children they could have. Less than half (only 6 of the 16 combinations) would be medium-skinned like their parents. Four each would be a shade darker or lighter. One in 16 of the children of medium-skinned parents (**AaBb**) would have the darkest possible skin color, while the chances are also 1/16 that a brother or sister will have the very lightest skin color (See Parker, Reynolds and Reynolds, 1977b).

Starting with medium-skinned parents (**AaBb**), how long would it take to produce all the variation we see in human skin color today? Merely one generation! In fact, this is the normal situation in India today. Some Indians are as dark as the darkest Africans, and some—perhaps a brother or sister in the family—as light as the lightest Europeans.

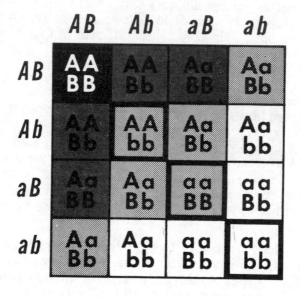

Figure 20. All human beings have *the same* basic skin color agent (melanin), just different amounts of it. From parents created with medium skin color, as diagrammed, all the variation we see today could be produced in just one generation. In the same way, plants and animals created with a mixture of genes could have filled all of the earth's ecologic and geographic variety.

But now notice what happens if human groups were isolated after creation. If those with very dark skins (**AABB**) migrate into the same areas and/or marry only those with very dark skins, then all their children will have very dark skins. (**AABB** is the only possible combinations of **AB** egg and sperm cells, which are the only types that can be produced by **AABB** parents.) Similarly, parents with very light skins (**aabb**) can have only very light-skinned children, since they don't have any **A** or **B** genes to pass on. Even certain medium-skinned parents (**AAbb** or **aaBB**) can get "locked-in" to having only medium-skinned children (since they always pass on one "capital" and one "lower case" gene).

Where people with different skin colors get together again (as they do in the West Indies, for example), you find the full range of variation again—nothing less, but nothing more either, than what you started with. Clearly, all this is variation within type.

"Gene pool" refers to all the different genes that are present in a population. There are at least four skin color genes in the human gene pool: **A, a, B, b**. That total human gene pool for skin color can be found in just one person with medium skin color (**AaBb**), or it can be "spread around" among many people with visibly different skin colors.

What happened as the descendants of medium-skinned parents themselves produced a variety of descendants? Evolution? Not at all. Except for albinism (the mutational loss of skin color), the human gene pool is no bigger and no different now than the gene pool present at creation. As people multiplied, the genetic variability *built right into* the first created human beings came to visible expression. The darkest Nigerian and the lightest Norwegian, the tallest Watusi and the shortest Pygmy, the highest soprano and the lowest bass could have been present right from the beginning in two quite average-looking people. Great variation in size, color, form, function, etc., would also be present in the created ancestors of all the other types as well.

Evolutionists *assume* that all life started from one or a

few chemically evolved life forms with an extremely small gene pool. For evolutionists, enlargement of the gene pool by selection of random mutations is a slow, tedious process that burdens each type with a "genetic load" of harmful mutations and evolutionary leftovers.

Neither creationist nor evolutionist was there at the beginning to see how it was done, but at least the creationist mechanism works, and it's consistent with what we observe. The evolutionist assumption *doesn't* work, and it's *not* consistent with what we presently know of genetics and reproduction. As a scientist, I tend to prefer ideas that do work and do help to explain what we can observe.

According to the creation concept, each type starts with a large gene pool present in created, probably "average-looking," parents. As descendants of these created types become isolated, each average-looking ("generalized") type would tend to break up into a variety of more "specialized" descendants adapted to different environments. Thus, the created ancestors of dogs, for example, have produced such varieties in nature as wolves, coyotes, and jackals. Human beings, of course, have divided into a great diversity of nationalities. (See Fig. 21.)

Varieties within a created type have the same genes, but in different percentages. Take my ancestors, for example, the Indians or Native Americans. Certain tribes have a high percentage of blood type **A**, but that type is quite rare among other tribes, including my branch of the Cherokee Nation. The differences just represent differences in the genes carried by the founders of each tribe as people migrated across the North American continent.

Differences from average gene percentages can come to expression quickly in small populations (a process called "genetic drift"). Take the Pennsylvania Amish, for example. Because they are descendants of only about 200 settlers who tended to marry among themselves, they have a greater percentage than the American average of genes for short fingers, short stature, a sixth finger, and a certain blood disease. For similar reasons, plants and animals on opposite sides of mountains, rivers, or canyons often have variations in size, color, ear-shape, or some such feature

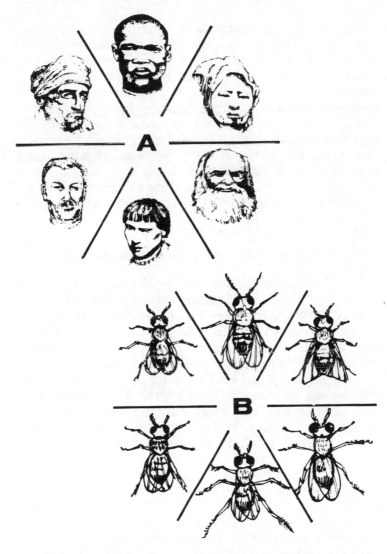

Figure 21. Descendants of created types tend to break up into different varieties. Even varieties that no longer interbreed (B) can be recognized as the same type because they possess only alternate forms (alleles) of the same genes. The existence of distinct types, both living and fossil, says Harvard's Stephen Gould, "fit splendidly with creationist tenets of a pre-Darwinian era," although Gould rejects creation. The facts seem to me to fit creation in our present "post-neo-Darwinian era" just as well.

that makes them recognizable as variations of a given type. All the different varieties of human beings can, of course, marry one another and have children. Many varieties of plants and animals also retain the ability to reproduce and trade genes—despite differences in appearance as great as those between collies and cocker spaniels, or wolves and wolfhounds. But varieties of one type may also lose the ability to interbreed with others of their type. For example, fruit flies multiplying through Central and South America have split up in many subgroups (Fig. 21). And since these subgroups no longer interbreed, each can be called a separate species.

"Species" and "Type"

Whoops! Two or more species from one type! Isn't that evolution???

Some evolutionists certainly think so. After I participated in a creation/evolution debate at Texas A & M, a biology professor got up and told everyone about the flies on certain islands that used to interbreed but no longer do. They've become separate species, and that, he said to a fair amount of applause, proves evolution is a fact—period!

Well, what about it? Barriers to reproduction do seem to arise among varieties that once interbred. Does that prove evolution? Or does that make it reasonable to extrapolate from such processes to real evolutionary changes from one type to others? I think the answer is simply, no, of course not. It doesn't even come close.

Real evolution (macroevolution) requires the *expansion* of the gene pool, the *additon* of new genes and new traits as life is supposed to move from simple beginnings to ever more varied and complex forms ("molecules to man" or "fish to philosopher"). Suppose there are islands where three varieties of flies that used to trade genes no longer interbreed. Is this evidence of evolution? No, just the opposite. Each variety now has a *smaller* gene pool than the original and a *restricted* ability to explore new environments with new trait combinations or to meet changes in their own environment. The long term result? Extinction would be much more likely than evolution.

Of course, if someone insists on defining evolution as "a change in gene frequency," then the fly example "proves evolution," but it also "proves creation," since varying the amounts of already existing genes is what creation is all about (Fig. 22).

If evolutionists really spoke and wrote only about observable variation within type, there would be no creation/evolution controversy. But as you know, textbooks, teachers, and television documentaries insist on extrapolating from simple variation within type to the wildest sorts of evolutionary changes. And, of course, as long as they insist on such extrapolation, creationists will point out the limits to such change and offer creation instead as the most logical inference from our observations. All we have ever observed is what evolutionists themselves call "subspeciation" (variation within type), never "transspeciation" (change from one type to others). (See Fig. 22.)

Evolutionists are often asked what they mean by "species," and creationists are often asked what they mean by "type." Both terms are hard to define. Evolutionists recognize certain bowerbirds as distinct species even though they interbreed, and they can't use the interbreeding criterion at all with asexual forms. Creationists sympathize with these problems, because they also associate "types" with groups that normally interbreed. However, both creationists and evolutionists are divided into "lumpers" and "splitters." "Splitters," for example, classify cats into 28 species; "lumpers" (creationist or evolutionist) classify them into only one!

Perhaps each created type is a unique combination of nonunique traits. Look at ourselves, for instance. Each of us has certain traits that we may admire (or abhor)—brown hair, tall stature, or even a magnificent nose like mine. Whatever the trait, someone else has exactly the same trait—but nobody has the same *combination* of traits that you do or I do. Each of us is a *unique combination* of *nonunique traits*. In a sense, that's why it's hard to classify people. If you break them up according to hair type, you'll come out with groups that won't fit with the eye type, and so on. Furthermore, we recognize each per-

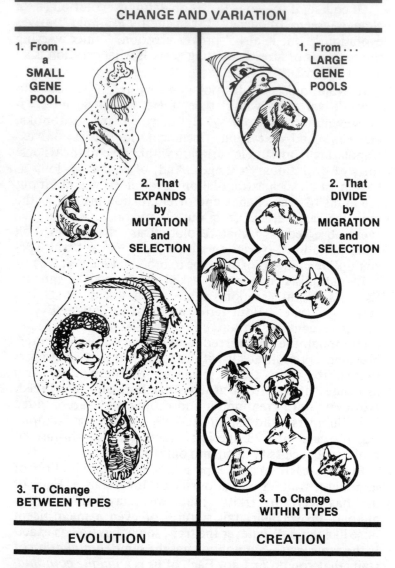

CHANGE AND VARIATION

1. From . . .
a
SMALL
GENE
POOL

1. From . . .
LARGE
GENE
POOLS

2. That
EXPANDS
by
MUTATION
and
SELECTION

2. That
DIVIDE
by
MIGRATION
and
SELECTION

3. To Change
BETWEEN TYPES

3. To Change
WITHIN TYPES

EVOLUTION   **CREATION**

Figure 22. Change? Yes—but which kind of change? What's the most logical inference, or the most reasonable extrapolation, from our observations: unlimited change from one type to others (evolution), or limited variation within types (creation)? Given the new knowledge of genetics and ecology, even Darwin, I believe, would be willing to "think about it."

son as distinct.

We see a similar pattern among living things. Each created type is a unique combination of traits that are individually shared with members of other groups. The platypus (Fig. 9), for example, was at first considered a hoax by evolutionists, since its "weird" set of traits made it difficult to even guess what it was evolving from or into. Creationists point out that each of its traits (including complex ones like its echo location mechanism, leathery egg, and milk glands) are complete, fully functional, and well-integrated into a distinctive and marvelous type of life.

Perhaps creation produced a design in living things similar to the one we find in the nonliving world. Only about a hundred different elements or atoms are combined in different ways to make a tremendous variety of nonliv ing molecules or compounds. Maybe creationists will one day identify a relatively few genes and gene sets that, in unique combinations, were used to make all the different types of life we see. It would take a tremendous amount of research to validate this "mosaic or modular concept of a created unit," but the results would be a truly objective taxonomy that would be welcomed by both creationists and evolutionists.

But why should we be able to classify plants and animals into types or species at all? In a fascinating editorial feature in *Natural History,* Stephen Gould (1979c) writes that biologists have been quite successful in dividing up the living world into distinct and discrete species. Furthermore, our modern, scientific classifications often agree in minute detail with the "folk classifications" of so-called primitive peoples, and the same criteria apply as well to fossils. In other words, says Gould, there is a recognizable reality and distinct boundaries between types at all times and all places—"A Quahog is a Quahog," as the title of his editorial reads.

"But," says Gould, "how could the existence of distinct species be justified by a theory [evolution] that proclaimed ceaseless change as the most fundamental fact of nature?" For an evolutionist, why should there be species at all? If all life forms have been produced by gradual expansion through selected mutations from a small beginning gene pool, organisms really should just grade into one another without distinct boundaries. Darwin also recognized the problem. He finally ended by denying the reality of species. But, as Gould points out, Darwin was an excellent classifier, and quite good at classifying the species whose ultimate reality he denied. And, says Gould, Darwin could take no comfort in fossils, since he was also successful in classifying them into distinct species. He used the same criteria we use to classify plants and animals today.

In one of the most brilliantly and perceptively developed themes in his book, *Evolution: A Theory in Crisis*, Denton (1985) shows how leaders in the science of classification—after a century of trying vainly to accommodate evolution—are returning to, and fleshing out, the creationist typological concepts of the pre-Darwinian era. Indeed, the study of biological classification was founded by Karl von Linne' (Carolus Linnaeus) on the basis of his conscious and explicit belief that living things were created to multiply after type, and that these created types could be rationally grouped in a hierarchical pattern reflecting themes and variations in the creator's mind.

"Actually," concludes Gould, "the existence of distinct species was quite consistent with *creationist* tenets of a pre-Darwinian era." (Emphasis added.) I would simply like to add that the evidence is also quite consistent with the creationist tenets of the present *post-neo-Darwinian* era. In Darwin's time as well as the present, "creation" seems to be the most logical inference from our observations.

But "What about Darwin?" He tried to explain "design without creation" on the basis of selection and the inheritance of traits acquired by use and disuse (pangenes), but pangenes failed. The neo-Darwinists tried to explain "design without creation" on the basis of selection and mutation, and mutations failed. The post-neo-Darwinists are turning to "hopeful monsters," instead of simple mutations, and to "survival of the luckiest" instead of selection. These new ideas have little basis in observation at all, and it remains to be seen if the evolutionist's faith in future discoveries will also fail.

But even as mutations and selection are being abandoned by some evolutionists, these same processes are being picked up and used by creationists—*not* as a means of creation at all, but as part of the process by which the created types vary around the earth. (See Fig. 22.) What would Darwin himself say about that? Would he object that creationists are now making more use of his ideas and observations than evolutionists are?

Darwin did muse occasionally about the role of a creator. But, of course, we'll never know whether or not he would be willing to consider creation as the more logical inference from our present knowledge of genetics and ecology. We can be sure of this, however: A man as thoughtful and devoted to detail and observation as Darwin was, would be willing to "think about it."

Chapter 4

The
Fossil Evidence

Fossils are the remains or traces of plants and animals preserved in sedimentary deposits. They represent the closest we can come to historical evidence in this matter of origins, so they are of prime importance in discussing creation and evolution.

Fossils are also fun. My family and I (that's two rock-hounds and four pebble-pups) have collected over 1,000 pounds of fossils from road cuts, creek beds, and quarries all over North America, and I even picked up a few in Australia.

When the modern version of creation-evolution dialogue got started in the middle of the last century, creationists and evolutionists had radically different ideas of the types of life they expected to find as fossils.

The evolutionist, of course, expected to find fossils that showed stages through which one type of animal or plant changed into a different type. According to evolution, the boundaries between types should blur as we look back at their fossil history. It should get more and more difficult, for example, to tell cats from dogs and then mammals from reptiles, land animals from water animals, and finally life from nonlife. They expected also that the criteria we use to classify plants and animals today would be less and less useful as older and older fossils show the in-between characteristics of presumed common ancestors for different groups.

But if the different types of life we see today are the

descendants of types created, as the creationist says, then all we ought to find as fossils are just variations of these types, with extinction evident among prehistoric life as it is among historic forms. The same kind of criteria we use to classify plants and animals today ought to work just as well with fossils. Fossils should be as easy to classify as modern forms (when evidence is complete enough), and each type should represent a mosaic of complete traits.

Certainly the evolutionist and creationist had radically different concepts of what would be found as the systematic study of fossils began in earnest in the middle of the last century. Let's now take a look at the evidence. Which concept does it support—evolution or creation?

Invertebrates: Animals Without Backbones

Take a look at Fig. 23. If you live near the seashore or like to visit marine aquaria, I'm sure most of the animals there are quite familiar to you. There are some jellyfish floating in the background. On the bottom you can find sea urchins and sea lilies, members of the starfish group; a couple of snails; sponges; lampshells; and members of the earthworm group. That large fellow stretched out along the right side is a nautiloid, a squid-like animal that is a member of the most complex group of invertebrate animals we know anything about (the cephalopod molluscs). The nautiloid belongs to the group of animals that has an eye somewhat like ours, as I mentioned in the first chapter.

What does this illustration show? A picture of present-day sea life off the California coast or around some tropical island? No, not at all. It pictures not sea life today, but the "first" or simplest community of plants and animals to leave abundant fossil remains. This illustration shows life in the so-called "Age of Trilobites" (what I'll later call the "Zone of Trilobites").

Trilobites, by the way, are fascinating creatures. Many trilobites, such as the one pictured in the inset in Fig. 23, had extremely complex eyes—the math to understand the lens structure was not even worked out until the middle of the last century. Trilobites belong to the same group that

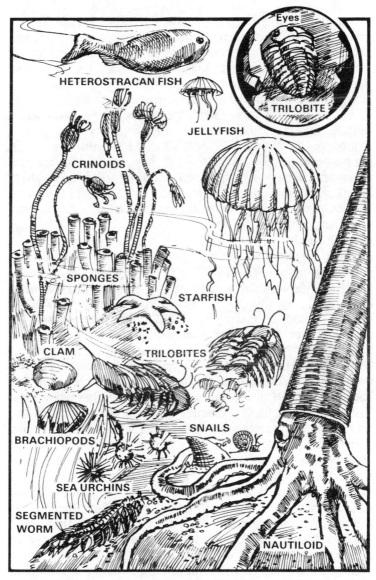

Figure 23. The simplest community of abundant fossils, the "Trilobite Seas" (Cambrian System), contains almost all the major groups of sea life, including the most complex invertebrates, the nautiloids, and the highly complex trilobites themselves (inset above). Darwin called the fossil evidence "perhaps the most obvious and serious objection to the theory" of evolution.

insects do (the arthropods), but apparently all trilobites are extinct. Trilobites are very famous as fossils, however, and are the "first" animals to leave abundant fossil remains. Suppose you like to scuba dive, as I do. Let's imagine we're diving in the ocean back when the trilobites were alive. If we compared life in the trilobite seas with what we see in the oceans today, what would we say? "Look at all the new forms of life, the increased variety and greater complexity!" No, that's not what we would say at all. Rather, we might say, "What happened? Where did everything go? What happened to all the trilobites? Where are all the lampshells?" There used to be several thousand species; now only a handful are left. We might also wonder what happened to the great nautiloids, with their long, straight shells reaching up to nine feet in length. Today the only shelled squid we have is the modest pearly nautilus.

Extinction, not evolution, is the rule when we compare fossil sea life with the sort of marine invertebrates we find living today. In fact, all major groups, except perhaps the groups including clams and snails, are represented by greater variety and more complex forms as *fossils* than today.

It's hard to imagine how absolutely crushing this evidence is to evolution. Suppose, for example, that you had a burning desire to find out where snails came from. You search the fossil evidence all over the world, all the way back to the "beginning," and sure enough, snails come from snails. Where did the most complex of all the invertebrates, members of the squid and octopus group, come from? Again, you search through all the fossil evidence, all the way back to the very "beginning," and sure enough, squids come from squids. In fact, the "first" squids, the nautiloids, are a bit more impressive than most modern forms. And, of course, trilobites seem only to come from trilobites.

In other words, you find snails and squids and trilobites as fossils; you don't find "snids" and "squails" and "squailobites," or some other in-between form or common ancestor. The "missing links" between these groups are still missing.

In fact, few scientists, if any, are still looking for fossil links between the major invertebrate groupts. The reason is simple. All the groups appear as separate, distinct, diversified lines in the deepest fossil-rich deposits (Valentine, 1978). Evolutionists are well aware of these facts, of course, and several have admitted that this "explosion" of life in Cambrian ("trilobite") rock seems to favor the concept of creation.

What about Precambrian rock that is found below Cambrian strata? Evolutionists used to say that they would have found the ancestors of Cambrian life there—if only the evidence hadn't been destroyed by heat in the rocks. That "excuse" no longer works. Although most Precambrian rock is the igneous and metamorphic type unsuitable for fossil preservation, we have now discovered great stretches of Precambrian sedimentary rocks that could and should have preserved the common ancestors of the diverse and complex Cambrian life—if any such evolutionary ancestors existed.

Actually, very few Precambrian fossils have been found, but those that have strongly support the creation concept. My wife and I have found soft-bodied jellyfish and members of the earthworm group (annelids) in the famous Ediacara Hills of South Australia, and they were separate and complex types like those living today. (Note, by the way, that claiming the supposed Precambrian ancestors were all soft-bodied does not explain their lack of existence either.) The "oldest" Precambrian fossils discovered so far are some marine blue-green algae that form rocky structures called stromatolites. Blue-green algae are biochemically quite complex forms with an elaborate solar-to-chemical energy transformation (photosynthesis), and their fossils have been found very near the same sort of algae living today along the west coast of Australia (between the towns of Geraldton and Canarvon, where I've spoken) and the south coast near Adelaide (where I've photographed specimens in the field).

Creation is also supported by our ability to use the same criteria to classify both living plants and animals and those found as fossils. Even among extinct types, we don't find "in-between forms," or forms that are any harder to classify (when the fossil evidence is complete enough) than plants and animals living today.

Let me emphasize that again. Most people just assume that fossils and evolution go hand in hand. Some people even seem to think that "believing" in fossils is almost the same as "believing" in evolution. We've been thoroughly indoctrinated with educational materials and entertainment touting evolution, and it's hard to even think that fossils argue so strongly *against* evolution and *for* creation.

Could I be right about that? Is there anyone else who thinks that the fossils argue against evolution? Yes, indeed . . . Charles Darwin, for one. That's right, Charles Darwin, the father of the modern concept of evolution. Darwin thought that the fossil evidence was "perhaps the most obvious and serious objection which could be urged against the theory [of evolution]." Why? Because he knew some of the same things we know about fossils.

Darwin's chapter on the fossil evidence was titled "On The Imperfection of the Geologic Record." In that chapter he dealt with "the sudden appearance" of groups of fossils in the lowest known fossil-bearing strata. When it came to intermediate links (those types of fossils supposed to show how one type of life evolved into others), Darwin wrote the following:

> . . . intermediate links? Geology assuredly does *not* reveal any such finely graduated organic change, and this is perhaps the *most obvious and serious objection* which can be urged against the theory [of evolution]. [Emphasis added.]

So, Darwin was faced with a conflict. Theory (evolution) and facts (fossils) didn't agree. Which was he going to throw out, the facts or the theory? Darwin chose to throw out the facts. Normally, of course, a scientist doesn't do that. But Darwin had reason, or at least hope, for doing so. He blamed the conflict between fact and theory on "the imperfection of the geologic record." In his time, the science of paleontology (fossil study) was just getting under way. He hoped that as new fossil evidence was unearthed around the world, the "missing links" would be found to support his theory.

Well, it's now over 120 years since Darwin made that statement, and we've unearthed thousands of tons of fossils from all over the world. What does all this massive amount of evidence show? Have we found the "missing links" required to support the theory of evolution, or have we merely unearthed further evidence of variation within the created types?

David Raup reviews the evidence for us. He has been the curator of the famous Field Museum of Natural History in Chicago. That museum houses 20% of all fossil species known, so Raup is in a position to speak with considerable knowledge about the fossil evidence. The title of his article in the January, 1979, issue of the *Field Museum Bulletin* is "Conflicts Between Darwin and Paleontology," and the thrust is repeated and expanded in a second article in March, 1983.

Raup starts by saying that "most people assume that fossils provide a very important part of the general argument made in favor of Darwinian interpretations of the history of life. Unfortunately, this is not strictly true." He then quotes the same passage from Darwin that I did, and points out that Darwin was "embarrassed" by the fossil evidence. He goes on to say that we now have a rich body of fossil knowledge, so that we can no longer blame the conflict between evolutionary theory and the fossil facts on the "imperfection of the geologic record." He mentions also, as I did, that Darwin expected those gaps in his theory, those missing links, to be unearthed by future discoveries. Then Raup summarizes those discoveries:

> Well, we are now about 120 years after Darwin, and knowledge of the fossil record has been greatly expanded . . . ironically, we have *even fewer examples* of evolutionary transition than we had in Darwin's time. By this I mean that some of the classic cases of Darwinian change in the fossil record, such as the evolution of the horse in North America, have had to be *dis-*

carded or modified as a result of more detailed
information. [Emphasis added.]

What a statement! Darwin said the fossil evidence was
perhaps the most obvious and serious objection against his
theory. Raup is saying that 120 years of research have
made the case for Darwinian evolution *even worse*. Raup
says we have "even fewer examples" now. Famous paleontologists at Harvard, the American Museum, and the
British Museum apparently indicate that we have *not a
single* example of evolutionary transition at all.

Raup goes on to say that "we still have a record which
does show change, but one that can hardly be looked upon
as the most reasonable consequence of natural selection."
In comparing fossil forms with modern forms, we do see
change all right, but it's *not* the kind of change associated
with natural selection. It's simply variation within type, the
kind of change that creationists expected all along.

Raup is still an evolutionist, but he's beginning to argue
for "survival of the luckiest," instead of "survival of the
fittest." Condemning with faint praise, he says, "natural
selection as a process is okay. We are also pretty sure that
it goes on in nature, although good examples are surprisingly rare." Genetic studies suggest that mutation-
selection *could not* lead to evolutionary change; the fossil
evidence seems to confirm that it *did not*.

Raup then tries to argue that "optimal engineering
design" is the best evidence of evolution—exactly the same
kind of evidence that Harvard geneticist Lewontin con-
cedes as the best evidence of creation! One of the reasons
that evolution continues to survive is that paleontologists
believe the geneticists have the real evidence, and
geneticists believe that paleontologists have the evidence,
and so on around the various specialties within biology—each man passing the buck for evidence to the next
man. Since professionals in different disciplines rarely talk
with one another about such matters, the myth of overwhelming support for evolution continues.

After he bemoaned the repeated failures of evolution
to come to grips with the fossil evidence, paleontologist
Niles Eldredge (1986) laments that the only alternative is

"Special Creation." As we have seen, the fossils of invertebrates, the most abundant by far of all fossils, do offer strong support for the concept of creation. But let's look now at fossil evidence from other groups.

Fossil Plants

Did you even wonder what kind of plants the dinosaurs tromped around on? The answer may surprise you. These unfamiliar animals, now extinct, wandered around among some very familiar plants: oak, willow, magnolia, sassafras, palms, and other such common flowering plants.

In the geologic sequence, the flowering plants first appear suddenly and in great diversity in Cretaceous ("dinosaur") rock. Darwin was aware of the situation and called the origin of these plants "an abominable mystery." As my professor of paleobotany summarized it, nothing has happened in the last 120 years to solve that mystery. As far as the fossil evidence is concerned, we simply find different varieties of the same types of plants we have today, plus extinction in many cases.

There is a tendency to give every different fossil fragment a different scientific genus-species name. Five different genus names were given to fossil specimens that later turned out to be parts of just one type of tree, the *Lepidodendron*. But many of the flowering plants are so easily recognizable that they are classified using the same scientific names we use today.

Other fossil plants are as easily classified as the flowering plants. The ferns and fern allies appear suddenly and simultaneously in Silurian/Devonian rock in far greater diversity than we have today (Fig. 24). Yet none of these fossil plants has any features of anatomy, morphology, or reproduction that are hard to understand in terms of what we observe among living plants. Even the algae are recognizable from their first appearance in the fossil sequence as greens, blue-greens, reds, browns, and yellow-browns—the same groups we have today.

My paleobotany professor (an evolutionist) started his class by saying he supposed we were there to learn about the evolution of plants. But then he told us that we weren't

going to learn much. What we *would* learn is that our
modern plant groups go way back in their fossil history.
Sure enough, all we studied was "petrified plant
anatomy," features already familiar to me from the study
of living plants. We encountered some difficulties in

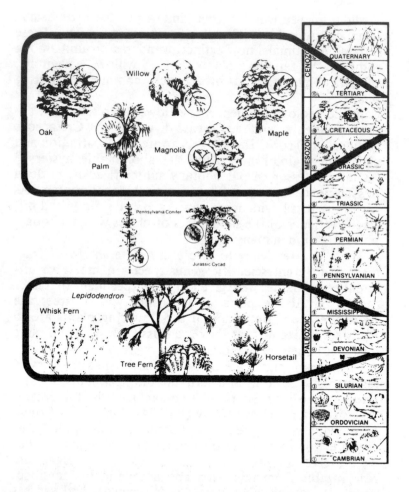

Figure 24. Fossil plants are easily classified using the same criteria we use today,
and, because of extinction, we find even greater variation among fossil plants
than we find now. As Professor Corner at Cambridge put it, " . . . to the un-
prejudiced, the fossil record of plants is in favor of special creation."

classificaton, of course, but only the same kinds which we encounter among the living plants. Summarizing the evidence of fossils plant studies, E. J. H. Corner, Professor of Botany at Cambridge University, once put it this way (even though he believed in their evolution):

> . . . to the unprejudiced, the fossil record of plants is in favor of special creation.

Vertebrates: Animals with Backbones

Now we come to the vertebrates, the animals with backbones. And here we run smack into the most powerful evidence of *evolution*. At least that's what I used to tell my students when I taught university biology as an evolutionist.

Sometimes I would run into a student who would ask me, "If evolution is true, where are the missing links?" "Missing links?" I'd say, "Glad you asked. It just so happens we have a perfect example: *Archaeopteryx,* the link that shows how birds evolved from reptiles."

Archaeopteryx is the showcase for evolution. There is only one really photogenic specimen, the Berlin specimen, which is pictured in essentially all biology books. That specimen, along with a reconstruction in the same position, is shown in Fig. 25.

At first, you may wonder what the fuss is all about. It has feathers, wings, and a beak, so it's a bird. But look closer. It has teeth in the bill, claws on the wings, no breast bone with a keel, an unfused backbone, and a long, bony tail. These are all characteristics we normally associate with reptiles. What's more, the existence of a creature like *Archaeopteryx* was predicted by evolutionists before any such specimen was found. What's a creationist going to say to a "perfect example of evolution" like *Archaeopteryx?*

Well, first of all, the reptile-like features are not really so reptile-like as you might suppose. The familiar ostrich, for example, has claws on its wings that are even more "reptile-like than those of *Archaeopteryx.* Several birds, such as the hoatzin, don't have much of a keel. No living birds have socketed teeth, but some fossil birds did. Besides, some

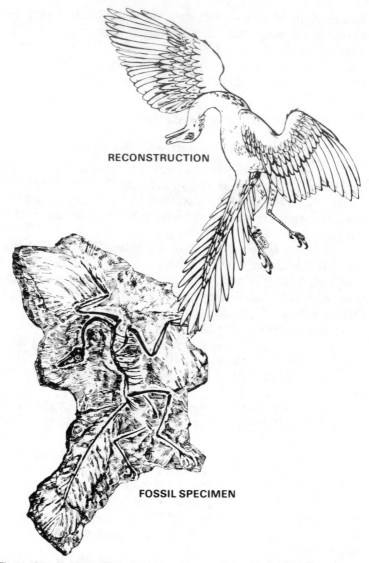

RECONSTRUCTION

FOSSIL SPECIMEN

Figure 25. At last—evidence of evolution! . . . *or is it?* The famous *Archaeopteryx* combines features most often found in reptiles (teeth, claws, unfused vertebrae, and a long bony tail) with features distinctive of birds (wings, feathers, and a furcula or wishbone). Does *Archaeopteryx* provide clues as to how scales evolved into feathers, or legs into wings? Is *Archaeopteryx* most likely an evolutionary link, or a mosaic of complete traits (a distinctive created type)? Read both sides and see what you think.

reptiles have teeth and some don't, so presence or absence of teeth is not particularly important in distinguishing the two groups.

More importantly, take a look at the individual features of *Archaeopteryx*. Is there any clue as to *how* legs evolved into wings? No, none at all. When we find wings as fossils, we find completely developed, fully functional wings. That's true of *Archaeopteryx*, and it's also true of the flying insects and the flying mammals (bats).

Is there any clue in *Archaeopteryx* as to *how* the reptilian scales evolved into feathers? No, none at all. When we find feathers as fossils, we find fully developed and functional feathers. Feathers are quite complex structures, with little hooks and eyelets for zippering and unzippering them. *Archaeopteryx* not only had complete and complex feathers, but feathers of several different types. As a matter of fact, it had the asymmetric feather characteristic of strong flyers.

What about a lack of a keel? Actually, muscles for the power stroke in flight attach to the wishbone or furcula, and *Archaeopteryx* had "an extremely robust furcula." As a matter of fact, a growing number of evolutionists, perhaps a consensus, now believe that *Archaeopteryx* was a strong flyer. Many now consider *Archaeopteryx* the first bird, and not a missing link between reptiles and birds (See Denton, 1985).

Actually the final piece in the *Archaeopteryx* puzzle (for the time being, anyway) has been put into place with the discovery in Texas of a quarry full of bird bones ("protoavis"), entombed in rock layers "deeper" than those which contain *Archaeopteryx* remains (Beardsley, 1986). What does that mean? It simply means that the *Archaeopteryx* specimens we have cannot have been the ancestors of birds, because birds already existed.

Creationists, by the way, are not forced to decide whether *Archaeopteryx* was a bird or a reptile. Creationists believe that many separate and distinct types were created. Because of its unique combination of *complete, functionally integrated traits, Archaeopteryx* would qualify as a created type (unless it turns out to be a hoax, as Sir Fred Hoyle has been claiming!). For creationists, it's the created type that is the real unit in nature. The higher categories are products of human thought, and difficulties with fitting organisms into these human categories represent only problems with human imagination, not with the reality of created types.

But imagination has always been evolution's strong suit. Evolutionists who accept *Archaeopteryx* as a bird must, of course, look elsewhere for the ancestors of birds. The new candidate is called "pro-avis" (which is *not* the same as the Texas birds loosely called "pro-avis"). In *American Scientist* for January-February, 1979, John Ostrom of Yale University discusses two possible pictures of this pro-avis, as redrawn in Fig. 26. One hypothesis has birds starting as partially feathered reptiles gliding down from trees. Ostrom points out a number of anatomical inconsistencies in that view. He then suggests that birds began as two-legged reptiles, with feathery baskets on their forearms, that jumped higher and higher to catch flying insects.

Take a look at the idea of pro-avis in Fig. 26-B. Can you see any problems in getting it off the ground? Perhaps you've seen children tie towels onto their arms and try to fly. If you ever tried it yourself (like I once did), you found out all that flapping created more drag than lift! Even though it's his idea, Ostrom acknowledges that the muscle action for catching insects is all wrong for flying. And eating insects out of the feathers would tear up the feathers anyway.

Besides these difficulties, Ostrom also points out that "No fossil evidence exists of any pro-avis. It is a purely hypothetical pre-bird, but one that must have existed . . . . " Apparently, where facts fail, faith avails. Ostrom, and other evolutionists, can be commended for their imagination. But their ideas cannot be presented in science classrooms as logical inferences from observed data, since they admit themselves the data simply do not exist.

As far as the fossil evidence is concerned, different types of invertebrates and plants have always been different types of invertebrates and plants... and birds have always been birds. The fossil evidence of creation is just as clear in

Figure 26. Two concepts of the evolutionary ancestor of birds, called "pro-avis," are redrawn here from an article by Yale's John Ostrom (1979). As Ostrom says, "No fossil evidence of any pro-avis exists. It is a purely hypothetical pre-bird, but one which must have existed." But this case for evolution is based on faith, not facts. The fossils found so far simply show that birds have always been birds, of many distinctive types.

the other vertebrate groups as well (See Gish, 1986; Bliss, Parker, and Gish, 1980).

The Debate Goes On

The evolutionist's problems with the fossil evidence are summarized by Ayala and Valentine in a textbook on evolution that came out in 1979. "In fact," they say, "there are no extinct fossil groups known that are the common ancestors of two or more living phyla . . . . Most taxa [groups] at these high levels appear abruptly in the fossil record, and we do not know their immediate ancestors."

On the positive side, the fossil evidence has provided the strongest support for creationists in the creation/evolution debates. These debates have been attracting students (in crowds up to 5,000!) at major universities in the U.S., Canada, Europe, Asia, and Australia. Thanks in large measure to the fossil evidence, the creationists have been winning these debates.

Joe Felsenstein, geneticist at the University of Washington, made some interesting observations about these debates in the *American Scientist* for March-April, 1978. He points out first that the study of fossils had "all but vanished from courses on evolution." (That's astonishing in itself! Most people think fossils and evolution go hand in hand. But apparently fossils and evolution have so little to do with each other that fossils are scarcely treated in university courses on evolution.) "The result," says Felsenstein, "has been a generation of evolutionary biologists who . . . can be reduced to babbling by any creationist debater in possession of more than two facts." But don't look in the yellow pages under "any creationist debater." When that was written, there were only two, Dr. Henry M. Morris and Dr. Duane T. Gish. Apparently all it took to level "mountains of fossil evidence for evolution" was Morris or Gish and three facts!

Largely because of the success of these two creationist debaters, creation science has attracted a great deal of attention from the news media. It started with a front page center column in the *Wall Street Journal* for June 15, 1979.

In September, 1979, *BioScience* carried a feature article by Robin Henig, "Evolution Called a 'Religion,' Creationism Defended as a 'Science.'" The article mentioned that creationists tend to win the debates, and it predicted that creation science would be around in scientific circles for a long time to come. Following on from the astute analysis in his captivating book, *Darwin Retried*, lawyer Norman Macbeth (1982) titled his summary judgment "Darwinism: A Time for Funerals."

Creation/evolution was featured on CBS "Sunday Morning" (Nov. 23, 1980) in a superb cover story put together by Richard Threlkeld (who ranks up there with CBC's Tom Kelly as a fair, honest, thoughtful, and thought-provoking TV journalist). The 20-minute piece starts with my students and me "in the act of discovery," hunting fossils in the desert east of San Diego; it continues with several evolutionists, other creationists, parents, students, and teachers in action; and it concludes with my favorite evolutionist, Stephen J. Gould, and with a clip from Carl Sagan's *Cosmos* TV series.

Threlkeld makes the inevitable trip to the site of the famous Scopes "monkey trial," but he doesn't allow his thinking to be buried there. "The debate goes on," he says, "and why not?" After all, nobody was there to see how life came into being, he says; at bottom both views are assumptions. But he doesn't stop thinking there, either. Instead, he treats the two ultimate assumptions as ideas which *can* be compared for their scientific merits and which *must* be compared before we can truly appreciate the origin of human beings.

In science, as well as the arts and humanities, then, the debate *does* go on, and it *should* go on. It should *not* be the kind of "winner take all" debate that generates more heat than light, of course, but rather the free exchange of ideas that helps each of us to better understand not only *what* we believe, but, more importantly, *why* we believe it.

When it comes to the scientific side of the debate, the news media and professional journals both credit creation with doing very well. *Science* (Lewin, 1981) and *The Washington Post* (Hilts, 1981) even called the historic

Gish/Doolittle television debate "a rout"—despite the fact that the evolutionist was an excellent speaker, highly qualified, and had both $5,000.00 and previous debating experience with Dr. Gish to help him prepare! Creation does so well, I think, simply because, like logical inference and the laws of science, the fossil evidence is so strongly in favor of creation.

Without giving creationists any credit, the world's leading evolutionists at that Chicago conference at least agreed on the same assessment of the fossil evidence reached (and predicted) by creationists long ago. As the summary in *Newsweek* (Nov. 3, 1980) put it (emphasis added):

> *Evidence from fossils now points overwhelmingly away from the classical Darwinism which most Americans learned in high school.*

In building up to that monumental conclusion (which should be posted as a plaque in all the nation's biology classrooms?), the writer starts with man:

> The missing link between man and the apes . . . is merely the most glamorous of a whole hierarchy of phantom creatures. In the fossil record, missing links are the rule . . . . The more scientists have searched for the transitional forms between species, the more they have been frustrated.

The concept of evolution touted in textbooks, then, is based on phantoms and figments of the imagination, *not* on fossils and the facts of science. Stephen Gould and Niles Eldredge (1977) put it this way: "Phyletic gradualism [gradual evolution] . . . was never 'seen' in the rocks." *Evolution was never seen in the rocks!* Evolution is *not* a logical inference from scientific observations, because the observations were contrary to the theory right from the start, even as Darwin said. If it wasn't based on evidence or logic, then, where did the concept of evolution come from? Gould and Eldredge supply the answer: "It [gradual evolution] expressed the cultural and political biases of

19th century liberalism." That's what has been passed off in our school systems for 100 years as the "fact of evolution"—"the cultural and political biases of 19th century liberalism."

When it comes to the fossil evidence, what are the facts? Believe it or not, when it comes to fossils, *evolutionists and creationists now agree on what the facts are.* The overwhelming pattern that emerges from fossils we have found is summarized in the word *stasis*. *Stasis* and *static* come from the same root word, a word that means "stay the same." Gould and Eldredge (1977) are simply saying that most kinds of fossilized life forms appear in the fossil sequence abruptly and distinctly as discrete types, then show relatively minor variation in their type, and finally abruptly disappear.

Steven Stanley (1981), fossil expert from Johns Hopkins University, provides several examples of stasis. Elephants *(Primelephas)* appear as a distinct group abruptly in the fossil sequence, diversify immediately into three subtypes, which then persist unchanged (except one which became extinct) without noticeably changing into anything else. Similarly, the modern horses *(Equus)* appear abruptly, Stanley says, "and their origin is not documented by known fossil evidence." Stanley also notes that the excellent fossil history of bowfin fishes shows only trivial changes and no basic shift of adaptation, making them very much like their descendants.

Stanley fully intends for the concept of stasis—sudden distinct appearance, minor variation, sudden disappearance—to stand out in stark contrast to the popular textbook and television picture of gradual, mutation-selection evolution. He singles out particularly the oft-taught "fact" of mammalian adaptive radiation, the idea that a mouse-like animal (without a mouse's gnawing front teeth) evolved into swimming whales and flying bats and all the other mammal types within about 12 million years. Trying to explain that on the basis of slow selection of minor mutational changes that would need a million years to transform just one species, he says, *"is clearly preposterous"* (emphasis added). Creationists only wish that evolutionists like Stanley were around decades ago, when creationists were pointing to the evidence, both genetic and fossil, that seemed even back then to make such an idea *"clearly preposterous!"*

The victory of stasis over gradualism did not come easily at the Chicago conference. As Lewin (1980) mentioned in his summary for *Science,* "the proceedings were at times unruly and even acrimonious," but, on the positive side, "many people suggested that the meeting was a turning point in the history of evolutionary thought."

Perhaps the most dramatic response came from Francisco Ayala. After admitting that neo-Darwinists "would not have predicted stasis from population genetics [extrapolation from mutation and selection]," he concluded, "but I am now convinced from what the paleontologists say that *small changes do not accumulate"* (emphasis added). No one finds it easy to change years of thinking, but a willingness to adapt theory to fact is the mark of a true scientist, and Ayala deserves a lot of credit for his stand.

When the dust finally settled, Gabriel Dover of Cambridge University summarized the Chicago conference by calling: "species stasis 'the single most important feature of macroevolution.'" Note again that at least the creationists and evolutionists agree on what the fossil facts represent, namely *stasis.*

But perhaps you also detected a note of irony in Dover's comment. If stasis means anything, it means staying the same; if evolution means anything, it means change. It seems to me, then, that evolutionists are actually saying (without quite meaning to, of course) that the most fundamental fact of their theory of change is that everything stays the same!

Creationists prefer a much more direct approach to the evidence. Each basic type of plant and animal life appears in the fossil sequence complete, fully formed, and functional; each classifies according to the criteria we use to distinguish groups today, with "boundary problems" generally no greater nor different for extinct forms than for those living today; and each type shows broad but quite finite ecologic and geographic variation within its type. The most direct and logical inference (to a heart and mind open to the possibility) appears to be, it seems to me, creation and variation within the basic created types.

When Darwin published his book back in 1859, no one knew what discoveries would be made or what patterns would emerge in the new science of paleontology. On the basis of their theory and the observations of heredity and reproduction, creationists predicted that only distinct types would be found, variation only within type, and persistence of the criteria for classification. Evolutionists predicted a series of links would be found to show how complex types today evolved slowly and gradually from common ancestral stocks that finally blurred into simple, indistinct, and difficult-to-classify early forms.

The real test of a scientific theory is its ability to predict in advance of observation. When it comes to fossils, *creation has passed the scientific test with flying colors*. The original Darwinian theory of evolution and the neo-Darwinist view have been disproven twice, both by genetics and the fossil evidence.

In his final chapter, as he reviews his reasons for calling his book "Evolution: A Theory in Crisis," Denton (1985) makes the following strong, sometimes harsh, statements:

> "We now know, as a result of discoveries made over the past thirty years, that not only is there a distinct break between the animate (living) and inanimate (non-living) worlds, but that it is one of the most dramatic in all nature, absolutely *unbridged by any series of transitional forms* ("missing links"), and like so many other major gaps of nature, *the transitional forms are not only empirically absent but are also conceptually impossible*" (p. 347, emphasis added).

> "Similarly, the sorts of scenarios conjured up by evolutionary biologists to bridge the great divisions of nature, *those strange realms of 'pro-avis' or the 'proto-cell' which are so utterly unrealistic to the skeptic*, are often viewed by the

believers (in evolution) as further powerful
confirmatory evidence of the truth of the
paradigm. Evolutionary thought today provides
many other instances where the priority of the
paradigm (i.e., the assumption that 'evolution is
fact') takes precedence over common sense" (p.
352, emphasis added).

"For the skeptic or indeed to anyone prepared
to step out of the circle of Darwinian belief, it
is not hard to find inversions of common sense
in modern evolutionary thought which are
strikingly reminiscent of the mental gymnastics
of the phlogiston chemists or the medieval
astronomers" (p. 351).

"In a very real sense, therefore, advocacy of
the doctrine of continuity (e.g., evolutionism) has
always necessitated a retreat from pure empiricism
(i.e., logic and observation), and contrary to what
is widely assumed by evolutionary biologists
today, *it has always been the anti-evolutionists
(e.g., creationists), not the evolutionists, in the
scientific community who have stuck rigidly to
the facts and adhered to a more strictly empirical
approach....* It was Darwin the evolutionist who
was retreating from the facts" (p. 353-354,
emphasis added).

On the positive side, Denton also notes that "there has
always existed a significant minority of first-rate biologists
who have never been able to bring themselves to accept
the validity of Darwinian claims" (p. 327). At a conference
in Sydney, Australia (April, 1987), where we appeared on
the platform together, Denton was willing to cautiously
extrapolate that "significant minority" to "perhaps a
majority" of first-rate biologists. And he stresses also that
those biologists willing to explore the design hypothesis do
so for scientific reasons, apart from particular religious
presuppositions (See p. 341).

Certainly, a growing number of university science majors
and graduate students are willing to consider creation a more

logical inference from our scientific observations. Most of the leading evolutionists, even those like Gould, Raup, Stanley, and others who have been debunking the old idea of gradualistic evolution, however, are only willing to try a new (or renewed) version of evolutionary theory: *"hopeful monsters."*

Hopeful Monsters and Punctuated Equilibria

A new concept of evolution is outlined by Stephen Gould in *Natural History* for June-July, 1977, in an article titled "The Return of Hopeful Monsters." Gould, who teaches paleontology at Harvard, says, "The fossil record with its abrupt transitions offers no support for gradual change . . . ." Then he goes on to propose that "Macroevolution proceeds by the rare success of these hopeful monsters, not by continuous small changes within populations." Actually, this new idea is quite like the idea Richard Goldschmidt had back in the 1930's, and Gould says, "I predict that during the next decade [the 80's] Goldschmidt will be largely vindicated in the world of evolutionary biology" (Fig. 27).

Now then, what is a hopeful monster? It's the supposed result of radical chromosome rearrangements or cataclysmic mutations in "super-genes" or regulatory genes that are crucial to early development. Why, for example, don't we find any gradual evolutionary transitions from reptiles to birds? Answer (according to the hopeful-monster concept): Because the first bird hatched out of a reptile egg (much to the surprise of its parents, no doubt!).

The reptile-bird example was the focus of an enthusiastic exchange between creationist Duane Gish and evolutionist Stephen Gould in *Discover* magazine for May and July, 1981. *Discover* had asked Dr. Richard Bliss and me to participate in a "magazine debate" with Stephen Gould and Carl Sagan, but Gould and/or Sagan declined. The magazine published instead an anti-creationist article by Gould and followed it with a letter by creationist Gish in which he mentioned that some evolutionists believe the first bird hatched out of a reptile egg. Gould responded that Gish was misrepresenting evolution and that anyone who believed that ought to be laughed off the intellectual stage. Gish responded by proving that the reptile-bird "jump" had indeed been used as a specific example quoted approvingly by Goldschmidt, whose ideas Gould is resurrecting. Stanley, in his book (1979), at least twice referred to the "hopeful monster" possibility in all seriousness.

And that's not the end of the story yet. There is a children's book called *The Wonderful Egg* (Ipcar, 1958) that achieved specific recommendation from the prestigious American Association for the Advancement of Science (AAAS) as well as from the American Council on Education and the Association for Childhood Education International. The book starts innocently enough with a mother dinosaur laying an egg. After asking, "Did a mother dinosaur lay that egg to hatch into a baby dinosaur?" the book answers "no" to brontosaur, stegosaur, and a list of other dinosaurs. Then comes the dramatic conclusion. The egg laid by the mother dinosaur wasn't a dinosaur egg at all: "It was a wonderful new kind of egg." And what did this dinosaur egg hatch into? "It hatched into a baby bird, the first baby bird in the whole world. And the baby bird grew up . . . with feathers . . . the first beautiful bird that ever sang a song high in the tree tops . . . of long, long, ago."

Now back when children grew up on farms and where science is based on fact, not fantasy, that idea would be pretty hard to sell! I realize, of course, that this "wonderful (reptile/bird) egg" is an extreme example, and I trust (or at least hope) that—despite the puzzling endorsement by the AAAS—no one takes it seriously.

But this admittedly far-fetched example does point up some genuinely serious problems with the hopeful-monster mechanism. Gould (1977b), of course, recognizes some of these himself. First, what are the chances, even given a vast amount of time, of producing a hopeful monster rather than a monstrosity? We have, unfortunately, observed many cases of monstrous changes as a result of mutations and chromosome rearrangements, but we have never yet observed a hopeful monster. Then, too, says Gould, with what would this hopeful monster mate? After all, to start

Figure 27. Harvard's Stephen Gould (1979b) says that, "The fossil record with its abrupt transitions offers no support for gradual change . . . " He proposes instead that evolution occurs in jumps by the "rare success of these hopeful monsters." Could a bird, for example, hatch from a reptile's egg? Gould (1975) assumes a materialistic philosophy for himself and all other scientists, however, and that does not permit him to consider creation as a more logical inference from the fossil evidence.

with, it's the only member of its species! Nevertheless, even while recognizing these difficulties, Eldredge (1978) said in a news interview that he is, in a sense, forced to look for some new mechanism of evolution, because, in all their searching, "no one has found any evidence of such in-between creatures" as gradual evolution requires.

Consider, further, the size and nature of the "jump" the hopeful monster makes. (The hopeful-monster concept is also called "saltatory [jumping] evolution" or "quantum evolution.") Even if animals don't go from reptile to bird in one jump, do they go from leg to wing in one jump? If the jump isn't big and dramatic, then what's the difference between the hopeful-monster mechanism and the discredited concept of the gradual accumulation of minor mutations?

Then there's Darwin's original problem: the origin of new traits. Gould (1980d) wants to believe that teratology, the study of embryonic defects, holds the key to understanding evolution. But all the examples of effects produced by "jumping genes," chromosomal rearrangements, and regular gene mutations are only shufflings of existing parts, e.g., insects with legs where their antennas normally are, or with the extra pair of wings thanks to duplication of the second thoracic segment. Duplicating, deleting, and shuffling around reptile parts might conceivably produce some weird new reptile, but such processes are fundamentally irrelevant to the origin of birds.

According to "punctuated equilibrium," the broadest and mildest and most reasonable evolutionary alternative to gradual evolution, there may have been several intermediate steps, but each stage involved organisms so *unfit* to survive that they existed only in small populations that left no fossil remains. Now at last we have the *chief advantage* of the hopeful-monster or punctuational approach: *it explains why the links are still missing.* Either they were so unfit to survive that they never multiplied in numbers sufficient to leave fossil remains, or else evolution simply jumped from one basic structural plan to another with no intermediate steps.

Here again we find the creationist and the modern evolutionist (the post-neo-Darwinian punctuationalist) at least *agreeing that the missing links are missing*. But what is the scientific difference between saying that the missing links can never be found (the "new" evolution) and saying that they never existed at all (creation)?

Sometimes it's kind of fun to be a creationist. The "rear guard" neo-Darwinian evolutionists like to point out the apparent absurdity of hopeful-monster evolution and claim that *evolution could not happen fast*. The punctuational evolutionists point to genetic limits and the fossil evidence to show that *evolution did not happen slowly*. The creationist simply agrees with both sides: evolution couldn't happen fast and it didn't happen slowly—because evolution can't and didn't happen at all! In terms of the kind of variation that *can* and *did* occur, the *creation* concept seems to be the more logical inference from our observations.

At least the hopeful monster concept avoids the problem of missing links. But notice: this new concept of evolution is based on the fossils we *don't* find and on genetic mechanisms that have *never* been observed. The case for creation is based on thousands of tons of fossils that we *have* found and on genetic mechanisms (variation within type) that we *do* observe and put into practice every day. As a scientist, I'm inclined to prefer a model that's based on what we *do* see and *can* explain (creation), rather than one that's based on what we don't see and cannot explain (evolution).

Human Beings

What about ourselves? What can we infer from the evidence regarding the origin of human beings? Evolutionists now give us two choices (Gliedman, 1982). Either human beings are the result of time, chance, and a ceaseless struggle for survival, or else we began as "a hopeful monster whose star was a bit more benevolent than most" *(Newsweek,* Nov. 3, 1980). According to creationists, the evidence suggests instead that we are here by creation.

Even some of the early evolutionists felt that human beings might be special. Alfred Wallace presented the theory of natural selection jointly with Darwin in 1859, but Wallace later argued that the human brain could not be explained by natural selection. Darwin disagreed. The difference between these two evolutionists is described by Isaac Asimov (1980) in the *T. V. Guide* preview of a special television series on Darwin, and the same topic is also explored by Stephen Gould (1980) and Colin Patterson (1981). Most evolutionists sided with Darwin. That is, they believed that man, like "other animals," was the result of time, chance, and evolutionary processes.

However, evolutionists chose to *believe* in the evolution of man for philosophical or "religious" reasons, not because of logical inference from the fossil evidence. In his book, *The Descent of Man,* Darwin did not cite a single reference to fossils in support of that belief. And there were several fossil specimens of human beings known when Darwin wrote, namely Neanderthal Man.

Neanderthal was originally portrayed as a "beetle-browed, barrel-chested, bow-legged brute" (a suitable ancestor for a mugger, if nothing else!). The creationists in those days responded, "Hey, wait a minute. Neanderthals are just plain people, some of whom suffered bone diseases." The first Neanderthals discovered came from harsh inland environments in Europe, where they could easily have (like many of our own American plains Indians) suffered skeletal abnormalities, especially from lack of iodine in the diet and shortage of sun-induced vitamin D necessary for calcium absorption during the long winters.

Neanderthals from the Palestine area don't show the more stooped and massive features. The brain volume of Neanderthals is slightly larger than the average brain volume of people today, and Neanderthal peoples had a well-developed culture, art, and religion. Nowadays, evolutionists agree completely with creationists: Neanderthals were just plain people, no more different from people living today than one living nation is different from another. What were the "cave men"? Just people who lived in caves. (And at today's prices, that may once again be a good idea!)

Tragically, Neanderthals have not been the only people once considered subhuman "missing links." In an article reprinted in *Natural History* for April, 1980 (as part of an issue on the history of evolutionary thought), there's a short but very sad article by Henry Fairfield Osborn. Osborn says that a hypothetical unbiased zoologist from Mars would classify people into several distinct genera and many species. Thus, said Osborn, Negroes would be classified as a separate species, not yet evolved to full human stature. "The standard of intelligence of the average adult Negro," wrote Osborn as a so-called fact of evolution, "is similar to that of the eleven-year-old youth of the species *Homo sapiens* [which, for Osborn, meant Caucasians only]." Osborn was a leading evolutionist of the 1920's, and it is easy to see how his kind of evolutionary thinking (rejected by modern evolutionists) helped to pave the way for the events of the 1940's. (See also Gould, 1981b, on the false science of "craniometry" and its terrible applications.)

In 1912, speculation about man's ancestry shifted to Piltdown Man, dignified by the scientific name *Eoanthropus dawsoni*. Almost everyone knows that Piltdown Man turned out to be a deliberate hoax. But Piltdown Man wasn't shown to be a hoax until the 1950's. For over 40 years, the subtle message of the textbooks was clear: You can believe in creation if you want to, but the facts are all on the side of evolution. The facts in this case turned out to be a bit of ape jaw and human skull stained to make them look older.

Piltdown was much in the news in 1979. One mystery is who perpetrated the hoax, but the real mystery is *why did anyone believe it?* It was *not* a particularly clever hoax. As Gould (1979b) points out, when people looked at the teeth with the right hypothesis in mind, "the evidences of artificial abrasion [filing] immediately sprang to the eye. Indeed so obvious did they seem it may well be asked—how was it that they had escaped notice before?" The age-stain was better done, but the imported mammalian fossils and handcrafted tools were again obvious frauds. People wanted to believe in evolution, so they were able to see what they wanted to believe. There's a lesson there in caution for both evolutionists and creationists, and a good reason for the two-model (creation/evolution) approach to origins. (Compare with the plea for pluralism by Washburn, 1978.)

Athough not an outright fraud, Java Man (*Pithecanthropus*) was not much better. (See Gish, 1986, for fascinating details on this and other human fossils.) The skull cap and femur were found quite far apart in a gravel deposit (which implies erosion and potential mixing). Eugene DuBois later dismissed his own find as the unrelated parts of a human and a giant gibbon, and since he had found—but kept secret for thirty years—a human skull discovered at the same level, he knew his other finds should not be called the ancestors of human beings. Although I'm completely unable to offer any reason why, Donald Johanson (1981) refers to Java Man as if it were still considered a valid fossil, and Richard Lewontin (1981) wants Java Man (*Pithecanthropus*) taught as one of five "facts of evolution" he cites. A better reason could hardly be cited for *not* teaching evolution as a fact!

Peking Man appears to be another "false fact" of evolution. Originally called *Sinanthropus*, it was re-classified Homo *erectus*, the group name later given to Java Man as well. But now, also like Java Man, it has changed from an illustration of evolution to an example of bad science instead.

Only the skulls of "Peking Man" were ever found, never the lower skeleton. And the skulls were all bashed in at the rear. The skulls were found in a cave outside Peking, China, before World War II, along with the bones of various other animals—and a few tools and evidence of human culture. The Peking skulls were very monkey-like, but, since no human remains were found, someone decided that the owners of those bashed-in skulls must have used the tools, thus making them "tool-using apes" or "ape men," some form of man's ancestor.

It now appears that "Peking Man" was *man's meal, not man's ancestor*! It seems the tools were used *on*, rather than *by*, the owners of those bashed-in skulls (Gish, 1981). Monkey meat is very tough and stringy, and quite difficult to eat. But monkey brains are a different story. Even to this day, natives of Southeast Asia will lop off the heads of monkeys, boil them, bash in the rear of the skulls, and enjoy that special delicacy once called our ancestor, a sort of monkey brains on the half skull.

Joining Piltdown Man, Java Man, and Peking Man as proposed witnesses for human evolution at the famous Scopes trial in 1925 was Nebraska Man.

Nebraska Man was dignified by the scientific name *Hesperopithecus haroldcookii*, but he was never known from anything but a tooth. By imagination, the tooth was put in a skull, the skull was put on a skeleton, and the skeleton was given flesh, hair, and a family! Fig. 28 includes a picture of Nebraska Man redrawn from a London newspaper published during the year of the Scopes trial.

Two years later, Nebraska Man was back to being just a tooth. The tooth was found in the real skull, attached to the real skeleton. It turned out not to be the tooth of man's ancestor, but the tooth of an extinct pig!

Most scientists have long since learned not to make so much of a tooth. Yet it was not until 1979 that *Ramapithecus*—"reconstructed as a biped on the basis of teeth and jaws alone"—was dropped as a "false start of the human parade" (Zihlman and Lowenstein, 1979). Yet even at present *Aegyptopithecus* is being suggested by Elwyn Simons (1980) as a "nasty little thing" whose social behavior and family life—conjured up largely from eye sockets and the canine teeth of the males—may make it a kind of psychological ancestor of man!

Modern speculation on man's ancestry centers on a group of fossils called *Australopithecus*. In the public mind, these fossils are associated especially with the work in Africa of the Leakey family and of Donald Johanson and his famous specimen, "Lucy" (Fig. 29).

The name *Australopithecus* means "southern ape," and there's a good chance that's just what they are. Johanson and Richard Leakey are presently engaged in a heated debate about the meaning of each other's specimens. (See

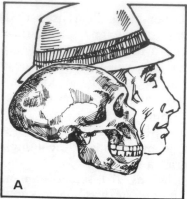

A. *Neanderthals* turned out to be just plain people, some of whom suffered from bone diseases. In proper attire, they would attract no particular attention today.

B. *Piltdown Man (Eoanthropus dawsoni)* was a deliberate (but not very clever) hoax palmed off as "proof of evolution" to students for more than two generations. It turned out to be a bit of ape jaw and human skull artificially aged.

C. *Nebraska Man (Hesperopithecus)* was reconstructed, family and all, from a tooth—a tooth that later was found to belong to an extinct pig!

Figure 28. Discarded candidates for man's ancestor.

Kern and Haupt in *Life,* Jan., 1982.) In their critique of
the Leakeys, Johanson and White (1980) noted: "Modern
chimpanzees, by this definition [Richard Leakey's] would
be classified as *A. africanus* [gracile australopithecines]."
Apes after all? And Johanson says Lucy and his Hadar
specimens are *more primitive* (i.e. more apelike) than the
Leakeys' finds, so much more so that Johanson gave them
a new species name, *Australopithecus afarensis* (see *Time,*
Jan. 27, 1979). Johanson likes to point out that where he
finds his australopithecine bones, he finds many of the
regular African animals (rhinos, boas, hippos, monkeys,
etc.), but never apes. Could it be that apes are exactly what
he has been finding all along?

If these australopithecine fragments are so primitive,
then what's all the fuss about? It's this: Did the
australopithecines walk upright? Johanson, the Leakeys,
and others say "yes," and therefore it belongs to the family history of man.

But how crucial to the definition of man is relatively
upright posture? Vincent Sarich at the University of
California in Berkeley and Adrienne Zihlman say that if
you want something that walks upright, consider the living
pygmy chimpanzee, *Pan paniscus.* This rare rain forest
chimpanzee is only slightly shorter than the average chimpanzee, but it spends a fair amount of time walking
upright. Since all the other features of the australopithecines are so apelike, perhaps Johanson and the
Leakeys have discovered the ancestor of the living pygmy
chimpanzee!

But did the australopithecines indeed walk upright? In
the *American Biology Teacher* (May, 1979), Charles Oxnard says, "In one sense you may think there is no problem. For most anthropologists are agreed that the gracile
australopithecines . . . are on the main human lineage .
. . . This is the view that is presented in almost all textbooks; I expect that it has been your teaching in the
classroom; and it is widely broadcast in such publications
as the 'Time-Life Series' and the beautiful [television]
story of 'The Ascent of Man.' However, anatomical
features in some of these fossils provide a warning against

a too-ready acceptance of this story . . . . " As part of his
warning, Oxnard reminds his readers of gross errors once
made in the cases of Piltdown Man and Nebraska Man.
Oxnard then proceeds to examine the evidence. And he's
well qualified to do so as Professor of Anatomy at the
University of Southern California. He points out first that
anatomical relationships can't be simply established by
subjective opinion. Viewed one way, for example, the
pelvic bones of australopithecines seem to be intermediate
between man and ape. But merely viewing the bones from
a different angle makes the specimen seem as far distant
from man as the apes are. "Yet another view," says Oxnard, "might suggest that the fossil arose from the African
apes via modern humans!"—in other words, that humans
were the missing link between the australopithecines and
the apes!

Because he is so sensitive to the serious problems of
subjective interpretations, Oxnard then goes on to describe
in fascinating detail a computer technique called "multivariate analysis." He goes into both its practical and its
theoretic applications and reaches two conclusions.

First, his scientific conclusion: if the australopithecines
walked upright, it was *not* in the human manner. If their
posture resembled that of any living creature, it was most
likely the orangutan. Oxnard also reaches a second conclusion for educators: *"Be critical."* That is, examine all the
relevant evidence. Look at it from different viewpoints.
Presumably, that's one of the chief skills and attitudes we
want to encourage in our science students. Certainly the
two-model (creation /evolution) approach can assist in
achieving that worthy goal. That admonition, "be
critical," applies also to the creation model, of course, and
that's just what I want you to be. Don't accept creation
only on my say so, but don't dismiss it either, until you
have examined the evidence to the best of your ability
(Fig. 29).

Louis Leakey started the modern interest in australopithecines (and captured the attention of *National
Geographic)* back in 1959 with his "ape man," *Zinjanthropus. Zinjanthropus* has since been reclassified as

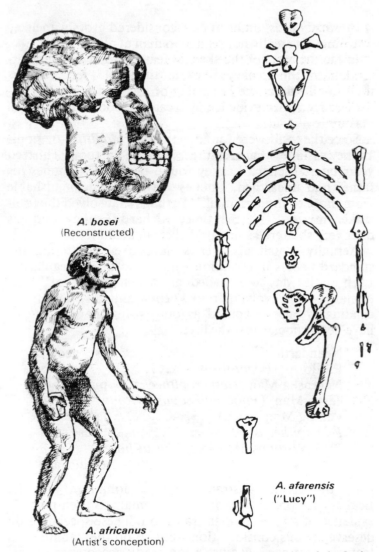

A. bosei
(Reconstructed)

A. africanus
(Artist's conception)

A. afarensis
("Lucy")

Figure 29. Australopithecines, including Johanson's "Lucy" and the Leakey finds in Africa, are the current candidates for man's ancestors. But USC's Charles Oxnard (1979) says the fossils "provide a warning against too ready acceptance of this view." He reaches two conclusions. One is scientific: "If the australopithecines walked upright, it was not in the human manner." The second is educational: "Be critical." We must encourage our science students to examine evidence more critically, he says—and, I might add, that's what the two-model creation/evolution concept is all about.

Australopithecus, and it is now considered grossly apelike, an extinct line really not related to man at all.

In fact, it was not the skeletal features that attracted attention to the Leakey finds in the first place. It was tools. As I said at the beginning of this book, every scientist can recognize evidence of creation. Tools imply a tool maker.

Since the tools were found with *Australopithecus,* Louis Leakey assumed that creature had made the tools. Thirteen years later, Richard Leakey found beneath the bones his father had unearthed, "bones virtually indistinguishable from those of modern man." Perhaps that solved the tool-maker mystery. At the time, Richard Leakey said his discovery shattered standard beliefs in evolution.

Actually, fossil discoveries have been shattering the standard beliefs in evolution with monotonous regularity. Each in its day was hailed as "scientific proof" that human beings evolved from apelike animals, yet all the candidates once proposed as our evolutionary ancestors have been knocked off the list:

Neanderthals.....................just people
Piltdown *(Eoanthropus)*.................hoax
Nebraska Man *(Hesperopithecus)*...pig's tooth
Java Man (*Pithecanthropus*; *Homo erectus*);
Peking Man.....................bad science
Ramapithecus.....................false start
Zinjanthropus *(Australopithecus bosei)* ....
.... extinct ape

Only the gracile australopithecines Johanson and the Leakeys are presently working on remain as even possible evidence of an ape/human transition. These specimens do deserve serious consideration—but so do the "anatomical features that warn against a too-ready acceptance of this story."

The australopithecines could not have been our ancestors, of course, if people were walking around *before* Lucy and her kin were fossilized—and there is some evidence to suggest just that. Fossils of ordinary people in Mid-Tertiary rock were found in Castenedolo, Italy, back in the late 1800's, and the evolutionist Sir Arthur Keith recognized that accepting these "pre-ape" finds would shatter his belief in evolution (or at least its scientific support). Oxnard (1979) calls attention to the *Kanapoi hominid,* a human upper arm bone found in rock strata in Africa laid down *before* those that entomb the australopithecine remains.

Then there's the footprint evidence. Actually, we have many features in common with the apes (as a trip to the zoo will verify), and it should not be surprising that some bones would be difficult to classify. But apes and human beings have quite different footprints. The apes have essentially four hands, with an opposable big toe, that makes their footprint quite different from ours. They also have a gait that's quite different and a tendency to drop to all fours and "knuckle walk."

In *National Geographic* for April, 1979, and *Science News* for February 9, 1980, Mary Leakey describes a trail of man-like prints in volcanic ash near Laetoli in east Africa. Fig. 30, redrawn from the former, shows Mary Leakey's concept of how the prints were formed and preserved and the kind of foot that made them. If you examine the article, you'll find that the foot looks pretty much like yours or mine.

In the center of the *National Geographic* article is a two-page foldout. Elephants, giraffes, guinea hens, and acacia trees dot the scene. Except for the volcano, it looks as if it could have been taken from a Tarzan movie. Then across the center is a line of very human-like tracks. You might be surprised, however, at what the artist put in the tracks. (An artist had to do it, by the way, since we have no foot bones connected to leg bones, etc., to tell us what really made the tracks.) Perhaps the most logical inference from these observations is that people made them. The stride is quite short, but perhaps the person was just very cautious about walking across the damp volcanic ash.

Most evolutionists, however, forbid themselves to believe these tracks could be made by people, because they don't believe people evolved until later. The Kanapoi hominid, however, suggests that people might very well have been around to make these prints. And living not far from that site in Africa today are people (the Pygmies) not much taller as adults than the Laetoli print makers.

Understanding the serious implications of the Laetoli finds, one scientist looked almost desperately for evidence that some animal, and not man, may have made those prints. He even had a dancing bear jump up and down in mud, hoping those tracks would resemble the Laetoli

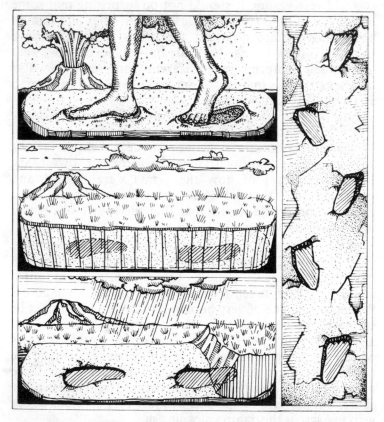

Figure 30. Footprints are more distinctive of man than most bone fragments are. If the footprints above are accepted as human, evolutionists would have to say that man existed "before" man's supposed ancestors. Creationists say that these footprints (and the Castenedolo and Kanapoi bones) simply suggest that people have always been people, beginning with the first created human beings.

prints! His conclusion? It was impossible to tell the Laetoli tracks from ordinary human footprints. As an evolutionist, he used such adjectives as "shocking," "disturbing," and "upsetting" to describe his results, since none of the popular evolutionary "links," including Lucy, could be man's ancestor, if people were already walking around before these so-called ancestors were fossilized. To the creationist, the evidence simply confirms that people have always been people, and apes always apes, as far back as the evidence goes.

Obviously, of course, the suggestion that man might have lived before man's supposed ancestors raises some fundamental questions about what we mean by the geologic sequence. So let's take a look now at that very important question.

Fossil Sequence: The "Geologic Column"

A cure for creationism, says the average evolutionist, is a walk from the bottom to the top of Grand Canyon. Here, he says, the story of evolution is laid out right before our eyes: marine creatures on the bottom, then the land plants and animals farther up.

Well, my family and I (and many other creationists) took up the challenge and made a four-day hike across the Canyon, North Rim to South (fantastic!). And, as we knew in advance, it's true enough that fossils are not found at random. They are found in groups called "geologic systems," and these geologic systems do have a tendency to be found in a certain vertical order. That order is represented in an idea called the "geologic column" (Fig. 31).

Now the geologic column is an idea, *not* an actual series of rock layers. Nowhere do we find the complete sequence. Even the walls of Grand Canyon included only five of the twelve major systems (one, five, six, and seven, with small portions here and there of the fourth system, the Devonian).

But still, the geologic column *does* represent a tendency for fossils to be found in groups and for those groups to be found in a certain vertical order. Cambrian trilobites and Cretaceous dinosaurs aren't usually found together. I

Figure 31. Two interpretations of fossil groups (geologic systems) and their sequence (the "geologic column").

Right. According to the evolution model, systems and the geologic column represent stages in the slow and gradual evolution of life over aeons of time.

Below. According to the creation model, groups of fossils are the remains of plants and animals once living in different ecological zones at the same time, and they were buried in rapid succession. (Drawings after Bliss, Gish, and Parker. 1980. *Fossils: Key to the Present.* CLP Pubs., San Diego.)

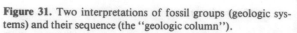

(1) CAMBRIAN (2) ORDOVICIAN (3) SILURIAN (4) DEVONIAN (5) MISSISSIPPIAN (6) PENNSYLVANIAN (7) PERMIAN (8) TRIASSIC (9) JURASSIC (10) CRETACEOUS (11) TERTIARY (12) QUATERNARY

found the trilobite I wear on my necktie, for instance, in Madison, Indiana, but our family's collection of dinosaur bones came from Alberta, Canada.

Why aren't trilobite and dinosaur fossils found together? According to evolution, the answer is easy. The Cambrian trilobites died out millions of years before the dinosaurs evolved. But there is another explanation that seems even more natural. After all, even if trilobites and dinosaurs were alive today, they still wouldn't be found together. Why? Because they live in different ecological zones. Dinosaurs are land animals, but trilobites are bottom-dwelling sea creatures.

According to creationists, the geological systems represent different ecological zones, the buried remains of plants and animals that once lived together in the same environment. A walk through Grand Canyon, then, is not like a walk through evolutionary time; instead, it's like a walk from the bottom of the ocean, across the tidal zone, over the shore, across the lowlands, and on into the upland regions. Several lines of evidence seem to favor this ecological view.

First, there's the matter of "misplaced fossils." Evolutionists believe, for example, that the land plants didn't appear until over 100 million years after the Cambrian trilobites died out. Yet over sixty genera of woody plants spores, pollen, and wood itself have been recovered from lowest "trilobite rock" (Cambrian) throughout the world. The evidence is so well known that it's even in standard college biology textbooks. A botany textbook by Weier, Stocking, and Barbour puts it this way: "Despite tempting fragments of evidence, such as cutinized [waxy] spores and bits of xylem [wood] dating back to the Cambrian period . . . ." most evolutionists still believe that land plants didn't evolve until much later. But notice, the evolutionist argues "in spite of the evidence."

The creationist doesn't argue, *"in spite* of the evidence." Rather, *"Because* of the evidence," the creationist says, "we think that land plants and Cambrian trilobites lived at the same time in different ecological zones. Normally, these sea animals and land plants would not be preserved together for ecological reasons. But a few plant specimens, escaping decay, could occasionally be entombed with trilobites in ocean sediment, and that's what we see." Footprints of man and dinosaurs together also represent "misplaced fossils." So does the long list of "living fossils"—forms of life once thought to be extinct for millions of years, but now found alive and well in certain restricted environments at the present time.

Misplaced fossils are common enough that evolutionists have a vocabulary to deal with them. A specimen found "too low" in the geologic column (before it was supposed to have evolved) is called a "stratigraphic leak," and a specimen found "too high" is called a "re-worked specimen." Oftentimes, of course, there is actual physical evidence for mixing of strata from two different sources. But sometimes such evidence is lacking. With such a handy vocabulary available, it's quite likely that the number of misplaced fossils found—without evidence of disturbance —is far greater than the number actually recorded (which is considerable anyway).

Sometimes whole geologic systems are misplaced. While I was a graduate student in stratigraphy class, we went on a field trip to find the missing 25 million years of the Silurian. We went to a quarry in southern Indiana that was famous for building quality limestone. The massive gray limestone was quite thick and exposed over many hundreds of yards. In the lower part of the formation, we found corals belonging to system No. 2, the Ordovician. But as we worked our way up the quarry wall, suddenly we began to find Devonian corals, those belonging to system No. 4. Where were the missing corals of system No. 3, the Silurian?

For an evolutionist, that's a crucial question. Evolutionists believe that Ordovician corals evolved into Silurian corals which evolved into Devonian corals. Skipping the Silurian would break the evolutionary chain, and for an evolutionist would be impossible.

What was there between the Ordovician and Devonian corals in the limestone quarry in Indiana? Only millimeters separated them, and there was no change in color, no change in texture, not even a bedding plane. There was no physical evidence at all for those hypothetical 25 million years of evolutionary time. As the professor emphasized, such a situation is a serious problem for evolution. We simply can't imagine land just lying there for 25 million years, neither eroding or depositing, then picking up exactly where it left off.

Again, evolutionists have coined a term to deal with the problem: *paraconformity*. A contact line between the two rock strata is called a "conformity" if the physical evidence indicates smooth continuous deposition with no time break. "Disconformity" is used where the physical evidence indicates erosion has removed part of the rock sequence. Disconformities are often represented by wavy lines in geologic diagrams, and they often appear in the field as *real* "wavy lines" in which erosion channels and stream beds can be seen cutting into the eroded rock layer. But in the case of paraconformity, there is no evidence of erosion nor any other physical evidence of a break in time. The name even means that it looks like a conformity. In fact, the only way to recognize a paraconformity is by prior commitment to evolutionary theory. There is no physical evidence. But if you believe in evolution, then you must believe there was some gap in the sequence, or else the evolutionary chain would be broken.

Creationists don't need the term paraconformity. Creationists can simply accept the physical evidence as it's found: smooth, continuous deposition with no time break.

Suppose the Ordovician and Devonian geologic systems represent different ecological zones of creatures living at the same time. Then a change in some ecological factor, such as saltiness or temperature, could cause one group of corals to replace the other ecologically, smoothly and continuously. Or sediment from one ecological zone could be deposited immediately on top of sediment from another zone, again producing smooth continuous deposition with no time break. Gould (1980a) laments that geologists are constantly reporting ecological interpretations of fossil deposits, but he says they should quit doing that, because the time scale is all wrong for evolution.

Paraconformities are quite common. In parts of Grand Canyon, for instance, Mississippian rock rests paraconformably on Cambrian rock—a gap of 125 million years of hypothetical evolutionary time with no evidence of a time break at all. (At some points, however, there is a disconformity between Devonian rock and Cambrian.) The widespread existence of paraconformities is one reason you need a local field guide to hunt fossils. Even when there's no physical evidence of any major disturbance, you often find yourself missing many millions of years of hypothetical evolutionary time and need the guidebook to remind you where you are.

Then there's the matter of *polystratic* fossils. As the name implies, polystrates are fossils that extend through many rock layers or strata. I first heard of polystratic fossils as a geology student. The professor, an evolutionist, was talking about zoning rocks on the basis of the microscopic fossils they contain. The usual assumption, of course, is that one microfossil evolved into another, which evolved into another, and so on. The rock unit he zoned was presumed to involve about 20 million years of evolutionary time. But, the professor said, "I followed the rock unit down the creek bed, and here was this ammonite [shellfish similar to nautiloid] sticking up through the whole 20 million years! How can that be?" That would indeed be a mystery for an evolutionist! But it would be no mystery at all, if the whole rock unit were deposited rapidly. Some things, like palm trees washed out in vegetation mats after a tropical storm, may float upright for a while, and they could be entombed in that upright position if burial occurred quickly enough (Fig. 32).

Polystrates are especially common in coal formations. For years and years, students have been taught that coal represents the remains of swamp plants slowly accumulated as peat and then even more slowly changed into coal. But there are many reasons that this swamp idea simply cannot be true: the type of plants involved, texture of deposits, and state of preservation are all wrong; the action of flowing water, not stagnation, is evident; etc., etc. (Nevins, 1976; Austin, 1979.)

A new concept of coal formation is being developed right now, thanks in part to the work of creationist geologists. One of the leaders in this field is Dr. Steven Austin. In his dissertation for the Ph.D. in coal geology from Penn State (Austin, 1979), Dr. Austin suggests that coal was formed from plant debris deposited under mats of

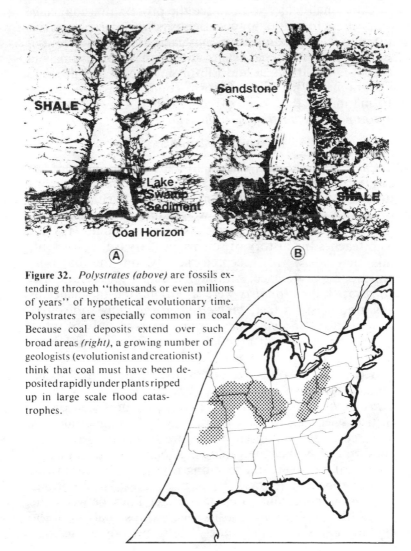

Figure 32. *Polystrates (above)* are fossils extending through "thousands or even millions of years" of hypothetical evolutionary time. Polystrates are especially common in coal. Because coal deposits extend over such broad areas *(right)*, a growing number of geologists (evolutionist and creationist) think that coal must have been deposited rapidly under plants ripped up in large scale flood catastrophes.

vegetation floating in sea water. His model, still in the developmental stage, already explains many features of coal that the swamp model cannot explain. Even more importantly, his theory—a real scientific breakthrough—is the first ever to be used to *predict* the location and quality of coal.

On a small scale, you can see the process that may have started the formation of coal deposits when a typhoon rips up mats of vegetation from an island and floats them out to sea. But some coal seams run from Pennsylvania out across Ohio, Indiana, and Illinois into Iowa and down to Oklahoma! What kind of storm could be involved in the formation of that kind of coal seam? Answer: *Massive flooding and catastrophic upheaval.*

Neo-Catastrophism

Catastrophism was originally an important part of creationist geology. In the 1800's, due especially to the influence of James Hutton and Charles Lyell, emphasis shifted to the concept of slow, gradual accumulation of sediment (uniformitarianism). As Stephen Gould (1977a), who teaches the history of science at Harvard, points out, this new idea was accepted largely on the basis of philosophic preference. Although Gould is an evolutionist, he says: *"Catastrophists* were as committed to science as any gradualist; in fact, *they adopted the more 'objective' view that one should believe what one sees* and not interpolate missing bits of gradual record into a literal tale of rapid change." (Emphasis added.)

Because of the objective evidence, a new group of evolutionary geologists has arisen. They call themselves *"neo-catastrophists."* Derek Ager (1976), past president of the British Geologic Association, says, "I have already declared myself an unrepentant 'neo-catastrophist.' " He goes on to say that the geologic evidence reminds him of the life of a soldier, full of "long periods of boredom and short periods of terror." It seems to me that the "long periods of boredom" are the contact lines between the strata (the *absence* of deposits where, presumably, all the evolution has occurred); the "short periods of terror" formed the fossil-bearing deposits themselves. It is rapid, large-scale processes that form the fossil-bearing deposits we actually observe.

Ager also interprets differences in geological formations as a result of "ecological expropriations," a rapid process involving replacement of one existing type by another— i.e., ecology *not* evolution. Ager knows that the creationists ("California sects," he calls them) are going to make use of his work, and he's absolutely right. We're not arguing our case on the strength of his opinion, however, but upon the evidence that he knows so well. The evidence suggests rapid deposition on a large scale—catastrophism.

In the *World Book Science Year 1980,* David Raup implies that the fossil evidence argues for "survival of the luckiest." The whims of statistics or catastrophe, he says— *not* "survival of the fittest"—explain the extinction we observe. The extinction of dinosaurs has been variously blamed on radiation from an exploding star, stupidity, and even chronic constipation from death of a laxative plant!

As I write this, evolutionists seem to be stepping all over themselves to see who can come up with the right worldwide catastrophe to explain the sudden, worldwide extinction of the dinosaurs and much of the rest of Cretaceous life. Many evolutionists think that the global cataclysm was caused by collision of an asteroid with the earth (see Russell, *Scientific American,* Jan. 1982), but they are divided on the secondary effects. Some say it hit the land and produced a dust cloud that reduced photosynthesis and starved the dinosaurs to extinction within 10 years; or alternately, that the dust blocked off the sun's heat and froze the dinosaurs out in 2 or 3 years. It is more likely, of course, that the hypothetical huge meteorite would strike the *oceans* covering 70% of the earth's surface, and a watery catastrophe would provide a means for preserving the dinosaurs as fossils. After surveying the many and varied theories of extinction, Norman Newell concluded way back in 1963 that the most consistent explanation for mass extinction is a catastrophe involving massive flooding.

Massive continental flooding runs contrary to the more

generally accepted evolutionary dogma of gradualism or uniformitarianism. But several scientists—still evolutionists—recognize that catastrophism, including massive flooding, mountain building, glaciation, and similar catastrophes, is the more logical inference from our scientific observations. Furthermore, catastrophism helps us to explain several features of the fossil evidence.

First of all, there's the very existence of fossils themselves. Fossils don't form when plants and animals simply die and rot away on the surface of the ground or on the bottom of the sea. To have any chance at all to be preserved as a fossil, a plant or animal must be buried rapidly under a relatively heavy load of sediment. Otherwise, scavengers or the forces of erosion will obliterate the specimen. That's one reason why there's scarcely a trace of the millions of bison slaughtered in America's move westward.

Once a plant or animal is buried deeply enough in the right kind of sediment, there's no special trick involved in turning it into a fossil, and no huge amount of time is required. Minerals simply accumulate in the specimen itself or in the cavity left by the specimen after it rots away. So, fossils could be formed in the laboratory, and they are probably forming here and there today.

But nowhere on earth today do we have fossils forming on the scale that we see in geologic deposits. The Karroo Beds in Africa, for example, contain the remains of perhaps 800 billion vertebrates! A million fish can be killed in red tides in the Gulf of Mexico today, but they simply decay away and do not become fossils. Similarly, debris from vegetation mats doesn't become coal unless it is buried under a heavy load of sediment.

Some geologic formations are spread out over vast areas of a whole continent. For example, there's the Morrison Formation, famous for its dinosaur remains, that covers much of the mountainous West, and there's the St. Peter's Sandstone, a glass sand that stretches from Canada to Texas and from the Rockies to the Appalachians. Sediment does build up slowly at the mouth of rivers, such as the Mississippi delta. But slow sediment build up could not possibly produce such widespread deposits, such broadly consistent sedimentary and paleontological features, as we see in the Morrison and St. Peter's formations. In this case, knowledge of the present tells us something happened on a much larger scale in the past than we see it happening anywhere today. That's not appealing to fancy; that's appealing to fact.

Catastrophes on a huge scale also help us to understand many of the earth's physical features. Take the channeled scablands in eastern Washington, for example. More than 15,000 square miles are deeply gouged by steep-walled canyons cutting into very hard, crystalline lava rock. What carved these channeled scablands? "The answer—the greatest flood documented by man." That's the conclusion published in a free booklet by the United States Geological Survey (USGS).

To start with, geologists assumed the channeled scablands were the result of slow stream erosion acting over millions of years. The actual field evidence, however, convinced a USGS team that the scablands were formed instead by the great "Spokane Flood." A tongue of ice blocked off the Columbia River, forming glacial Lake Missoula. The ice dam broke, cutting the basic features of the scablands over much of eastern Washington—*not* in 1 or 2 million years, but in 1 or 2 *days!* The dramatic story can be read in the free USGS booklet, "The Channeled Scablands of Eastern Washington," or in an article by Stephen Gould (1978), "The Great Scablands Debate."

Creationists are pleased, of course, that more and more evolutionists are finally recognizing the evidence of catastrophism that has been an important part of creationist thinking for over 300 years. Because of his research on the scablands, geologists gave their highest award (the Penrose Medal) to Harlan Bretz (1980), who said his major contribution was reviving and de-mystifying legendary catastrophism.

The scablands, incidentally, were formed "merely" by the overflow of one lake over a period of one or two days. Imagine the effect of massive continent-wide flooding, lasting for a longer period! Beds of huge boulders ("megabreccias") requiring catastrophic flooding to deposit them are found in areas all over the world (Chadwick, 1978). For further discussion, see Chapter 6.

Catastrophism also helps us to understand the patterns of extinction we see when we compare living forms with their fossil relatives. A catastrophe would wipe out creatures regardless of their environmental fitness. Only those that happen to be in the right place at the right time when the catastrophe hit would survive (Raup's "survival of the luckiest?"). That would explain why present forms appear to be no more fit to survive than their fossil relatives. At best only a few of each type would survive, and these would possess less of the original created gene pool. That would help to explain why most groups existed in greater variety in times past than they do now.

Giant forms seem to have been particularly hard hit by extinction. As fossils, we find giant dragonflies with wingspreads of some 27 inches; giant fusilinids among the one-celled creatures (½ inch is giant for them); the giant reptiles, including some of the dinosaurs; even a giant beaver that reached six feet in length. (Imagine looking up into the face of a beaver; when he says, "I want that tree," you respond, "Take it. It's yours!") Perhaps the giant beavers were for cutting down the giant trees. Plants such as the club mosses or ground pines (lycopods), which grow only a few inches tall today, are represented as fossils (with the same kind of stem and "leaf" anatomy and reproductive structures) by trees reaching 120 feet in height (the lepidodendrons). The fossil evidence shows the existence of worldwide mild climates in all geologic systems except the most recent. Since some life forms continue to grow indefinitely in a favorable environment, that may have been at least partly responsible for giantism.

Worldwide climate changes, brought on by massive flooding and other catastrophes, might also help us to explain patterns of survival. Fossil plants and living plants include both spore-bearing and seed-bearing types. Both types have been hit by extinction, but the spore-bearing plants have been much more hard hit by extinction, and those are the types of plants that would find it harder to migrate throughout an earth with climate extremes like we have today. Similarly, animals can be described as warm-blooded or cold-blooded. Again, it's the cold-blooded, those less likely to adapt to climate extremes like we have today, that have been most strongly devastated by extinction.

I am not saying by any means that catastrophism answers all the questions you might have about fossil deposits. But I am saying that it, as a model related to the creation model, offers the promise of fruitful research.

Creation Science: The Promise of Fruitful Research

Concepts of catastrophism have stimulated much research, both in the laboratory and in the field (Fig. 33). Thanks to research, many of the questions that bothered me when I was an evolutionist considering becoming a creationist have been solved. And there is the promise of fruitful answers in such areas as cave formation, so-called "evaporite' deposits, petrified forests, animal tracks in Grand Canyon's Coconino Sandstone, cooling rates of molten rock, etc., etc. I have already mentioned the research Dr. Austin and his students have in progress. Prof. Harold Slusher and his graduate students in geo/astrophysics at the Institute for Creation Research are working on magma cooling rates, break up times for star clusters, and a dozen other projects.

All this research means three things:

First, creationists don't have all the answers. In teaching university biology, I work with the Institute for Creation Research—that's the Institute for Creation *Research,* not the Institute for Creation *Answers!* There are many questions that you could ask me, questions that have probably already occurred to you, where I'd simply have to say in all honesty, "I don't know." In at least some of the cases, no one else will know either. The facts and concepts simply aren't in yet to answer some of the questions that rightfully interest us as scientists, students, or other curious people.

Second, creation is a scientific concept. It's based on testable hypotheses and stimulates research. When Galileo first presented the evidence against Ptolemy's earth-

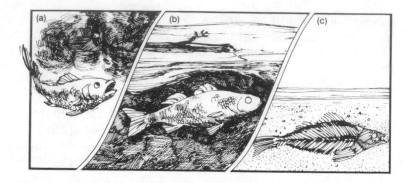

Figure 33. Because massive flooding seems to be the most logical inference from our observations of fossil deposits, a number of evolutionary geologists are now calling themselves "neo-catastrophists." Catastrophist geology, originally a creationist idea, has stimulated a great deal of research, and it helps us to understand how fossils form *(above)* and why such huge numbers are spread over such broad areas *(below)*.

centered view of astronomy, leaders of "the establishment" refused to even look through his telescope. The leaders in those days were both churchmen and scientists who had, unfortunately, made the thinking of an early Egyptian astronomer an article of faith (a warning against making a particular theory an "article of faith" in the "establishment" today?). Today it's too often the evolutionist who hides behind thought-stifling ridicule and cliche (e.g., misinterpreted "separation of church and state") and refuses to even "look through the telescope" (or microscope!) at the evidence of creation.

If it was wrong in Galileo's day to suppress evidence, wrong of the Inquisition to ban books, and wrong at the Scopes trial to present only one view of origins, how can it be right (with hands covering eyes, ears, and mouth) to suppress the evidence of creation, to ban books and a major history-shaping system of thought from the classroom (and from the hearts and minds of young people), and to establish one view of origins as the official tax-supported "state view"? Fortunately, several evolutionists agree with us that the scientific case for creation has been developed using the ordinary tools of science, logic and observation, and that it deserves to be defended—or defeated—on the basis of free and objective comparison of its scientific merits with those of evolution.

Finally, however, it is the scientific aspect of origins which means that the creation/evolution debate can never be completely settled by scientific study alone. There will always be new evidence to investigate and new concepts to apply. Each generation will have to reevaluate its concept of origins in terms of current knowledge. "The debate goes on."

The debate need not, of course, be hostile or unfriendly. In the description of his visit to the site of the Scopes trial, for example, Gould (1981c) mentions that the townspeople were very open and friendly and enjoyed exchanging ideas (even though, he says, they were not successful in changing his mind, nor he theirs). Yet Gould calls creationists "yahoos" and "latter-day antediluvians," and he calls scientific creationism "the nonsense term of the century."

If only Gould would sit down and chat with creationists whose scientific knowledge equals his own (an opportunity he has so far declined), I really think he would come away with a sense of intellectual exhilaration, a deepened respect for the diversity of human thought, and perhaps even a willingness (contrary to his present position as a leading anti-creationist crusader) to let young people in high schools and universities "think about it."

If creationists "win" the public school debate, by the way, Dr. Gould and *the evolutionists will still be able to present all their arguments.* It's just that *students will also be able to hear the rest of the story.* They will be told everything the evolutionists say about Miller's spark chamber, for example, but they will also be told that the amino acids he produced were both right and left handed, long and short chain, and likely to react with non-amino acids in the mixture, all of which makes their conversion into discrete and consistently coiled proteins most unlikely. They will be told about mutations and natural selection, but they will also be allowed to explore the logical, mathematical, genetic, and ecological limits to extrapolating from these processes to "macroevolution." They will hear all about *Archaeopteryx* and "Lucy" as possible evolutionary links, but they will also hear about both the "hopeful-monster" approach to evolution and about the complexity and diversity of Cambrian life, the Kanapoi hominid, and the fact of fossil stasis that all make the creation concept a very reasonable and scientific alternate inference from our observations. Most importantly, they will be told that human beings have the ability to distinguish the kind of order found in a tumbled pebble from the kind we see in an arrowhead, and that—in the science classroom more than anywhere else—they will be not only free, but also encouraged, to use all their science process skills in considering which kind of order is reflected in living systems—time and chance operating on the inherent properties of matter . . . or, design and creation resulting in irreducible properties of organization.

Scientists, whether creationist or evolutionist, must be willing to follow the evidence wherever it might lead. All must recognize, however, that the scientific case is likely to see-saw back and forth because of the very nature of science, which is an exciting and self-correcting, but also sharply limited approach to knowledge—limited both by an always incomplete knowledge of the facts and by a very finite ability of the human mind to put together what facts we have in a meaningful pattern.

The Creation Model

We have looked at the pattern of evidence as the creationist sees it, and, by comparison, as the evolutionist sees it, as well. The creation model can be simplified in terms of three logical inferences from our scientific observations.

I present this to you as a brief summary of the creation model. It's a model based on logical inference from scientific observations, and it's a model that must be discussed and defended on the basis of evidence and experiments.

Our knowledge of . . .	Suggests that . . .
1. DNA and protein in living cells, biochemistry, and mathematical probability...	1. Life is the result of design and creation *(not* time and chance acting on the inherent properties of matter).
2. Genetics, ecology, homology, embryology, and the types of life we find as fossils . . .	2. Many separate and distinct types were created, each a mosaic of complete traits, with each showing broad but limited variation and some genetic burden resulting from time and chance mutations.
3. The fossil evidence and the geologic sequence . . .	3. Groups of fossils are ecological zones of created types living in different environments at the same time, whose preservation reflects catastrophism.

It's not a model to end discussion, but to begin it. I'm not saying, "Here it is—believe it or else." I'm saying instead, "Here it is. Examine the concepts in terms of what you know about life science and what you can find out from reading and talking with others." I am also saying, "Don't make up your mind ahead of time. And don't just probe for weak spots; consider the *merits* of creation, as well." Even if you can't accept creation, see if you can understand what creationists believe and why they believe it. Creationists, of course, should do not less with evolution.

I want you to read the evolutionary literature, too. That's really why I have included so many references to the "latest and greatest" in evolutionary thought. (I don't mean to be mean, but I actually think that nothing is more likely to get you interested in creation science than finding out what evolutionists *really believe*—though I know the references I cited contain strong arguments for evolution, as well.) I have only just touched the tip of the mountains of evidence for creation, though, so I also hope you look into other creation science books and articles that go more into the details.

But there is still one problem left to consider in the case for creation.

Can Creation Be Science?

Many evolutionists attempt to settle the origins issue by defining science to exclude creation, and then they draw from their own definition the conclusion that creation cannot even be considered on its scientific merits. The noted British anthropologist, Sr. Arthur Keith, for example, summarized it this way, "The only alternative to some form of evolution is special creation, which is unthinkable." For Keith, creation (which he acknowledged as the only alternative to evolution) was simply "unthinkable," so he would not even permit himself to look at the evidence one way or the other.

The Russian biochemist, A. I. Oparin, is the "father" of the current concept of chemical evolution. He put it this way: "Engels' materialistic philosophy shows that the origin of life could have followed only a single path. It could not have existed eternally, nor could it have arisen [instantaneously]. It must have, therefore, resulted from a long evolution of matter . . . . " Note the logical chain in his argument: *"Materialistic philosophy . . . therefore . . . evolution."* Materialistic philosophy is belief that matter (mass-energy) is the only reality, and that there is nothing more than matter.

Oparin states his philosophic beliefs in the first chapter of his famous book on life's origin; the rest of the book is his attempt to muster facts to fit that faith. Notice, by the way, that his materialistic philosophy did not even permit him to consider the possibility of creation. At least he's consistent: if matter is the only reality, then there is no creation.

But what's his basis for ruling out creation? The scientific facts? Not at all. Oparin states his acceptance of the "matter-only philosophy" *before* he even begins to examine the scientific evidence.

In his articles as editor of *Natural History,* Stephen Gould often compares evolution with creation. He acknowledges that pre-Darwinian creationists were objective scientists, and that certain facts fit splendidly with creationist interpretations. But he never considers the possibility that the creationists might actually be correct. Why not? Because he assumes that matter-only philosophy for himself, and assumes also—*quite incorrectly*—that "all scientists accept materialism (at least in their workplace)" (Gould, 1975).

Sometimes people ask me, "If the evidence for evolution is so weak, and the scientific case for creation is as strong as you say, then why do so many scientists still believe in evolution?" For many, it's simply that evolution is the only idea they ever heard. For others, the answer is as simple as the one I used to give myself: *Creation can't be true if there's nothing more than matter.*

When I first began teaching university biology, I just assumed—without even knowing I assumed it—that science could only deal with *inherent properties of matter* and not with *created properties of organization.* I assumed, too, that evolution was a "fact," and I taught it as a fact—even though, when pressed, I acknowledged it was only a theory or model (the best substantiated theory in the history of science, I thought then!). Without realizing it, I was practicing materialism. I assumed, without even being conscious of it, that everything in science had to be explained in terms of time, chance, and the inherent properties of matter.

If materialist philosophy is confused with science, the search for truth is sharply limited. If science is considered only a search for materialist explanations instead of part of the search for truth, then evolution would still be the only theory taught even if it were known to be completely false. At best, one would be free only to explore *how* evolution occurred, but not *whether* evolution occurred (Wieland, 1979). Believe it or not, I used to pass that off as "academic freedom!"

But for one whose mind is open to the possibility of creation, there is freedom indeed! Nature becomes a scientist's dream. Everyone, scientists included, can tell the difference between a pebble and an arrowhead—one shaped by time and chance acting on the inherent properties of matter, the other with irreducible properties of organization resulting from design and creation. If scientists can't study created objects, they can't study arrowheads or airplanes. If they are open to creation as a possibility, then they are free to explore both kinds of order, and to test predictions and inferences against observations.

At bottom, there are only two possibilities regarding the ultimate origin of any pattern of order. Either mass-energy is the only reality, and *all* order results from time and chance acting on the inherent properties of matter (evolution); or more than matter is involved, and there are irreducible properties of organization that result from design and creation. The famous evolutionary astronomer, Harlow Shapley, put it more simply:

> Some piously record, "In the beginning God," but I say, "In the beginning hydrogen."

In more scientific terms, the choice is between *matter only* and *more than matter* as the fundamental explanation for the origin of the basic orderliness in our universe. *Time, chance, and the inherent properties of matter* . . . or *design, creation, and the irreducible properties of organization?* These are the two, and only two, ultimate choices.

Some will object, of course, that there must be more choices than just these two. Indeed, there are people of various religious persuasions who see evolution as compatible with their philosophic outlook, and there are scientists with no religious or even anti-religious sentiment who see scientific merit in the case for creation. *Clearly it is not a choice between science and religion,* since some see evolution as compatible with their religion and some without religion see creation compatible with science.

People are, and should be, free to mix various sentiments about how creation and evolution should or should not be related, and science is prohibited by its own methodology from making any statements about ultimate purpose. When it comes down to any particular case, however, there are two and only two possible scientific explanations for the origin of order: the order was either *imposed on* matter, or it *resides within* matter. We can distinguish these two kinds of order when it comes to artifacts of human creation; the same tools of science, logic and observation, also allow us to distinguish those two kinds of order even when the creative agency is unknown.

We are so humbly limited in both space and time that we can never finally prove or disprove either of these two ultimate models. We owe it to each other as fellow human beings to examine the evidence honestly and to constantly check our assumptions against all the relevant information.

But that's not easy! Looking into origins forces us to face ourselves and our foundations. What about ourselves, our families, and our friends and neighbors? "Only through the deaths of an immense number of slightly maladapted organisms are we, brains and all, here today," said Shapley's famous protege ', Carl Sagan (1980).

Is it true that we are, like the tumbled pebble, the products of time and chance acting on the properties of matter, destined, like the pebble, to be washed away by the same river of time that somehow brought us into being? Or, do we, like the arrowhead, bear the marks of creation?

Regardless of our personal preferences and philosophic perspectives, which view is more consistent with the weight of our knowledge? Science, like other approaches to knowing, can help us with this ultimately very personal decision. But, as finite beings, we must look at the world with eyes wide open . . . and a heart that listens to the other fellow. *Think about it!*

Part III

The
Physical
Sciences

By Henry M. Morris

Chapter 5

Creation and the
Laws of Science

The Relation of the Life Sciences
to the Physical Sciences

In the first part of this book, Dr. Gary Parker has demonstrated that biology, paleontology, and the other life sciences point clearly to direct creation by a living Creator as the ultimate source of life and all the basic types of living things. Both in the living world and the fossil world, there is much evidence of horizontal variation within types, but not one bit of real evidence for vertical change from any one type to a higher, more complex type. There are no genetic mechanisms yet known which are capable of generating any such vertical transmutations; all changes observed are either "horizontal" (recombinations, variations) or "downward" (harmful mutations, extinctions).

Dr. Parker, of course, is unusually well qualified to make such judgments, having had much training and experience as an evolutionary biologist, even to the extent of teaching evolution dogmatically in college biology classes. His own studies, however, led him finally to see that creation was a much more rational explanation of all the facts of the life sciences than evolution, and he now teaches biology in a creationist framework—the same *facts,* but more realistically interpreted and explained.

Now *living* systems must all function in a *physical* world. Biological processes, while far more complex than physical processes, nevertheless must operate also in conformity to the physico-chemical laws which govern nonliving systems. In fact, most materialistic biologists would themselves argue that biological systems are merely very complex physical systems, and that ultimate explanations of life processes must be in physico-chemical terms.

So the question of origins is not merely a biological question, to be resolved by biologists. The origin of life and the origin of the various kinds of life must be related ultimately to the origin of the earth and the universe and the laws which govern them. The creation/evolution issue is one of cosmic dimensions.

Consequently, any exposition of scientific creationism must deal with the physical sciences (physics, chemistry, astronomy, geology, hydrology, etc.), as well as the life sciences (biology, paleontology, genetics, physiology, embryology, etc.). My own background is in the physical sciences, but is similar to that of Dr. Parker's in one respect. Like him, I once was an evolutionist, and it was while teaching in a university that I became a creationist.

Creationism and Engineering

My undergraduate training had been in civil engineering, which is the broadest of the various engineering disciplines. Engineers are "applied scientists"—that is, they not only must *understand* the sciences, but also be able to *use* them in the design of various systems for man's use. A typical civil engineering curriculum covers a broad spectrum of training—not only physics and chemistry, but also geology, astronomy, biology, and other sciences, as well as economics, history, sociology, and various other social sciences and humanities. These are not merely "broadening" courses, for all of them are actually used in the design of engineering structures and systems.

In fact it was while teaching civil engineering courses that I became convinced of the inadequacies of evolutionism. Teaching structural design made me intensely conscious of the fact that the marvelous structural design of plants and animals could not be the result of chance. Teaching surveying, which included the determination of longitude, latitude, and time by careful observations of the sun and stars, impressed me with the majesty and the precision of all the components of the cosmos. With my special interest in hydrology and hydraulics (the study and control of water in earth processes), I could see clearly the overwhelming evidences of hydraulic catastrophism in the rocks of the earth's crust, which themselves were of paramount importance in numerous engineering applications (dams, highways, etc.). I also taught water and sewage treatment courses, which got into the remarkable world of microorganisms and their behavior.

All of this stimulated me to spend untold hours reading evolutionist books and articles on geology, astronomy, biology, etc., trying to see if the evolutionary beliefs with which I had been indoctrinated as a student could really yield satisfactory explanations of all these phenomena. The more I read, the more I became convinced that they could not.

The so-called evidences for evolution crumbled away when closely examined and critically analyzed. They certainly were not comparable to the evidence supporting the laws and principles upon which engineers must base their designs. These must all be empirically tested and proven before use. The design of a dam or a bridge cannot be based on armchair philosophizing or leap-of-faith extrapolating, as is true of macroevolutionary theory. On the other hand, the concept of a creator as the explanation of the scientific evidence was eminently satisfying, both intellectually and emotionally, and so I became a creationist.

That was a long time ago (in 1943, to be exact), and all my studies since then have merely further confirmed in my own thinking the superiority of the creation model over the evolution model in explaining, organizing, and applying the data of the physical sciences. Furthermore, there are today thousands of other physical scientists—both engineers and the "pure scientists" such as physicists and chemists—who would express similar convictions. Even though we may still represent a minority position, the minority is growing, and our convictions are strengthened by the fact that most of us were indoctrinated in evolutionary thought as students and therefore have had to study and think our way through to creationism, going against the tide, as it were, impelled by the facts to stand against the heavy weight of media propaganda and peer pressure. It is not easy to be a creationist scientist in a humanistic society, but commitment to *true* science demands it for many of us.

The Two Models of Origins

Evolutionists frequently try to avoid the issue by raising the question: "Which creation story do you want in the schools? What about the Buddhist and Hindu cosmogonies, and all the rest?"

The fact is, however, that there are *only two* possible models of origins, evolution or creation. The Buddhist, Hindu, Confucianist, Taoist, and many other cosmogonies are based on evolution; the Orthodox Jewish, Muslim, and Christian cosmogonies are based on creation. Either the space/mass/time universe is eternal, self-existent, and self-contained, or it is not. If it is, then evolution is the true explanation of its various components. If it is not, then it must have been created by a Creator.

These are the only two possibilities—simply stated, either it happened by accident (chance) . . . *or it didn't* (design). Putting it another way, the origin and development of all things can either be explained in terms of natural processes which are continuing to operate today—or they cannot. If not, then non-natural processes (or extra-natural, preternatural, or supra-natural, if you prefer) must have operated in the past to originate and develop at least some of the components of the universe, as well as the universe itself.

There are only these two possibilities. There may be many evolutionary submodels (e.g., different evolutionary mechanisms or sequences) and various creationist submodels (e.g., different dates of creation or events of creation), but there can be only two basic models—evolution or creation.

And to say that one of these (evolution) is the scientific

model while the other (creation) is the religious model is nothing but self-serving evolutionary pretense. Are not Buddhism and Taoism—not to mention humanism and atheism—religions? The definition of science is *truth,* not "mechanistic philosophy." The very word "science" comes from a Latin word meaning "knowledge," and so properly refers only to that which is *known*—that is, to demonstrated *facts.*

Both evolution and creation are properly called scientific models, since they can both be used to explain and predict scientific facts. The one which does the best job of this is probably the better scientific model, though that does not prove it to be true. The "facts" may be true facts, and thus real "science," but the explanation of how those facts come to be facts is a different matter altogether. If evolution is *true,* then it is science; if creation is true, then *it* is science. At this point in time, the scientific verdict is not yet in, but there are at least many scientists—and the number is growing—who are convinced that the facts of science point to creation, not evolution.

What we need to do, therefore, is to define the two basic models in broad, general terms, and then to compare their effectiveness in explaining and predicting various types of scientific data. Since it is not possible to repeat history, it is not possible to *prove* which model is *true* in the ultimate scientific sense of direct observation. That means that it will always be possible to modify either model to make it fit any set of data, merely by expanding it to accommodate every special case that arises. However, that model which, in its general form, does the best job of explaining the data, without having to be so modified and particularized, is the best model, and probably the true model. Creationists, of course, are convinced that when the two models are compared on this basis, the general creation model will always fit the facts directly, while the general evolutionary model must continually be expanded and specialized to *make* it fit the facts. That is why evolutionists are continually modifying their model (e.g., gradualism to punctuationalism), while the simple, straightforward creation model continues year after year to function satisfactorily

just as it is, even though creationist scientists are quite willing to modify their scientific model to conform better to
new evidence.

In this chapter we wish particularly to look at the two
models and their implications concerning the basic laws of
the physical universe, especially those which govern the
nature of the possible changes which can occur in the
systems and processes of the universe. First we must define
the two models in their broad, general form.

In the *evolution model,* the entire universe is considered
to have evolved by natural processes into its present state
of high organization and complexity. Since natural laws
and processes are believed to operate uniformly, such
evolutionary developments are interpreted in an over-all
context of *uniformitarianism.*

The *creation model,* on the other hand, defines at least
one period of direct creation in the beginning, during
which the basic systems of nature were brought into existence in completed, functioning form right from the
start. Since "natural" processes do not accomplish such
things at present, these creative processes must have been
processes requiring a Creator for their implementation.

In the evolutionary model, the universe in its present
form began in a state of randomness and has been gradually becoming more ordered and complex over the ages, as illustrated in Figure 34.

In order for the complex structure of the universe to
have been produced by present natural processes, tremendous aeons of time would have been required. Current
estimates range up to 3×10^{10} (30 billion) years, with the
earth evolving about 5×10^9 (5 billion) years ago.

The creation model (Figure 35), on the other hand,
shows the universe created in perfect organization. Particles, chemicals, planets, stars, organisms, and people
were all created, so that long ages were not required for
their development.

Although the universe was thereafter to be maintained
by the continuing processes of conservation, it is conceivable that its "degree of organization" would change.
If so, however, the organization could not increase (having

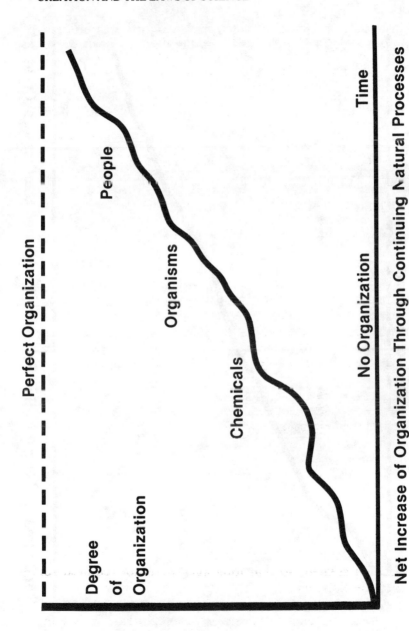

Figure 34. The Evolution Model

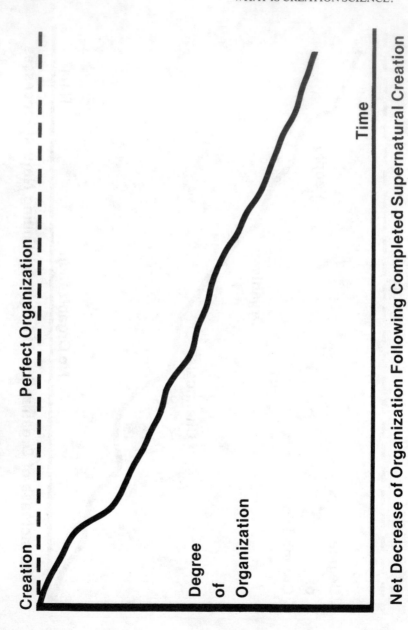

Figure 35. The Creation Model

begun in perfection); it could only decrease.

Unlike the evolution model, which permits both increases and decreases in organization in the universe through natural processes (with the net effect being an increase), the creation model predicts only net decreases (for the universe as a whole) through natural processes, since only extra-natural processes could generate net increases in complexity. The creation model stipulates nothing concerning the *rate* of decrease, however. This may be almost zero in times of peace and calm and very high during great catastrophes.

It should be recognized by everyone—both evolutionists and creationists—that neither model can be *proven* scientifically. As admitted by Matthews in the Foreword to the 1971 edition of Darwin's *Origin of Species:*

> The fact of evolution is the backbone of biology, and biology is thus in the peculiar position of being a science founded on an unproved theory—is it then a science or a faith? Belief in the theory of evolution is thus exactly parallel to belief in special creation—both are concepts which believers know to be true but neither, up to the present, has been capable of proof (Matthews, 1971).

In a similar vein, Leon Harris has said:

> First, the axiomatic nature of the neo-Darwinian theory places the debate between evolutionists and creationists in a new perspective. Evolutionists have often challenged creationists to provide experimental proof that species have been fashioned *de novo*. Creationists have often demanded that evolutionists show how chance mutations can lead to adaptability, or to explain why natural selection has favored some species but not others with special adaptations, or why natural selection allows apparently detrimental organs to persist. We may now recognize that neither challenge is fair. If

the neo-Darwinian theory is axiomatic, it is not
valid for creationists to demand proof of the ax-
ioms, and it is not valid for evolutionists to
dismiss special creation as unproved so long as it
is stated as an axiom (Leon Harris, 1975).

Therefore, since we cannot repeat history, it is impossible to prove scientifically which model is correct. Creation
is not taking place now, and thus it is not subject to experimental observation. Evolution takes place so slowly (in
the sense of increasing order) that it could not be observed
either, even if it were true. Consequently, a decision as to
which to believe must be made on the basis of which model
explains the data better.

In any case, both evolutionists and creationists should
be aware of the arguments and evidences for both models.
To the extent that it is possible, the scientist should continually and consciously try to evaluate all new data that
come to hand in light of both models.

Since there are only two possible models, and they are
diametrically opposed, it is clear that evidence against
evolution constitutes positive evidence for creation and
evidence against creation is evidence for evolution. Of
course, either model can be modified to accommodate any
set of data, so that neither can be firmly proved or
falsified. However, the model which fits the larger number
of data with the smaller number of secondary modifica-
tions is the one which is more likely to be true and,
therefore, scientific.

What Changes Are Possible?

An important and obvious test of the two models is to
compare them in terms of the types of changes which they
would predict for the various systems and processes of the
universe. This, in fact, is the very essence of the conflict
between evolutionism and creationism.

As Dr. Parker has already shown, there is no experimental evidence of any "upward" evolutionary changes taking
place in the living world at present. Could this fact be
related to some fundamental physical law which prevents

such changes? Creationists are convinced this actually is the case. Instead of a universal law of development operating in the cosmos, there is a universal law of degeneration.

If evolution is true, then there must be some innovational and integrative principle operating in the natural world which develops structure out of randomness and higher organization from lower. Since, by uniformitarianism, this principle is still in effect, scientists should be able to observe and measure it.

The creation model, on the other hand, suggests that there should be a conservational and disintegrative principle operating in nature. Since the total quantity of matter and energy, as well as the highest degree of organization, were created preternaturally in the beginning, we could not expect to see naturalistic processes of innovation and integration, as required by evolution, working today.

From the creation model, in fact, one would quickly predict two universal natural laws: (1) a law of conservation, tending to preserve the basic categories created in the beginning (laws of nature, matter, energy, basic types of organisms, etc.), in order to enable them to accomplish that function for which they were created; (2) a law of decay, tending to reduce the *useful* matter, energy, types, etc., as the original organization of the created cosmos runs down to chaos. As far as *changes* are concerned, one would expect from the creation model that there would be "horizontal" changes within limits (that is, energy conversions, variation within biologic types, etc.), and even "vertically-downward" changes in accordance with the law of decay (for example, mutations, wear, extinction, etc.), but never any *net* "vertically-upward" changes, as required by evolution.

Testing the Predictions

These two contrary sets of predictions from the two models should be testable in terms of structures and processes in the real world. It is noteworthy, then, that no one has ever *observed* any phenomenon requiring a universal principle of innovation or integration to explain it.

Localized temporary phenomena of *apparent* increasing order (e.g., a growing organism) are only superficial, developing within broader systems of decreasing order which always "win out" in the end.

On the other hand, universal laws of conservation and decay *have* been observed. In fact, these principles are called the First and Second Laws of Thermodynamics—the law of conservation of mass/energy and the law of increasing entropy (or disorder). All scientific measurements ever made to date confirm the validity of these two laws. They govern all processes of any sort, so far as known. These laws of thermodynamics apply not only in physics and chemistry, but also in biology and geology. Furthermore, there seem to be similar principles operating at the scale of living complexes. That is, "like begets like." Many varieties of dogs can be produced, but never can one breed a dog from some other *type* of animal. The same restraint operates throughout the entire realm of life, so far as observations go. Similarly, certain organs in animals may atrophy and become "vestigial," or even entire groups become extinct, but never do scientists observe either "nascent" organs or new types evolving.

The Second Law of Thermodynamics is especially significant in its support of the creation model and, correspondingly, its contradiction of the evolution model. Its nature and universality are well recognized:

> As far as we know, all changes are in the direction of increasing entropy, of increasing disorder, of increasing randomness, of running down (Isaac Asimov, 1973).

This principle is exceedingly important. Its operation is experienced in everyday human life, as well as in the most sophisticated machine and most complex process. If you let anything go, it deteriorates. If you let your desk go, it becomes cluttered (like mine); if you let your automobile go, it runs down; if you let your body go, it gets sick. If you let anything just *go,* with no attention or care, it will disintegrate, wear out, run down.

And even if you don't let them go, but do your best to

take care of them, they will eventually wear out anyhow! The Second Law inevitably triumphs, sooner or later. This experience of deterioration is so universal and so common that it is surprising that anyone could ever believe in evolution at all.

On a more formal basis, the Second Law of Thermodynamics (also known as the Law of Increasing Entropy) can be expressed in several different ways, all of which can be shown to be equivalent. The three most important applications are as follows:

1. **Classical Thermodynamics:** The energy available for useful work in a functioning system tends to decrease, even though the total energy remains constant.
2. **Statistical Thermodynamics:** The organized complexity (order) of a structured system tends to become disorganized and random (disorder).
3. **Informational Thermodynamics:** The information conveyed by a communicating system tends to become distorted and incomplete.

In each case, *entropy* (from a Greek word meaning "inturning") is a measure of the lost usefulness of the system. In classical thermodynamics, it measures the useful energy which must be converted into nonusable heat energy to overcome friction and keep the system running. In statistical thermodynamics, it measures the probability of the structured arrangement of the system, with a state of complete disorganization being most probable. In informational thermodynamics, it measures the amount of garbled information, or "noise," that accompanies the transmission of information by the system. The same mathematical equations can be shown to apply to all three types of situations, so that all are equivalent to each other. Any system can be treated as a working system in which some of the energy required to operate it is deployed into nonrecoverable heat energy, or as a structured system which tends to break up and become less organized, or as an information system in which some of the information built into the system tends to become distorted or irretrievable. In each case, the entropy of the system always tends to increase. Note Figure 36.

ENTROPY ("in-turning")

measures:

(1) Deterioration of Energy in a Working System

(2) Degree of Disorder in a Structured System

(3) Loss of information in a Programmed System

Entropy always tends to increase in any system.

Figure 36. Varied Applications of Entropy Concept

One of the interesting things about this Second Law is that it is so universal that many scientists seem to think it belongs only to their particular fields. I frequently encounter physicists and chemists, for example, who think of it only as an equation involving the flow of heat, or the direction of a chemical reaction. In my own field of hydraulics, it is a fundamental equation of water flow. Many biologists are apparently unaware that it is basic in all biological processes. It is being frequently applied today even to economic and social systems.

As a matter of fact—so far as all studies have shown to date—it applies to the whole universe. As the socialist Jeremy Rifkin (himself an evolutionist) points out:

> The Entropy Law will preside as the ruling paradigm over the next period of history. Albert Einstein said that it is the premier law of all science; Sir Arthur Eddington referred to it as the supreme metaphysical law of the entire universe. (Jeremy Rifkin, 1980a)

Eddington also originated the term "Time's Arrow" to describe the Second Law, noting that the arrow points downward. If present processes continue to function into the indefinite future, eventually *all* energy will become useless, uniform, heat energy; all structures will have disintegrated into maximum disorder, their state of maximum probability; and all information will have become meaningless noise. The sun and stars will burn out, all processes will stop, and the universe will die an ultimate "heat death." It will still exist (by the First Law), but will be dead (by the Second Law).

The First Law of Thermodynamics (also known as the Law of Conservation of Energy—which in our nuclear age, is known also to include Mass or Matter) states that there can be no creation or annihilation of Mass/Energy. One form of Energy can be converted into another, one state of Matter can be converted into another, and there can even be Matter/Energy interconversions, but the totality of Mass/Energy in the universe remains constant. The Two Laws of Thermodynamics are the most universal and best-proved laws which science has, and they do indeed point to a gloomy future for the cosmos, which is the main theme of Rifkin's book. Even though he believes in evolution, he does see the fundamental clash between evolution and entropy.

> We believe that evolution somehow magically creates greater overall value and order on earth. Now that the environment we live in is becoming so dissipated and disordered that it is apparent to the naked eye, we are beginning for the first time to have second thoughts about our views on evolution, progress, and the creation of things of material value . . . . Evolution means the creation of larger and larger islands of order at the expense of ever greater seas of disorder in the world. There is not a single biologist or physicist who can deny this central truth. Yet, who is willing to stand up in a classroom or before a public forum and admit it? (Jeremy Rifkin, 1980b)

Testimony to Primeval Creation

Of course, Rifkin's pessimism about the world's future would be justified if evolution were true, as he assumes. The fact is, however, that there is no evidence whatever that evolution is really proceeding in any such manner, even at the cost of great increase in entropy. The entropy principle actually seems to *preclude* evolution from taking place at all on any significant scale.

Furthermore, the gloomy prediction of Time's Arrow concerning the future heat death of the universe is valid only if there is no Creator. But the two Laws, rightly viewed, point *back* to creation just as they seem to point *forward* to death. This remarkable fact dispels the gloom!

Consider the implications of Figure 37.

Here the Two Laws are expressed graphically in the terms of classical thermodynamics, with the horizontal scale representing "Time" and the vertical scale representing the "Energy (including Matter) of the Universe."

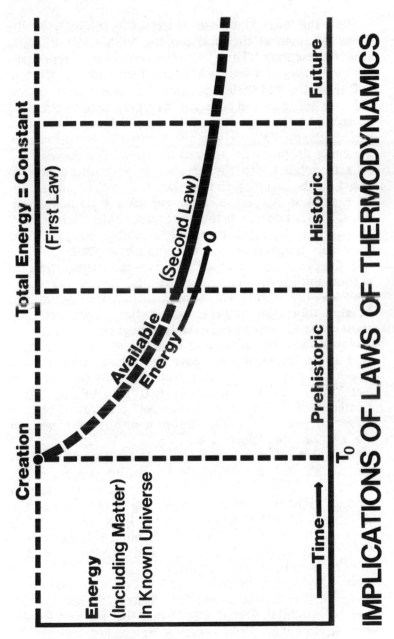

Figure 37. Implications of Laws of Thermodynamics

Here the Two Laws are expressed graphically in the terms of classical thermodynamics, with the horizontal scale representing "Time" and the vertical scale representing the "Energy (including Matter) of the Universe."

During the "historic" period, the *total energy* of the universe has remained constant, as represented by the solid horizontal line at the top of the graph. During this same period, the *available energy* has decreased, as indicated by the curve dropping off toward the right. The curves must be extrapolated into the prehistoric and future periods based on the assumption that they follow the same trends as in the historic period, as shown by the dashed extensions. This, of course, is the most reasonable, "scientific," assumption. In the future, the available energy would eventually approach zero, the ultimate heat death.

In the past, however, the two curves must come together at some initial time (T_0), when the total energy was totally available, like a great watch that had just been wound up. At this time, the universe would have been perfectly organized and "informed," ready to begin operations.

Now, since the universe is destined to "die" at some time in the future, it must have had a beginning at some time in the past—otherwise, it would already be dead. The First Law, however, indicates that it could not have created itself. It must, therefore, have been created by processes of creation which are not now occurring, *exactly as the creation model postulates!*

Now, this still does not *prove* creation to be true. It is conceivable that a naturalistic integrative process might have occurred in the time before time T_0, or that such a process might even today be occurring in that part of the universe outside the *known* universe. In *observable* space and time, however, there is no such thing. Science is what we *see,* and we see only a universal disintegrative process pointing back to an initial creation.

Not only does the Second Law point back to creation; it also directly contradicts evolution. Systems do not naturally go toward higher order, but toward lower order. Evolution requires a universal principle of upward change; the entropy law is a universal principle of downward change.

If language is meaningful, evolution and the Second Law cannot both be true. The Second Law, however, has been confirmed by all sorts of scientific tests, while evolution is a model not even capable of being tested scientifically. If one must make a choice, it would seem better to go with science!

The Open-System Argument

Even though evolution and entropy cannot both be universal laws, many evolutionists insist that evolution could take place locally and temporarily. The earth is an open system, and there is energy enough from the sun to sustain evolution during the geologic ages, even if the process will eventually cease when the sun dies.

The laws of thermodynamics are defined in terms of closed systems, they say (a closed system is one that neither gains nor gives up energy to its surroundings), and so the apparent conflict is resolved.

This very common evolutionist argument is inexcusably naive. An influx of heat energy into an open system (such as solar heat entering the earth-system) does not decrease entropy (i.e., increase order)—it *increases* entropy! The standard thermodynamic equation for the change in entropy resulting from heat flow into a system is:

$$\Delta S \quad = \quad \int \frac{dQ}{T}$$

where $\int dQ$ is the total influx of heat energy, T is the absolute temperature and ΔS is the increase of entropy in the system.

Thus, the greater the outside heat energy that enters the system, the more will be the increase in its entropy and disorder. It is absurd to claim that the mere availability of solar energy to the earth resolves the fundamental conflict of evolution and entropy; in fact, it aggravates it!

Figure 38 illustrates what happens in a closed system as time goes on. At time T_1 the system is "ordered," as represented by the hexagons inside the system. Later, at time T_2, the structure in the system has disintegrated. No one would question this, of course, as even evolutionists acknowledge that entropy increases with time in a closed system. "But," they will say, "the earth is an open system, and so there is no problem."

There *is* a problem, however, as illustrated in Figure 39. Opening the system to external heat energy will increase the entropy in that system even more rapidly than if it remained closed. Any "structure" that might exist in the system will be destroyed, not improved or upgraded. *This* is certainly no resolution of the evolution/entropy problem!

This is not to say, of course, that *all* open systems always exhibit a decrease in organization. Evolutionists frequently charge creationists with saying that the Second Law makes all systems go downhill. They then triumphantly point to a crystal or to a growing plant and say: "See! If the system is open, it can increase in order and complexity."

Now, despite such evolutionist allegations, no knowledgeable creationist ever says that all systems go downhill. One can even make *water* flow uphill—by putting a pump in the line. There are many systems, especially artificial systems (e.g., buildings, machinery) and living systems (e.g., plants, animals) which do indeed manifest, for a time, an increasing degree of complexity or information, and they somehow are able to do this without in any way breaking the Second Law. They are open systems, of course, and do draw on external sources of energy, or information, or order, to build up their own structure. Even though their (internal) entropy is decreased (for a while), it is at the expense of an overall increase of entropy in the larger system outside, all fully in accord with the Second Law.

But these cases are exceptions, and thus require particular explanations. Most open systems do *not* increase in order. Having an open system is a necessary, but not a sufficient, condition. Merely to have an open system and energy available from the sun does not automatically generate higher order in that system. All *real* systems are

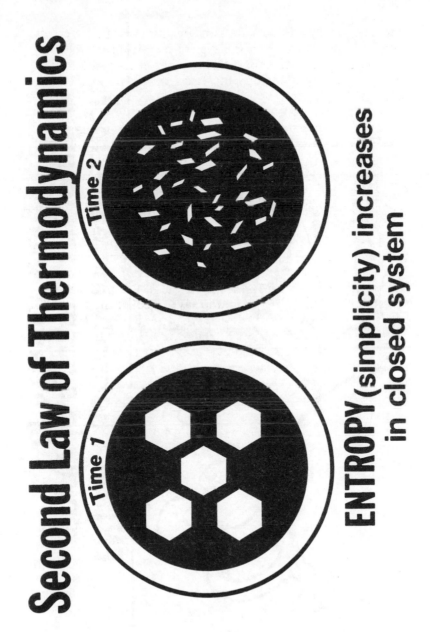

Figure 38. Increasing Entropy in Closed System

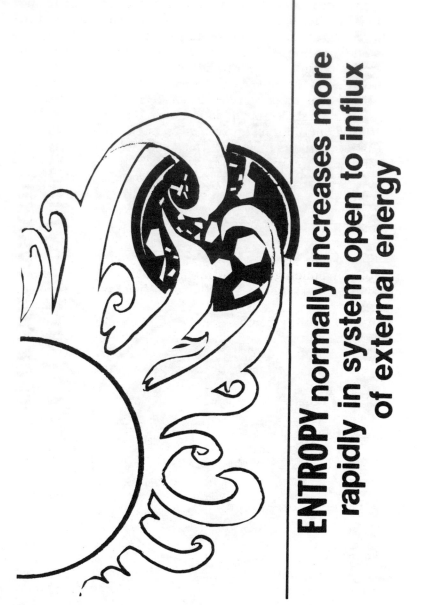

Figure 39. Increasing Entropy in Open System

open systems and are open in one way or another to the sun's energy, but most such systems normally proceed to lower degrees of order in accord with the law of entropy. The question is: What conditions must be satisfied to cause any finite system to advance to a higher degree of order, when the universe as a whole is decreasing in order? Careful analysis of all types of local systems of increasing order (e.g., seed growing into a tree, building being constructed out of bricks and other components) shows that at least four criteria must be fulfilled in every case. These are outlined in Figures 40 and 41.

As far as the earth is concerned, every real system is an open system and is open either directly or indirectly to the sun's energy. Yet no system shows an increasing order unless it also possesses a highly specific program to direct its growth and a complex mechanism (or "motor," or "membrane") to convert the sun's energy into the specific work of building its growth. As noted in Figure 42-A, a typical living system and a typical artificial system do meet these criteria. One case often cited—formation of a crystal out of a cooling liquid—is not a valid example, however, since the energy or information contained in the liquid is higher than in the crystal which develops from it. In any case, the program and the mechanism required to increase the organization in a system must have been provided somehow beforehand, and no accidental or random phenomenon is capable of generating either such a program or such a mechanism.

With this in mind, the question is whether the biosphere as a whole can evolve into higher order. Figure 42-B outlines the problem.

Every stage of real organic evolution represents an increase in complexity of a living system. In each case, the system is an open system with energy available in the form of sunlight. The problem is: What are the programs and the mechanisms? What is the pre-existing program that directs the inorganic chemicals of the primeval soup how to become the first replicating chemicals? As yet there is no answer. Also, what is the complex energy converter that transforms the solar energy into the infinitely intricate

Conditions for Increasing Complexity in Open System

1. Open system
2. Available energy

NOTE

These two conditions are satisfied by all systems on earth. Therefore, though "necessary," they are not "sufficient" conditions.

Figure 40. Necessary Conditions

Additional Necessary Conditions

3. Program (to "direct" the growth in complexity)

Examples:

a. "Genetic Code" in DNA of living systems
b. "Plans and specifications" for construction of artificial system

4. Mechanism for storing and converting incoming energy

Examples:

a. Photosynthesis in plants
b. Metabolism in animals
c. Machinery in artificial construction

Figure 41. Necessity of Program and Conversion Mechanism for Decrease in Entropy

CRITERIA	GROWING PLANT	BUILDING CONSTRUCTION
	SYSTEM	
Open System	Seed	Materials
Available Energy	Sun	Sun
Directing Program	Genetic Code	Blueprint
Conversion Mechanism	Photosynthesis	Workmen

Figure 42-A. Criteria for Increasing Order

CRITERIA TO BE SATISFIED	SYSTEM	
	FIRST LIVING CELL	POPULATION OF COMPLEX ORGANISMS
Open System	Complex Inanimate Molecule	Population of Simple Organisms
Available Energy	Sun	Sun
Directing Program	None	None (Natural Selection?)
Conversion Mechanism	None	None (Mutations?)

Figure 42-B. Absence of Ordering Criteria in Evolution

structures required for life? Merely saying that the sun's energy is adequate to sustain evolution without saying *how* it sustains evolution is like saying there is enough energy in a waterfall to fly an airplane. Even if correct, it is irrelevant to the problem.

Once simple life has appeared, however, is it possible for a population of simple organisms to be transformed into a population of more complex organisms? What is the conversion mechanism that converts the sun's energy into the specific work required to build up this more complex system? The phenomenon of mutation may be a response to environmental radiations, of course, but never do genes mutate in such a way as to increase the *organization* of the genetic system. Mutations are random changes and, *so far as all observations go,* random changes in ordered systems inevitably decrease the order in those systems. Also, what is the directing program that instructs a population of worms to develop themselves into a population of, say, crocodiles? Natural selection serves as a conservational "program," weeding out harmful mutations, but it cannot specify the development of more complex systems.

Thus, it seems that evolution in the vertically upward sense is impossible in the light of the Second Law of Thermodynamics. If even such a simple system as a seed requires a previously available program and mechanism (genetic code and photosynthesis) to grow in complexity, much more must this be true of the gigantic space-time continuum which constitutes the supposedly evolving biosphere.

Evolutionists, for the most part, have ignored this problem. A few evolutionists, mostly in the physical sciences, have recognized it and are trying to solve it—so far, mainly by speculative suggestions. Prigogine, for example, proposed that "fluctuations" or "instabilities" in what he calls "dissipative structures" can generate higher order in an open system. However, he acknowledges that there is no evidence that life originated by any such means.

> The probability that at ordinary temperatures
> a macroscopic number of molecules is assembled

to give rise to the highly ordered structures and to the coordinated functions characterizing living organisms is vanishingly small. The idea of spontaneous generation of life in its present form is therefore highly improbable, even on the scale of the billions of years during which prebiotic evolution occurred. (Ilya Prigogine, 1972)

In another paper Prigogine holds out some hope that his theory may eventually be able to provide the missing ordering mechanism. He cautions, however:

But it is not just one instability that makes it possible to cross the threshold between life and non-life; it is, rather a succession of instabilities of which we are only now beginning to identify certain stages. (Ilya Prigogine, 1973)

It is the same old problem. How can an increase of order (or "information") be produced in a system (whether open or closed) by any kind of random process? All experience, as well as any probabilistic or mathematical analysis, indicates that *random* changes lead only to a *decrease* of order.

Prigogine's suggestion, essentially, was that in a system where a high degree of energy dissipation is taking place, a small sub-region may exist where a higher degree of structure is somehow generated by the dissipative field. An example might be the generation of a trail of vortices in the wake behind an object around which a fluid is flowing rapidly, or the cyclonic movements in the atmosphere generated by the sun's heat. In such instances, a large amount of energy is being dissipated into nonusable heat in the large flow-through of energy, but in the process, order of a sort is developed in the vortex systems so produced. Prigogine's hope was that this sub-region of higher order might then provide the "sub-strate" for the development of a still higher degree of order by a similar dissipative field through which *it* would pass—and so on, until living systems finally are generated.

He recognized, as noted above, that his own accomplishments (which were strictly theoretical, not experimental) had come nowhere near to generating life or
any higher form of life, but he simply expressed hope that
his "discovery" of "dissipative structures" and "order
through instabilities" might eventually breach the hitherto
impenetrable barrier erected by entropy against evolution.
This is a vain hope; the very idea of a vast succession of
catastrophic instabilities, each of which has to be maintained by a continuous flow of high-gradient energy,
operating on successively smaller and smaller sub-regions
in a complex space-grid of dissipative fields, is itself an ap-
palling testimonial to the futility and gullibility of evolutionary faith. The desperate need of evolutionary theory
for an answer to the entropy problem is pointed out by the
eagerness with which the scientific establishment seized on
Prigogine's mathematics as their answer. It is now common for evolutionists to respond to creationist debaters on
the implications of entropy merely by stating that Prigogine has solved the problem. The fact is, of course, he has
done no such thing, and he himself has refused to debate
with creationists on this issue.

There have been a few other writers who have at least
recognized the problem (most evolutionists, unfortunately,
still simply dismiss the problem as irrelevant, since "the
earth is an open system") and attempted to work out some
kind of analysis which would equate entropy with evolution. This is impossible, of course, since both are supposed
to express universal laws—one a universal law of upward
change, the other a universal law of downward change.
Two recent writers who have made such attempts are
David Layzer and Jeffrey Wicken.

David Layzer, of Harvard, in attempting to deal with
this problem, has first redefined "time's arrow" (a term
coined for the Second Law by Sir Arthur Eddington) in
terms of two arrows, one pointing up and one pointing
down (see Figure 43).

The processes that define the historical and
the thermodynamic arrows of time generate in-

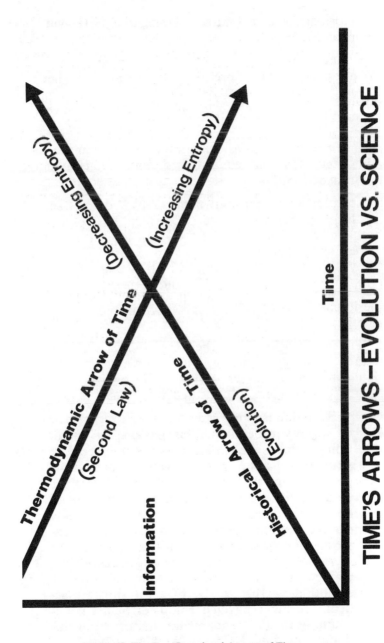

Figure 43. The Two Postulated Arrows of Time

formation and entropy, respectively. (David
Layzer, 1975)

By the "historical arrow," Layzer means the evolutionary process, which presumably generates a higher and
higher degree of "information" (or "order" or "complexity") in the world. This can only be done at the cost of
decreasing entropy.

Thus a gain of information is always compen-
sated for by an equal loss of entropy. (David
Layzer, 1975)

However, the "thermodynamic arrow" defines entropy
as always increasing. Layzer, in effect, has restated the
problem, but he hasn't solved it. That is, just *how* is this
increasing information generated at the cost of a loss of entropy? What is the code that directs it and where is the
mechanism that actuates it? Without these, the naturally
increasing entropy simply precludes an increase of information. The vacuous statement that "the earth is an open
system" is no answer.

Jeffrey S. Wicken is another recent writer who has tried
to face this problem, dealing with it in a manner somewhat
similar to that of Layzer. He clearly recognizes that there
is, indeed, a problem, as indicated in the following:

Evolutionary processes are *anamorphic,* or
complexity generating. The passage of evolutionary time is accompanied by the emergence of
structures having progressively greater mor-
phological and functional complexity. But the
essential feature of evolutionary anamorphosis
remains enigmatic. It has not been successfully
derived from or identified with more fundamental physico-chemical laws, particularly those of
thermodynamics; nor has it been adequately explained at its own phenomenological level by
evolutionary theory. Neo-Darwinism in particular seems to have enormous difficulty in accounting for this fundamental feature of evolutionary process. (Jeffrey S. Wicken, 1979)

To the contention that mutations and natural selection could generate the higher degrees of complexity required by evolution, Wicken says:

> As a generative principle, providing the raw material for natural selection, random mutation is inadequate, both in scope and theoretical grounding. (Jeffrey S. Wicken, 1979)

That is mutations, being random, cannot "order" anything, or make anything more complex. Natural selection can serve only to weed out those mutations that are harmful, thus at best preserving the status quo.

Wicken points out quite incisively that use of the term "order" to correspond with low entropy and "disorder" with high entropy may be misleading if order merely refers to geometric regularity, as in a crystal. The "information" required to specify a simple geometric structure may be much less than that required to specify a highly complex network that may not exhibit geometric regularity but that does involve functional relationships between its various components.

> "Organized" systems are to be carefully distinguished from "ordered" systems. Neither kind of system is "random," but whereas ordered systems are generated according to simple algorithms and therefore lack complexity, organized systems must be assembled element by element according to an external "wiring diagram" with a high information content. (Jeffrey S. Wicken, 1979)

Thus, in describing the Second Law, it is usually better to speak of "decreasing information" or "decreasing complexity" instead of "decreasing order." When using "order" or "disorder" (as most scientists do when referring to the Second Law) it should be made clear in context that "order" is synonymous with "organized complexity" or "functional information," rather than merely "geometric regularity."

> Organization, then, is functional complexity and carries functional information. It is non-random by *design* or by *selection,* rather than by the *a priori* necessity of crystallographic "order." (Jeffrey S. Wicken, 1979)

Wicken thus recognizes that *design* can add information to an open system, and this would, of course, imply a Designer. Unfortunately, he also assumes that *selection* can likewise add information, but this is entirely gratuitous. He hypothesizes that natural selection can, in effect, perform the function of a Designer, by merely selecting from among the various systems submitted to it those that will increase the information content. But this idea presupposes that some mechanism is available which will generate systems of higher organization from lower, and for this notion there is no evidence whatever. He has already recognized that mutation is not an adequate mechanism for this purpose, but he thinks that somehow it can be accomplished by some unknown process following the laws of thermodynamics.

Like Layzer, he arbitrarily assumes that evolution can be derived from entropy, since both involve continual change.

> The cosmological arrow generates randomness or disorder, whereas the evolutionary arrow generates complexity. A fully reductionist theory of evolution must demonstrate that the evolutionary arrow can be derived from the cosmological arrow. (Jeffrey S. Wicken, 1979)

Wishing, however, does not make it so, except in children's fairy tales! How can a universal principle which generates complexity ever be derived from a universal principle which continually generates disorder? The very statement of this idea is its own rebuttal!

A number of other evolutionists (Weisskopf, Dickerson, Eigen, *et al*) have also tried to deal with this subject. They at least have acknowledged that the entropy problem requires more than the usual "open system" cliche, but they are all as unable to solve the problem as Prigogine, Layzer, and Wicken have been.

Summary

To summarize, the two most basic and universal laws of science, the First and Second Laws of Thermodynamics, can legitimately be regarded as direct predictions from the creation model, speaking of a cosmos which is being conserved quantitatively, but which is decaying qualitatively. Not only do these laws point directly to a primeval creation, but also they seem to preclude any significant amount of "upward" evolution at any stage of history, assuming only that they have been operational in past history the same as at present.

The pat rejoinder by evolutionists to this obvious conflict between evolution and entropy is that the earth is an open system and there is enough energy from the sun to energize the evolutionary process throughout geologic time. This rejoinder, however, ignores the elemental fact that an influx of heat energy into an open system directly corresponds to an increase of entropy (and, therefore, a decrease in "functional information") in that system. There must, therefore, be certain other constraints applied to an open system before the information or organization of that system can ever be increased. Creationists have maintained that the necessary additional constraints include at least a directing program and a conversion mechanism. These are available in such cases as the growth of a plant or the erection of a building, but not in the supposed billion-year evolution of the biosphere.

Those occasional evolutionists who have not ignored this problem have used various other terminologies of their own to try to bridge the gap, but so far such attempts have all been futile. Without some kind of biochemical predestinating code to direct the hypothetical evolutionary growth of the biosphere, it would become a heterogeneous blob if it grows at all. And without some kind of complex global energy conversion mechanism to store and transform the incoming solar energy, the sun's heat would destroy, not build up, any organized systems that might exist on the earth. Without such a code and such a mechanism, the naturally increasing entropy simply precludes a naturalistic increase of complexity on the earth, even though the earth is, indeed, an "open system" and even though there is, indeed, enough energy coming in from the sun to initiate and sustain evolution. The evolutionist Charles Smith (1975) recognizes the inadequacy of the "open system," rejoinder calling this conflict between evolution and thermodynamics "one of the most fundamental unsolved problems in biology."

Now, even if Prigogine or Eigen or some other worker in this field could ever conceive a possible worldwide, agelong, code and mechanism by which evolutionary increases in order might be produced, in spite of a universe of increasing entropy, the evolution model still would not be as good as the creation model. At best the evolution model might be imagined to be able to *accommodate* the Second Law, but it would never *predict* it. The creation model, however, in effect *predicts* both the First and Second Laws, the most basic laws in all science.

Unfortunately, evolutionists often respond to the powerful Second Law argument for creation by asserting (without justification or explanation) that creationists do not understand the Law. Surely they will not apply this unsupported opinion to the work of the two internationally acknowledged authorities on thermodynamics, Sonntag and Van Wylen. In their widely used two-volume textbook, these experts say:

> . . . the authors see the second law of thermodynamics as man's description of the prior and continuing work of a creator, who also holds the answer to the future destiny of man and the universe. (Sonntag and Van Wylen, Vol. 1, 1973.)

Thus, the present laws of science point directly to the fact of a primeval creation and profoundly conflict with the philosophy of a continuing naturalistic evolution. The creation model is, therefore, much more "scientific" than the evolution model.

Chapter 6

Catastrophism in Geology

Did Evolution Occur in the Past?

Evolution in the "upward" sense is not observed to be occurring today. In fact, it even seems to be impossible at present, in light of the empirically proved Second Law of Thermodynamics. Is it possible, however, that conditions were different in past ages, so that evolution could have occurred throughout the geological ages, even though we cannot see it occurring at present?

There are no records of vertically upward evolution occurring since the beginning of written history, so it is necessary to study records of the pre-history of the earth to answer this question. These records are found almost exclusively in the rocks of the earth's crust, especially the fossil-bearing sedimentary rocks that have been laid down above its "basement complex" of primeval crystalline rocks—that is, in the "geologic column." (See Figure 31 and Dr. Parker's discussion of the geologic column in Chapter 3.)

It is well known that the local geologic column at any given place is usually quite different from that at any other place. However, these all are summed to fit somewhere in the standard geologic time table, which is believed by evolutionists to constitute the buried record of all the earth's evolutionary geological ages, from the Precambrian up to the Recent. The physical interpretation of the processes that formed these rocks is based on the principle of *uniformitarianism*—that is, the principle that present laws and processes, operating essentially as they do at present, are sufficient to account for all these great rock systems. (This would certainly include the laws of thermodynamics!)

If the Evolution Model is correct, present processes have produced not only the rocks but also the various forms of life preserved as fossils in the rocks. Thus, uniformitarianism is an essential component of the model. These processes operate slowly—in fact, so slowly in the case of vertically upward evolutionary changes that we cannot see them operating at all in the present historical period.

Similarly, if evolution was operating through these past geological ages, then all the present complex forms of life were slowly developing from primeval simple forms of life, and this should be documented by the fossils found in the rock record of these ages. The fossil record should show an abundance of intermediate, transitional forms of plants and animals, showing how the various phyla, classes, orders, and families developed through the ages.

The Creation Model, on the other hand, postulates that all the basic types of plants and animals were directly created and did not evolve from other types at all. Consequently the Creationist predicts that no transitional sequences (except within each created type) will ever be found, either in the present array of organisms or in the fossil record.

That this prediction is borne out in the present assemblage of plants and animals is obvious to all. If it were not so, it would not even be possible to have a taxonomic system—one could never determine the dividing lines between similar organisms.

> In other words, the living world is not a single array of individuals in which any two variants are connected by unbroken series of intergrades, but an array of more or less distinctly separate arrays, intermediates between which are absent or rare. (Theodosius Dobzhansky, 1951)

This in itself is strange. It would be much better

confirmation of the Evolution Model if all variants *were* connected by unbroken series of intergrades. Creationists would be hard pressed to explain *that* sort of thing. As it stands, however, the present array of organisms (abundant variation within limited categories, clear-cut gaps between categories) fits precisely the expectations of the Creation Model.

The fossil record is the key test, however. Transitional series *must* have existed in the past, if evolution is true, and the fossil record should reveal at least some of these.

The fact is, however, that no such transitional series—or even any clearly transitional forms—have ever been found in the fossil record. The leading paleontologist, George G. Simpson, recognizes this, as does another prominent paleontologist (and student of Simpson's), David Kitts.

> . . . every paleontologist knows, that *most* new species, genera, and families, and that nearly all categories above the level of families, appear in the record suddenly and are not led up to by known, gradual, completely continuous transitional sequences. (George Gaylord Simpson, 1953)

> Despite the bright promise that paleontology provides a means of "seeing" evolution, it has presented some nasty difficulties for evolutionists, the most notorious of which is the presence of "gaps" in the fossil record. Evolution requires intermediate forms between species and paleontology does not provide them. The gaps must therefore be a contingent feature of the record. (David B. Kitts, 1974b)

Two University of California scientists add their testimony:

> The abrupt appearance of higher taxa in the fossil record has been a perennial puzzle. Not only do characteristic and distinctive remains of phyla appear suddenly, without known ancestors, but several classes of a phylum, orders of a

class, and so on, commonly appear at approximately the same time, without known intermediates. (James W. Valentine and Cathryn A. Campbell, 1975)

Dr. Parker has already discussed in Chapter 3 this phenomenon of the ubiquitous absence of transitional forms in the fossil record. Evolutionists have suggested various explanations—the inadequacy of the fossil record, explosive evolution in small populations, and others. All such explanations are based upon the *absence* of evidence, a strange situation in science. Actual fossils of transitional forms would be much better evidence of evolution than their absence!

The Creation Model, on the other hand, is not embarrassed by these gaps in the fossil record. Evolutionists have to try to *explain* the gaps, whereas the gaps are precisely predicted from the Creation Model.

There is, therefore, no evidence that the laws of nature were different in the past than they are at present. The Second Law of Thermodynamics seems to prevent upward evolutionary change in the present, and it apparently did the same in the past.

Abandonment of the Fossils as Evidence for Evolution

It is interesting to note the recent change in attitude of evolutionists toward the geologic record. For a long time, the fossils have been regarded as the essential evidence for evolution, the only noncircumstantial evidence, since they presumably documented the actual course of evolutionary history through the ages. For example, Pierre Grasse ', the leading French zoologist, said:

"Naturalists must remember that the process of evolution is revealed only through fossil forms. A knowledge of paleontology is, therefore, a prerequisite; only paleontology can provide them with the evidence of evolution and reveal its course or mechanisms." (Pierre P. Grasse', 1977b)

In recent years, however, evolutionists have finally taken serious notice of the universal absence of transitional forms in the fossil record.

> The known fossil record fails to document a single example of phyletic evolution accomplishing a major morphologic transition and hence offers no evidence that the gradualistic model can be valid. (Steven M. Stanley, 1979a)

As Dr. Parker has already pointed out, however, this does not at all mean that evolutionists are about to become creationists, even though creationists had been emphasizing for decades the fossil gaps as evidence of creation. Instead they have changed their model to one called by Gould "punctuated equilibrium," by Stanley "quantum speciation," and by Goldschmidt "hopeful monsters." Dr. Parker has already called attention to Stephen Gould's revival of the latter concept (p. 147). Steven Stanley, one of the nation's leading modern paleontologists, professor at Johns Hopkins University, also takes the Goldschmidt "hopeful monster" concept (which a generation ago was merely ridiculed) quite seriously.

> . . . there has recently been renewed expression of support for the importance in macroevolution of what Goldschmidt (1940) termed the hopeful monster . . . . At least in principle, Goldschmidt accepted Schindewolf's extreme example of the first bird hatching from a reptile egg. The problem with Goldschmidt's radical concept is the low probability that a totally monstrous form will find a mate and produce fertile offspring. (Stanley, 1979b)

To avoid the notion that a single animal could generate a completely new type, Stanley's quantum speciation idea allows several animals to be involved.

> Evidence is also mounting that quantum speciation events themselves may span rather few generations . . . . it is generally agreed that

quantum speciation takes place within very small populations—some would say populations involving fewer than 10 individuals. (Stanley, 1979c)

Whether one or several are postulated, the fact is that there are *no* truly transitional forms that have ever been found, either in the living world or fossil world. This fact conforms explicitly to a key prediction from the Creation Model. Consequently, more and more evolutionists are now abandoning the fossil record altogether in their idealistic search for some kind of scientific evidence of evolution. Says Mark Ridley, for example, a professor in Oxford University's Zoology Department:

> In any case, no real evolutionist, whether gradualist or punctuationist, uses the fossil record as evidence in favor of the theory of evolution as opposed to special creation. (Mark Ridley, 1981)

Similarly, David Kitts, a long-time specialist in paleontology and the philosophy of geology, has admitted:

> Few paleontologists have, I think, ever supposed that fossils, by themselves, provide grounds for the conclusion that evolution has occurred . . . . The fossil record doesn't even provide any evidence in support of Darwinian theory except in the weak sense that the fossil record is compatible with it, just as it is compatible with other evolutionary theories, and revolutionary theories, and special creationist theories, and even ahistorical theories. (David B. Kitts, 1979)

David Raup, Curator of Geology at Chicago's Field Museum, goes even further:

> So, the geological time scale and the basic facts of biological changes over time are totally independent of evolutionary theory . . . . One of the ironies of the evolution-creation debate is

that the creationists have accepted the mistaken notion that the fossil record shows a detailed and orderly progression and they have gone to great lengths to accommodate this "fact" in their Flood geology. (David Raup, 1981)

Here, indeed, is a remarkable situation. Grasse' and many others have pointed out that fossils must provide the *only* real evidence for evolution. Yet Kitts and others are now saying that fossils provide *no* real evidence for evolution.

Well, creationists think they are *both* right! The only *real* evidence is the fossil record, and it *doesn't* support evolution. It is interesting also that Ridley, Kitts, and Raup all place these remarkable admissions in the context of the creation/evolution debate. The real reason for going to these exotic new concepts of sudden evolution, for which not the slightest genetic evidence exists, is because the only alternative is creation, and this is out of the question altogether for men committed to a naturalistic faith.

The Shaky Foundations of the Geologic Column

If the fossil record does not give evidence for evolution, then what exactly is its testimony? What is the meaning of the billions of fossils buried in the sedimentary rocks of the earth's crust? How come there are different types of life forms in the different geologic ages if there is no fossil evidence that any one group evolved into any other group? How are these different ages recognized in the first place, since they all antedate any historical records by alleged millions and billions of years?

As a matter of fact, the rejection of the evolutionary implications of the fossil record is tantamount to rejecting the geologic column itself, as we shall see. Most people do not realize today that the very existence of the geological ages is based on the unrecognized—perhaps even subconscious—assumption of evolution.

Before we discuss this subject, however, it should be stressed that this is a secondary issue. I have frequently found in debating the subject of creation versus evolution that the evolutionist prefers to attack the concept of flood geology or the idea of recent creation, rather than giving any evidence for evolution. The question of the nature and duration of earth history is, indeed, an important related issue, but it is *not* the *main* issue. Whether or not all things were created is the basic issue. I am convinced that the scientific evidence strongly favors recent creation and catastrophism, but each question should be discussed on its own merits. The evidence for creation and against evolution is quite independent of whether the earth is old or young and whether the geologic data should be interpreted in terms of uniformitarianism or catastrophism. There are, as a matter of fact, some evolutionists who believe in a young earth and geological catastrophism, and there are some creationists who believe in an old earth and geological uniformitarianism.

In spite of recent questionings, however, the geologic age system still is accepted by most evolutionists as the basic framework for interpreting the earth's assumed evolutionary history. Consequently the problem of establishing and identifying the various geologic ages is an important related issue. How, then, does one identify the geologic age of any particular rock system? Further, how can one confirm the correctness of the standard geologic column? The column is supposed to represent a vertical cross-section through the earth's crust, with the most recently deposited (therefore youngest) rocks at the surface and the oldest, earliest rocks deposited on the crystalline "basement" rocks at the bottom. If one wishes to check out this standard column (or standard geologic age system), where can he go to see it for himself?

There is only one place in all the world to see the standard geologic column. *That's in the textbook!* . . . almost any textbook, in fact, that deals with evolution or earth history. A typical textbook rendering of the standard column is shown in Figure 44.

This standard column is supposed to be at least 100 miles thick (some writers say up to 200), representing the total sedimentary activity of all the geologic ages. However, the average thickness of each *local* geologic column is about

MAIN DIVISION AND EVENTS OF GEOLOGICAL TIME

ERAS	PERIODS	CHARACTERISTIC LIFE	ESTIMATED YEARS AGO
	Quaternary: Recent Epoch Pleistocene Epoch	Rise of modern plants and animals, and man.	25,000 975,000
CENOZOIC	Tertiary: Pliocene Epoch Miocene " Oligocene " Eocene " Paleocene "	Rise of mammals and development of highest plants.	12,000,000 25,000,000 35,000,000 60,000,000 70,000,000
MESOZOIC	Cretaceous	Modernized angiosperms and insects abundant. Foraminifers profuse. Extinction of dinosaurs, flying reptiles, and ammonites.	70,000,000 to 200,000,000
	Jurassic	First (reptilian) birds. First of highest forms of insects. First (primitive) angiosperms.	
	Triassic	Earliest dinosaurs, flying reptiles, marine reptiles, and primitive mammals. Cycads and conifers common. Modern corals common. Earliest ammonites.	
PALEOZOIC	Permian	Rise of primitive reptiles. Earliest cycads and conifers. Extinction of trilobites. First modern corals.	200,000,000 to 500,000,000
	Pennsylvanian	Earliest known insects. Spore plants abundant.	
	Mississippian	Rise of amphibians. Culmination of crinoids.	
	Devonian	First known seed plants. Great variety of boneless fishes. First evidence of amphibians.	
	Silurian	Earliest known land animals. Primitive land plants. Rise of fishes. Brachiopods, trilobites, and corals abundant.	
	Ordovician	Earliest known vertebrates. Graptolites, corals, brachiopods, cephalopods, and trilobites abundant. Oldest primitive land plants.	
	Cambrian	All subkingdoms of invertebrate animals represented. Brachiopods and trilobites common.	
PROTEROZOIC	Keweenawan Huronian	Primitive water-dwelling plants and animals.	500,000,000 to 1,000,000,000
ARCHEOZOIC	Timiskaming Keewatin	Oldest known life (mostly indirect evidence).	1,000,000,000 to 1,800,000,000

Figure 44. Standard Geologic Column and System of Geologic "Ages"

one mile (in some places, the column has essentially zero thickness, in a few places it may be up to 16 or so miles, but the worldwide average is about one mile). The standard column has been built up by superposition of local columns from many different localities.

On what basis was this done? The classic summarization in an older textbook describes this process:

> By application of the principle of superposition, lithologic identification, recognition of unconformities, and reference to fossil successions, both the thick and the thin masses are correlated with other beds at other sites. Thus there is established in detail the stratigraphic succession for all the geologic ages. (O. D. von Engeln and K. E. Caster, 1952)

At first this seems like a reasonable procedure, in accord with sound principles of induction. When each of these criteria is examined individually, however, the resulting system is much less impressive. Consider briefly each criterion in turn.

(1) *Principle of Superposition*. The fundamental principle of stratigraphy is that the sediments on the bottom were deposited first and are therefore older. This seems obvious.

And yet there are many, many regions where "old" formations are found deposited on top of "young" formations, as sketched in Figure 45. Such situations are commonly explained away by saying that great earth movements (especially so-called "overthrusts," also called "thrust faults," "nappes," or "low-angle faults") have somehow gotten the original order inverted. Much of the Cordilleran Range is in this condition, especially in the so-called "overthrust belt" of the Rockies, and the same is true of the Alps and of practically every major mountain range in the world.

A surprising recent addition to this list is the Appalachian range. These are supposed to be very old mountains, mostly dated in the Paleozoic Era.

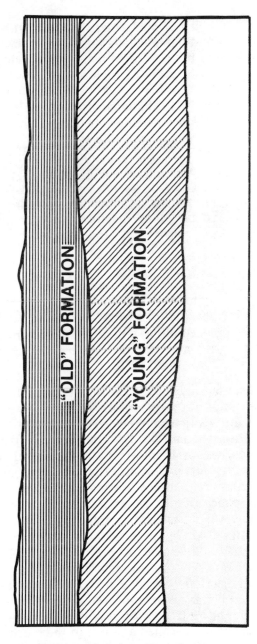

Figure 45. Inadequacy of Stratigraphic Order to Determine Age

> The Appalachians, which run from New-
> foundland to Alabama, were probably formed
> not by upward thrusting, as previously believed,
> but by a thick conglomerate of oceanic and con-
> tinental rock that was shoved horizontally at
> least 250 kilometers over existing sediments.
> . . . But beneath that jumble of rock . . . lies a
> younger, flat, thin (1-5 km thick) layer of
> sediments that "no one thought existed." The
> unbroken, wide extent of the layer—researchers
> estimate it covers 150,000 km^2 . . . and its
> similarity to sediments found on the East Coast
> indicate that the mountains "could not have
> been pushed up." (Science News, 1979a)

The researchers who have investigated this tremendous
out-of-order complex of formations say:

> The only explanation for the buried strata is
> that the overlying crystalline rocks were em-
> placed along a major subhorizontal thrust fault
> (a horizontal fault below the surface). (F. A.
> Cook, *et al,* 1980)

That is, this may be the only explanation if the formations
are indeed out of order. But then, where was the original
region from which they were pushed?

Many such out-of-order stratigraphic series do give
evidence of involvement in intense deformations of the
crust, folds and fractures as well as thrust-faulting. On the
other hand, there are many of them where there is no
evidence of significant movement at all—they are simply
out of sequence stratigraphically.

Even where there is some real physical indication of
relative movement between adjacent formations, it is extremely difficult to demonstrate that these movements
were actually capable of translating vast blocks of rock
great distances up and over underlying systems, against the
tremendous forces of gravity and friction. This is not the
place for a detailed analysis of the mechanics involved, except to say that the translation of many of these great over-

thrust blocks still seems mechanically impossible.

The most widely used explanation is that of abnormally high fluid pressures entrapped in the sediments at the time of deposition, which in effect buoyed up the blocks and, so to speak, "floated" them into place in an out-of-order sequence. This mechanism, however, seems completely unrealistic. The attainment and maintenance of such abnormally high pressures large enough to float a great thickness of rock over a large area would require impossible conditions.

> If we assume that rocks have no tensile strength . . . then when the pore fluid pressure exceeds the least compressive stress, fractures will form normal to that stress direction. These fractures limit pore pressure . . . . we suggest that pore pressure may never get high enough to allow gravity gliding . . . ; the rocks might fail in vertical hydrofracture first. (J. H. Willemin, *et al*, 1980)

If such gigantic overthrusts really have taken place, they would have required extremely unusual, probably catastrophic, conditions. In any case, whatever the cause, and whether the strata have really been moved out of their original depositional order or not, it is clear that the simple principle of superposition is not adequate to determine geologic age.

(2) *Lithologic Identification.* At one time it was believed that different types of rock (granite, sandstone, shale, etc.) were formed in different ages, but no one believes this today. It has been known for over a hundred years that rocks of all kinds can be found from all geologic "ages." Furthermore, minerals and metals of all kinds can be found in all ages. All sorts of geologic structures can be found in all ages. Even coal and oil have been found in rock systems from almost every so-called geologic age. All this is summarized in Figure 46.

In other words, nothing about the type of rock or the contents of the rock can determine the age of the rock. Not even radioactive minerals which the rock may contain will

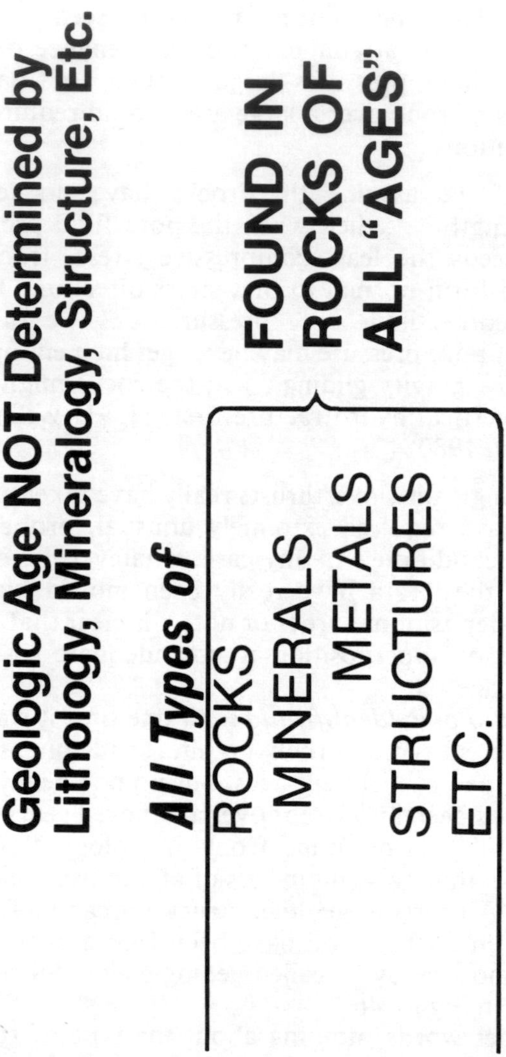

Geologic Age NOT Determined by Lithology, Mineralogy, Structure, Etc.

FOUND IN ROCKS OF ALL "AGES"

All Types of

ROCKS
MINERALS
METALS
STRUCTURES
ETC.

Figure 46. Inadequacy of Lithology to Determine Age

determine its geologic age, for the whole geologic age system had been completely worked out before the discovery of radioactivity. Furthermore, as will be shown in the next chapter, there are numerous sources of error in radioactive age measurements, so that whenever a radiometric age disagrees with the geologic age, the latter will govern.

(3) *Recognition of Unconformities.* An unconformity is an interface between adjacent formations marked by "nonconformable" strata above and below (note Figure 47). As long as successive sedimentary strata (that is "layers") are parallel (i.e., "conformable"), the deposition process which formed them can be assumed to have been continuous. An unconformity, however, indicates a significant interruption in the deposition process, with a period of erosion in between. The unconformable strata above and below the interface probably result from an uplift and tilting of the lower formation, before the beginning of the sedimentary deposition of the strata of the upper formation. The unconformity obviously represents a gap in time of unknown duration, at least in the local geologic column.

Nevertheless, such local unconformities cannot be used to identify the boundary between geologic ages, even locally. Chang points out this fact, as follows:

> Many unconformity-bounded units have been erroneously regarded as lithostratigraphic units, even though they are characterized not by lithologic unity but by the fact of being bounded by unconformities . . . . Similarly, many unconformity-bounded units have been erroneously considered to be chronostratigraphic units, in spite of the fact that unconformity surfaces are apt to be diachronous and hence cannot constitute true chronostratigraphic boundaries. (K. Hong Chang, 1981)

If an unconformity surface is "diachronous," that means it cannot be an "isochronous" surface ("diachronous" means "across time;" "isochronous" means "equal

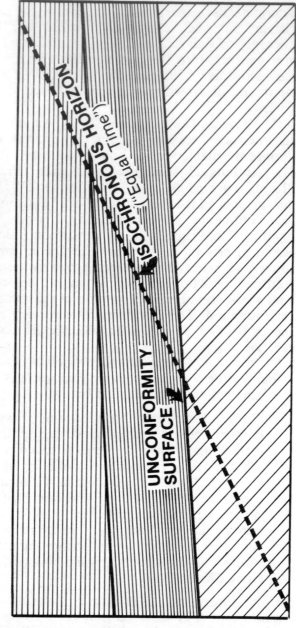

Figure 47. Inadequacy of Unconformities to Determine Age

time"). Thus, as shown on Figure 47, the unconformity surface cuts across the isochronous surface, which is the true time-marker. As Chang says, unconformity surfaces "cannot be true chronostratigraphic boundaries."

Thus, neither the principle of superposition nor lithologic identification nor recognition of unconformities can suffice to determine geologic age. Of these four criteria listed by von Engeln and Caster (p. 198), only one is left—"reference to fossil successions."

All of the others—superposition, lithology, and unconformities—can help to identify particular formations on a local basis, but only the fossils can really settle the question of "geologic age." Not all fossils, of course, but the so-called "index fossils" and the particular assemblage of fossils in a formation do indeed determine the age supposed age.

> Each taxon represents a definite time unit and so provides an accurate, even "infallible" date. If you doubt it, bring in a suite of good index fossils, and the specialist, without asking where or in what order they were collected, will lay them out on the table in chronological order. (J. E. O'Rourke, 1976)

The term "taxon" refers to a taxonomic unit—that is, any particular species, genus, family, etc., found as fossils in the strata. Some organisms, of course, cannot be used as index fossils for a particular "age," since they supposedly lived through many such ages, but others—particularly "suites" or "assemblages" of fossils—are believed to be specific indicators of specific ages, or "index fossils."

But how do such fossils determine the age of a rock? Dr. H. D. Hedberg, then president of the Geological Society of America, answers:

> . . . fossils have furnished, through their record of the evolution of life on this planet, an amazingly effective key to the relative positioning of strata in widely separated regions and from continent to continent. (H. D. Hedberg, 1961)

A leading European paleontologist likewise says:

> The only chronometric scale applicable in geologic history for the stratigraphic classification of rocks and for dating geologic events exactly is furnished by the fossils. Owing to the irreversibility of evolution, they offer an unambiguous time-scale for relative age determinations and for worldwide correlations of rocks. (O. H. Schindewolf, 1957)

That is, since evolution takes place worldwide, rocks containing fossils representing a certain stage of evolution are assumed to have been formed during the age when that evolutionary stage was attained. This would certainly be the best way of dating rocks, if we knew for certain—say, by divine revelation—that evolution were true.

But this is the very question. If the Creation Model is a better model than the Evolution Model, as creationists believe, then evolution is *not* true, and there is no way to distinguish one geologic age from another. In fact, they may all be essentially the *same* age!

This criticism of the Evolution Model is all the more cogent in light of the fact that most evolutionists still think the fossil record is the best evidence for evolution. As Dunbar has said:

> . . . fossils provide the only historical, documentary evidence that life has evolved from simpler to more and more complex forms. (C. O. Dunbar, 1960)

How can the fossil sequence prove evolution if the rocks containing the fossils have been dated by those fossils on the basis of the assumed stage of evolution of those same fossils? This is pure circular reasoning, based on the arbitrary assumption that the Evolution Model is true. (See Figure 48.)

Some evolutionists recognize this problem. David Kitts, of the University of Oklahoma, admits:

> But the danger of circularity is still present.

Figure 48. Circular Reasoning and Use of Fossils to Determine Age

For most biologists the strongest reason for accepting the evolutionary hypothesis is their acceptance of some theory that entails it. There is another difficulty. The temporal ordering of biological events beyond the local section may critically involve paleontological correlation which necessarily presupposes the nonrepeatability of organic events in geologic history. There are various justifications for this assumption but for almost all contemporary paleontologists it rests upon the acceptance of the evolutionary hypothesis. (David B. Kitts, 1974a)

Similarly, and more recently, he says:

. . . the record of evolution, like any other historical record, must be construed within a complex of particular and general preconceptions, not the least of which is the hypothesis that evolution has occurred. (David B. Kitts, 1979)

In other words, evolution must be assumed before the fossil record is used to establish geologic ages. Ronald West concurs:

Contrary to what most scientists write, the fossil record does not support the Darwinian theory of evolution because it is this theory (there are several) which we use to interpret the fossil record. By doing so, we are guilty of circular reasoning if we then say the fossil record supports this theory. (Ronald R. West, 1968)

There seems really no objective reason, therefore, why the entire range of organic life preserved in the fossils could not have been living concurrently in one age. If so, it is reasonable to give serious consideration to a return to *catastrophism,* rather than uniformitarianism, as the explanation of the geologic column. In this model, the great beds of sedimentary rocks were formed mainly by a great worldwide hydraulic cataclysm, as believed by the found-

ing fathers of geology (Steno, Woodward, *et al)* before the
rise of the uniformitarians (Hutton, Lyell, Darwin). Some
(e.g., Cuvier) believed in several such cataclysms

The Catastrophic Model

With all the above considerations in mind, it is well
worthwhile to consider an alternative to the widely accepted uniformitarian model of earth history. As already
stressed, this issue is not as fundamental as the basic crea-
tion/evolution issue, and both questions can be argued independently on their own respective merits. Furthermore,
both can be discussed completely on the basis of scientific
data, without reference to their philosophic implications,
and thus both issues (i.e., creation/evolution and
catastrophism/uniformitarianism) can appropriately be
discussed and evaluated in public schools, solely in terms
of their respective abilities to explain the scientific data.

Even though they *can* be treated independently,
however, it is obvious that the two issues are closely
related. If the evolution model *requires* a long expanse of
geologic time to be feasible at all (as most evolutionists
believe), then the concept of geologic ages becomes a very
important asset to evolutionism. On the other hand, if the
only real basis for believing in different geologic ages is a
prior belief in evolution, as shown in the previous section,
then scientists ought to be willing to take a critical second
look at the whole idea of great geological ages to see if
there is any real substance to the concept, other than this
need to support evolution. By the same token, if creationists can show not only that there is strong independent
evidence for creation, but also that most of the geologic
column is essentially a unit, deposited catastrophically at a
recent period in earth history, then the whole chronologi-
cal framework of evolution will be undermined and its
foundations destroyed. Die-hard evolutionists would have
to retreat to some concept of cataclysmic evolution (*a la*
Velikovsky) in order to retain their faith in evolution at all.

As a matter of fact, that is essentially what the "punctuationists" are already doing, except that they are still
hanging on to the geologic ages. Since they recognize that

there is no evidence of gradual evolution, they postulate episodes of very rapid evolution in very small populations, leaving no transitional fossils to mark these transmutations. And then, since there is no known genetic or ecologic mechanism to produce such quantum jumps in evolution, many are turning to the concept of environmental catastrophes as the means of triggering and energizing some yet-undiscovered genetic reaction which can somehow generate these hopeful monsters. Prigogine's notion of "dissipative structures" and "order through perturbations" is also becoming a part of this scenario.

In the modern context, old-fashioned uniformitarianism now seems to be passing off the stage, along with old-fashioned Darwinian or neo-Darwinian evolutionism. Ironically, most public schools are still teaching the "old fashioned" evolution now being discredited by the leading evolutionists. Gould and other punctuationists are attempting to retain the time-honored framework of Darwinism just as Ager and other neo-catastrophists are likewise paying lip-service to the venerable tenets of uniformitarianism, but they have really been converted to a radical new concept that might well be called "revolutionary evolutionism."

Derek Ager, past-president of the British Geological Association, ties his catastrophism to Gould's punctuationism in the following words:

> I am now coming more and more to the opinion that most evolution proceeds by sudden short steps or *quanta* and I was pleased to see the same views recently expressed by S. J. Gould in America. (Derek V. Ager, 1973a)

Gould, in turn, has clearly repudiated the older uniformitarianism established by Sir Charles Lyell and which served as the basis for Charles Darwin's concept of unlimited natural selection.

> Lyell relied upon true bits of cunning to establish his uniformitarian views as the only true geology . . . . In fact, the catastrophists were much more empirically minded than Lyell.

> The geologic record does seem to require catastrophes: rocks are fractured and contorted; whole faunas are wiped out. To circumvent this literal appearance, Lyell imposed his imagination upon the evidence. (Stephen J. Gould, 1975)

Both Ager and Gould are vitriolic anti-creationists, so their repudiation of uniformitarianism and neo-Darwinism is certainly not because of any conversion to creationism. In spite of the fact that they are now using the same evidence and arguments that creationists were previously using, they are both still committed to the geologic age system and to materialistic evolutionism, as are the many younger geologists, biologists, and paleontologists who are today following their system of intermittent catastrophes and accompanying punctuational evolution.

Gould and many like-minded colleagues, in fact, clearly have political motives as well. These latter-day fantasies of improvement by quantum jumps, order by perturbation, structure through dissipation, hope through monsters, advance through catastrophes, and evolution by revolution are beautifully consistent with Marxian dialectics, and have long been advocated in Soviet Russia. Gould, with his colleague Niles Eldredge, has said:

> Alternate conceptions of change have respectable pedigrees in philosophy. Hegel's dialectical laws, translated into a materialist context, have become the official "state philosophy" of many socialist nations. These laws of change are explicitly punctuational, as befits a theory of revolutionary transformation in human society. . . . In the light of this official philosophy, it is not at all surprising that a punctuational view of speciation, much like our own, . . . has long been favored by many Russian paleontologists. It may also not be irrelevant to our personal preferences that one of us learned his Marxism, literally, at his daddy's knee. (Gould and Eldredge, 1977)

Not all evolutionists have become converts to these new concepts. The old guard (quite as committed to evolutionary naturalism as the punctuationists, but still believing in gradual, rather than sudden, changes) is now becoming aware of the political implications. One of these men, Professor of Zoology and Geology at the University of Reading in England, has expressed his concern as follows:

> If it could be established that the pattern of evolution is a saltatory one after all, then at long last the Marxists would indeed be able to claim that the theoretical basis of their approach was supported by scientific evidence. Just as there are "scientific" creationists seeking to falsify the concept of gradual change through time in favor of creationism, so too there are the Marxists who for different motives are equally concerned to discredit gradualism. (L. B. Halstead, 1980)

Political motives aside, there is no question that Gould, Ager, and their colleagues have been adducing much evidence in favor of catastrophism and against slow-and-gradual evolution. Their position certainly seems to be the "wave of the future" as far as evolutionary theory is concerned. Creationists who have long been arguing against Lyellian uniformitarianism and Darwinian evolutionism suddenly have found unexpected, unwilling, and unwanted allies among these younger "revolutionary evolutionists."

Thus the creation/evolution battle may soon be shifting to a different front, and it may well center around the geologic-ages question. Everyone now recognizes that there is much evidence for catastrophism, but these are assumed to be intermittent events which punctuate long periods of uniformity when essentially nothing happens. The concept of a single global hydraulic cataclysm accounting for all or most of the geologic column, on the other hand, would in effect not only eliminate the geologic-ages concept, but destroy the entire chronologic framework of the basic Evolution Model. Such a global hydraulic cataclysm would necessarily be accompanied by worldwide volcanism, mountain building, and other catastrophic phenomena, followed possibly by continental shifts and large-scale glaciation. Consequently, evolutionists of all stripes vigorously resist the idea of a worldwide hydraulic cataclysm, even though they are now quite amenable to any number of intermittent regional catastrophes.

Nevertheless, the Cataclysmic Model can be shown to be a very effective model for explaining all the real data of the geologic column. I have been rather intensively studying this model for forty years and am firmly convinced it is a far better model than uniformitarianism for correlating the factual, scientific data of all the earth sciences.

In fact, my main motivation in going to graduate school back in 1946 was to become prepared to deal effectively with this great issue. As I mentioned in the preceding chapter, I had become a creationist as a young engineering instructor, but I soon realized that the critical question was the matter of the geologic ages. Since the fossil beds which supposedly identified these ages were all in sedimentary deposits and these had almost all been formed by water action, it was obvious that a real understanding of the column and the geologic ages would require a comprehensive understanding of both hydraulics and geology. As it happened, both disciplines were also important in my academic field of civil engineering, so they would contribute to professional development, as well.

Accordingly, I enrolled in 1946 in the University of Minnesota, which I concluded (after investigating many possibilities) had the nation's best graduate program in hydraulics and hydrology, and one of the best in geology. I received the M.S. in 1948 and the Ph.D. in 1950, both with majors in hydraulics and minors in geology and mathematics (the latter being an essential for a hydraulics major). I am still convinced that this is one of the best combinations for someone wanting to deal incisively with the geologic age question, to critique the uniformitarian model of earth history, and to develop a coherent system of catastrophic geology.

Although other geological processes (volcanism, earth movements, etc.) are very important in the cataclysmic model, hydraulic processes are by far the most significant, since most of the earth's fossil-bearing rocks are sedimentaries, formed by hydraulic deposition. It may be significant that there are traditions of such a primeval cataclysm found in practically every ancient nation and tribe. However, discussion of this model need not refer to these traditions.

The question is simply whether the model of a single global cataclysm, primarily hydraulic in nature, can explain the data of geology better than the uniformitarian/multiple local catastrophe model. This Cataclysmic Model of geology can be examined in terms of five major predictions:

(1) Most or all formations should be explainable in terms of catastrophic intensities of the processes which formed them;

(2) Evidence should exist of continuous deposition, without significant time gaps, of most or all of the geologic column;

(3) The order of deposition in any local column should usually be in terms of the elevation of ecological habitat of the organisms preserved as fossils in that column;

(4) The order of deposition in any given formation should usually be the order implied by the hydraulic processes producing it as a single depositional unit;

(5) Because of the cataclysmic and complex geophysical phenomena associated with such a catastrophe, there would be occasional exceptions to the order of fossil deposition specified as "usual" in predictions (3) and (4).

Now, even if one prefers to believe in the basic uniformitarian interpretation of geology, he should recognize that each of the five predictions above are fulfilled in the actual facts of geology. In the first place, it has become obvious in recent years that normal, slow processes of sedimentation, tectonism, volcanism, etc., could never produce the formations and structures found in the earth's crust, not to mention the coal, oil, and metal deposits. Dr. Parker has already reviewed many evidences of catastrophism in Chapter 3.

Dr. Derek Ager, Head of the Geology Department at Swansea University in England, has published an entire book demonstrating that every formation requires a catastrophic explanation. He concludes his book as follows:

> In other words, the history of any one part of the earth, like the life of a soldier, consists of long periods of boredom and short periods of terror. (Derek V. Ager, 1973b)

That is, everything we can actually see in the geologic column is the result of geologic catastrophes. However, although there is no visible evidence of the supposed vast periods of time in between, Dr. Ager does not believe in a worldwide cataclysm, but rather in a succession of regional catastrophes, each separated from the next by a long time gap of unknown duration. Such time gaps presumably were times of slow erosion, marked by unconformities in the geologic column.

In the second place, however, it should be emphasized that there are no worldwide unconformities and therefore no worldwide time gaps in the column. That is, even though formation **A** may be separated from formation **B** in locality **1** by a clear unconformity, it will be found to rest conformably on the same formation in locality 2, as sketched in Figure 49. There may have been a period of uplift and erosion in region **1**, while deposition was continuous in region **2**.

In any case, whatever the specific physical sequences may have been, there is no worldwide unconformity, and thus no worldwide time gap. Some have suggested a global unconformity below the Cambrian system, but this is doubtful, except at the so-called "crystalline basement" below all sedimentary rocks.

> In the early history of stratigraphy, unconformities were overestimated in that they were believed to represent coeval diastrophism over areas of infinitely wide extent. (K. Hong Chang, 1975b)

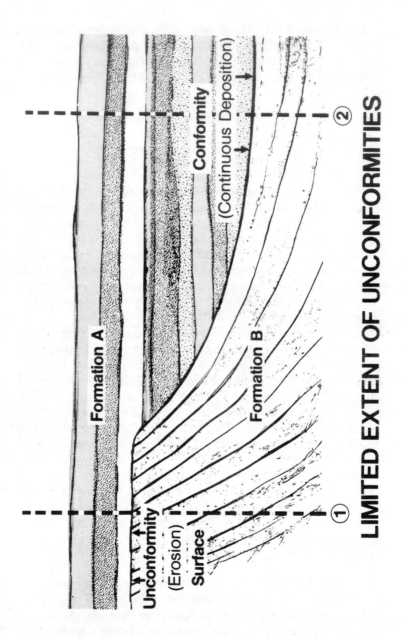

Figure 49. Limited Extent of Unconformities

Even if there should prove to be a global unconformity somewhere in the Precambrian sedimentary rocks, the fact still remains that the great bulk of the geologic column, including *all* the fossil-bearing rocks, represents continuous deposition, with no worldwide time gap.

The ideas of worldwide "revolutions" and mountain-building upheavals at the end of each geological epoch are still reflected in the terminology of the standard geologic time-table, but they correspond to no real chronology in the real geologic column.

> Many unconformity-bounded units are considered to be chronostratigraphic units in spite of the fact that unconformity surfaces inevitably cut across isochronous horizons and hence cannot be true chronostratigraphic boundaries. (Chang, 1975a)

The obvious conclusion is that there is no clear physically demarked worldwide time boundary anywhere in the geologic column. That can only mean that, since each unit in the column was deposited rapidly, as noted by Ager, the entire column was formed rapidly. The entire sedimentary crust, therefore, fits the prediction of the Catastrophic Model—continuous, cataclysmic hydraulic sedimentary activity throughout the column.

The last three predictions from this Model also are obviously confirmed, since the order of deposition which they suggest for the fossils is from the simpler on the bottom to the complex on top (with occasional exceptions), and it is this very order which has been appropriated by the evolutionist in support of his own model. This aspect of global hydraulic sedimentary catastrophism has already been discussed in some detail in Chapter 4. The occasional exceptions (inverted sequences in the geologic column and fossils from different "ages" in the same formation) are easy enough to understand in a cataclysm, but very difficult to explain in terms of simple uniformitarianism.

The Cataclysmic Model of the earth's geologic crust, as a supplement and corollary of the basic Creation Model of origins, thus clearly does fit all the facts of geology at least as well as the Uniformitarian Model, with fewer unsolved problems, and so should be seriously considered by scientists. As a matter of fact, many young scientists now *are* taking it seriously, and the Model has already stimulated much fruitful research, showing real promise of becoming a very effective tool in geological exploration and development.

Chapter 7

How and When Did the World Begin?

Significance of the Time Question

The question of the *date* of creation is separate and distinct from the question of the *fact* of creation. The basic evidences supporting the Creation Model—for example, the laws of thermodynamics, the complex structures of living organisms, the universal gaps between types in both the living world and the fossil record—are all quite independent of the time of creation. Whether the world is ten thousand years old or ten trillion years old, these and other such evidences all point to creation, not to evolution, as the best explanation of origins.

Unfortunately, evolutionists commonly confuse the issue, apparently believing that an ancient earth would prove evolution and a young earth would prove creation. The critics of the creation movement commonly focus their attacks not on creation in general, but on *recent* creation.

The fact is, however, that the question of the age of the earth and the universe, while an important question in its own right, is quite independent of the question of creation or evolution, at least as far as the facts of science are concerned. For evolutionists to concentrate their criticisms of creationism mostly on this independent issue is merely an admission of the weakness of evolutionism.

On the other hand, the concept of evolution does suggest an *old* earth. Creationism is free to consider *all* evidences regarding the earth's age, whether old or young, whereas *evolutionism is bound to an old earth.* Practically all evolutionary systems require immense amounts of time. Since there are no evidences of real "vertical" evolution occurring in all the thousands of years of recorded history, it is obvious that evolution—if it is taking place at all—is proceeding so slowly as to require immense aeons of time for its accomplishments. Evolutionists therefore must categorically reject all evidences of a young earth.

Consequently, even though scientific creationism does not necessarily specify a recent creation, the question of the date of creation, like the question of catastrophism, is an important related issue. That is, there is only one basic question, that of creation or evolution, but there are two important corollary questions: (1) catastrophism or uniformitarianism; (2) recent or old origin. All three of these are important questions that can be evaluated strictly as scientific models, without reference to their theological, philosophical, or moral implications. Each can be treated independently of the other two, even though they all deal with the history and character of the cosmos and are obviously related to each other.

The preceding chapter dealt with the first of these two related issues, demonstrating that global catastrophism is a better model than uniformitarianism for correlating the data of historical geology. In this chapter we want to look at the second corollary issue and see whether the actual scientific data really do support the great ages required by evolution.

It will never be possible to *prove* the age of the earth or the universe, of course, since these are matters of history (or "prehistory"), rather than science. Just like the question of creation or evolution, we cannot repeat the origin of the earth in the laboratory. The essential aspect of the scientific method (experimental repeatability) can never be applied to either the nature or date of ultimate origins. Nevertheless, there are many physical processes and systems which can provide clues and estimates of age, and all of these should be considered before making a decision. The present practice of considering only the handful of indicators of an old origin, while ignoring the scores of evidences of young age, is certainly unworthy of a true scientific attitude. A much more honest approach would be to consider and teach openly all the evidences of age, whether old or young, allowing students and others to judge their relative merits for themselves.

Origin of the Cosmos

When I first became interested in the subject of cosmogony almost forty years ago, it was widely held that the universe was two billion years old. The most persuasive "proof" of this age was the convergence of several independent calculations on this date. The argument went like this: "Although questions can be raised about the reliability of any one method, the fact that several independent methods 'agree' must prove that they are all basically correct. The decay of lead into uranium, the expansion of the universe, and several other calculations all yield an age of two billion years, so this is undoubtedly the true age!"

It is now known, of course, that all these calculations were wrong. In each of the methods, certain assumptions had been made which were later proved wrong.

However, the line of reasoning still has a familiar ring. Even though all currently popular geochronometers involve certain very questionable assumptions, the apparent agreement in their results (or, at least, in *some* of their results) is taken as proof that they are correct.

It is currently fashionable to believe that the earth is about 4.5 to 5.0 billion years old, the universe in its present form is somewhere between 10 and 30 billion years old, and the space/mass/time cosmos in some form existed from eternity.

Forty years ago I was taught that the expansion of the universe (as deduced from the "red-shift" in the light spectra from distant galaxies) indicated that the present form of the universe must have originated in the explosion of a "primeval atom" two billion years ago.

This "Big-Bang Theory," in somewhat more sophisticated form, is still the dominant cosmogonic model today. However, for a considerable period of time between then

and now, it experienced strong competition from the
"Steady-State Theory," first widely advocated by the
British astronomer, Sir Fred Hoyle, in the early fifties.
This theory was not based on any empirical observations,
but on what its advocates called "the perfect cosmological
principle," the assumption that the universe must always
be essentially uniform in both time and space. Because of
the continuing expansion of the universe, as well as the
continuing decay of the universe described by the Second
Law of Thermodynamics, Hoyle and his followers postulated a "continuous creation" of matter (i.e., atoms of
hydrogen) out of nothing. The "creation" term was a
misnomer, of course, since as an atheist, Hoyle did not
believe in a Creator; a better term would have been "continuous evolution out of nothing."

The Steady-State Theory, of course, contradicted both
the First and Second Laws of Thermodynamics, and it was
criticized on many other counts as well. Probably the most
cogent criticism came from the eminent cosmologist and
philosopher of science, Sir Herbert Dingle:

> We are told that matter is being continually
> created, but in such a way that the process is im-
> perceptible—that is, the statement cannot be
> disproved. When we ask why we should believe
> this, the answer is that the "perfect cosmological
> principle" requires it. And when we ask why we
> should accept this principle, the answer is that
> the fundamental axiom of science requires it.
> This we have seen to be false, and the only other
> answer that one can gather is that the principle
> must be true because it seems fitting to the peo-
> ple who assert it. With all respect, I find this in-
> adequate. (Herbert Dingle, 1954)

There is no need at this point for a detailed critique of the
Steady-State Theory, since it has now been completely
abandoned by cosmologists—even by Fred Hoyle himself.
The final and conclusive "proof" of the Big-Bang Theory,
its competitor, was the discovery in 1965 of the supposedly
uniform "background radiation" left over from the

primeval explosion, a discovery which produced a Nobel Prize for the Bell Telephone scientists who recognized it. For over a decade now, practically all cosmologists have been disciples of the Big-Bang Theory, with the only significant disagreement having to do with whether or not the Big Bang is a cyclic phenomenon, with the universe alternately expanding and contracting. Although there still are many unresolved problems, the supposed uniformity and homogeneity of the low-temperature background radiation (corresponding to 3 degrees on the Kelvin scale, measured above absolute zero) is believed to have provided compelling evidence for the Big Bang.

Now, however, it is beginning to become evident that this commitment to the Big Bang was premature:

> Coincidence of prediction and observation made the big bang seem the most plausible of cosmological theories. From plausible it became predominant and then virtually an orthodoxy. . . . But now its decade of total dominance may be starting to close. (Dietrick V. Thomsen, 1978)

One of the long-time opponents of the Big Bang idea is Dr. Hannes Alfven, Professor of Physics at the University of California (San Diego) and one of the world's leading astrophysicists. He has shown conclusively that, even if the background radiation were indeed isotropic and homogeneous, the Big Bang is only one of several possible explanations for such a phenomenon.

> The observed cosmic microwave background radiation, which has a high degree of spatial isotropy and which closely fits a 2.7K black body spectrum, is generally claimed to be the strongest piece of evidence in support of hot big bang cosmologies by its proponents . . . . The claim that this radiation lends strong support to hot big bang cosmologies is without foundation. (Hannes Alfven and Asoka Mendis, 1977)

As a matter of fact, the supposed uniformity of the

background radiation has recently been called into serious question.

> Cosmologists would like to believe that the universe is homogeneous and isotropic, that it is relatively smooth over-all and the same in all directions . . . . Our evidence for isotropy is the microwave radio radiation, the so-called 3K black-body that pervades space and seems to be a relic of the very beginning of time. It used to seem to be the same in all directions.
> Not any more. Five or six years ago we began to hear of a possible dipole anisotropy. Then at the beginning of 1980 came hints of a quadrupole anisotropy . . . . A quadrupole anisotropy (difference in four directions at right angles to each other) has to belong to the substance of the radiation of the universe itself. (*Science News,* 1981)

In other words, not only is the radiation not uniform in all directions, it is not even uniform in any direction! The Big Bang explosion, if it really happened, must have exploded heterogeneously rather than homogeneously, splaying radiation selectively in certain directions.

Not only is the radiation nonuniform, however, but so is the matter which presumably was formed out of the primordial explosive energies. It has never been adequately explained how cosmic "lumps" such as stars and galaxies could be generated from the homogeneous energies of the hypothetical explosion.

> Few cosmologists today would dispute the view that our expanding universe began with a bang—a big hot bang—about 18 billion years ago. Paradoxically, no cosmologist could now tell you how the Big Bang—the explosion of a superhot, superdense atom—ultimately gave rise to galaxies, stars, and other cosmic lumps.
> As one sky scientist, IBM's Philip E. Seiden, put it, "The standard Big Bang model does not give rise to lumpiness. That model assumes the

universe started out as a globally smooth, homogeneous expanding gas. If you apply the laws of physics to this model, you get a universe that is uniform, a cosmic vastness of evenly distributed atoms with no organization of any kind . . . . ''

How then did the lumps get there? No one can say, at least not yet and perhaps not ever. (Ben Patrusky, 1981)

But that is not all. Not only do such lumps as stars and galaxies occur in the universe, but they occur in nonuniform fashion, contrary to the so-called cosmological principle. There are significant "empty spaces" in the universe, as well as regions where the aggregation of galaxies is far greater than the average density for the universe as a whole. Speaking of a supercluster of galaxies in the constellation Virgo, a recent article points out that:

. . . there has not been enough time since the beginning for such an agglomeration to gather together out of an originally homogeneous universe. Therefore the clump must have been present at the beginning, a lump in the leaven, so to speak. *(Science News,* 1979b)

Thus, if the Big Bang really occurred, it could hardly have been isotropic and homogeneous, as the theory requires. It would be a "lumpy Big Bang," as some have called it, as well as anisotropic and heterogeneous. Such an explosion is exceedingly unlikely.

If the evidence gets too strong that the beginning of the universe was more like chicken soup with dumplings than a smooth gruel, it could be disturbing to most cosmologists. (*Science News,* 1979b)

There are other problems with the Big Bang, perhaps even more serious than even these which are now admitted. The primeval explosion is supposed to have resulted in a uniform radial expansion of energy and matter. One of the most basic conservation laws of physics is the principle of conservation of angular momentum, which states, among other things, that uniform radial motion could never give rise to curvilinear motion. How, then, could the linearly expanding gas soon be converted into orbiting galaxies and planetary systems?

The Big Bang and the Second Law

An even more basic problem exists. The Big-Bang Theory flatly contradicts the Second Law of Thermodynamics. The very idea that a primeval cosmic explosion could somehow generate a highly ordered and complex universe seems preposterous on the very face of it. Explosions produce disorder, and this ultimate explosion would surely have generated the ultimate in disorder, as the primeval state of the universe.

This hypothetical initial state of the universe may have been highly energized, but it was also totally unorganized. There is no "information" in randomly moving particles, and no "structure" in an explosion. To the evolutionist, the universe is a closed system, with no external agent to organize it into its present infinite array of complex galaxies and suns and, at least on one planet, a marvelous variety of living systems. By the Second Law of Thermodynamics, there is absolutely no natural way that such a completely isolated system as the universe could increase in information and organized complexity. As the British astronomer, Paul Davies, has said:

> The greatest puzzle is where all the order in the universe came from originally. How did the cosmos get wound up, if the second law of thermodynamics predicts asymmetric unwinding towards disorder? . . .
> There is good evidence that the primeval universe was not ordered, but highly chaotic; a relic of the primordial chaos survives in a curious radiation from space, believed to be the last fading remnant of the primeval heat, and the characteristics of its spectrum reveal that in the earliest moments of the universe the

cosmological material was completely unstruc-
tured. (Paul C. W. Davies, 1979)

There is apparently no solution to this puzzle, at least on
any naturalistic basis. In fact, Professor Davies is forced to
call it "the miracle of the big bang."

Thus the Big-Bang Theory, no less than the late-
lamented Steady-State Theory, is repudiated by one of the
most basic principles of science, the Second Law of Thermodynamics. In fact, it now becomes evident that these
two "theories" constitute the only two basic speculations
by which humanistic philosophers can hope to escape the
creationist testimony of the two laws of thermodynamics.

As noted in Chapter 4, and illustrated in Figure 36, these
two best-proved laws of science point directly to creation.
The Second Law indicates that, since the universe is now
"running down," it must have been "wound up," or
created. The First Law testifies that the universe could not
have created itself. The conclusion must be that the
universe was created by a Creator able to create the
marvelously complex, highly organized cosmic continuum
of Space, Time, and Mass/Energy which constitutes the
universe.

The only way of escaping this conclusion is to deny the
validity of the two laws of thermodynamics when applied
to the origin of the universe. Since they are known to be
valid when applied to all mass/energy systems and processes in *observable* space and time, the denial of their ap-
plicability must apply either to nonobservable space or
nonobservable time.

This is exactly the function of these two "theories" of
cosmic origins. The Steady-State Theory assumes that matter and "information" are somehow being continuously
brought into existence far out in nonobservable space. The
Big-Bang Theory assumes that matter and information
were somehow brought into existence way back in nonobservable time. These ideas are illustrated in Figure 50,
which is the same as Figure 36, except that the two trends
suggested by these two cosmogonic theories have been
superimposed on the curves represented by the two laws of

thermodynamics. The Big-Bang Theory attempts to balance the Second Law by increasing the organization of the cosmos in the imaginary time before time T_0, when the decay began. The Steady-State Theory attempts to balance the decay by increasing the information in the cosmos somewhere out in space where it cannot be observed.

In the one case, the Second Law is circumvented in nonobservable time; in the other case, it is circumvented in nonobservable space. In *observable* space and time, however, the organization of the universe always decays in accord with the Second Law. The laws of thermodynamics are *science;* these evolutionary theories of cosmic origins are mere philosophical speculations which have been devised essentially for avoiding the testimony of true science, which points specifically and directly to true primeval creation. And yet evolutionists have the nerve to say that creation is based only on religion, while evolution is based on science! The real situation is exactly the reverse.

The testimony of the true facts of science is thus in full support of the Creation Model. That is, at some point of time, say T_0, the Space/Mass/Time cosmos was simply *created,* brought into existence in fully developed and functioning form right at the beginning. The complex structures of its immense variety of stars and galaxies did not *evolve* at all. They were simply created, with any changes since that time limited to processes of decay, not development.

This assumption of the Creation Model is supported by three obvious facts: (1) the universe is immensely vast and complex; (2) as long as men have been observing the stars and galaxies, they have been stable, with no evolutionary changes ever observed since the beginning of recorded history; (3) all *observed* changes (e.g., novas, meteorites, etc.) represent disintegration processes, not evolutionary processes. Figure 51 is a typical photograph of a portion of the stellar heavens, illustrating their immensity, complexity, stability, and variety—all fully in accord with the Creation Model.

Any difficulties in the Creation Model, as far as astronomy and cosmogony are concerned, are philosophi-

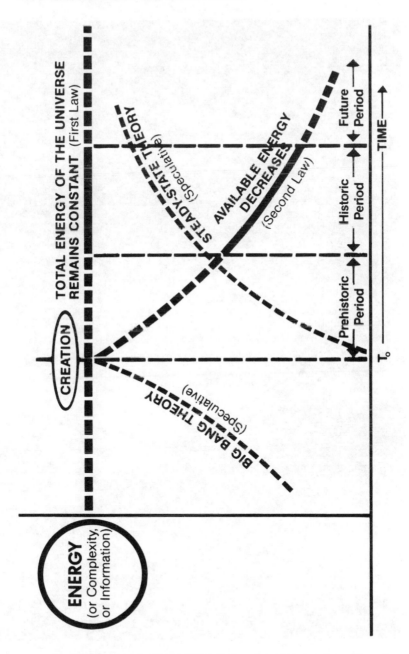

Figure 50. Changes in Cosmic Organization: Speculative vs. Scientific

Figure 51. Complexity and Stability of the Cosmos

cal—not scientific. Questions can be asked as to *why* there are different types of stars and galaxies, *why* novas occur and meteorites break up, etc., but all "Why?" questions are, in the very nature of things, theological or philosophical, not scientific. If our discussion is to be limited strictly to scientific data and their implications, then the Creation Model fits these data far better than the Evolution Model does.

Origin of the Solar System

As far as the earth and the solar system are concerned, creation likewise is a better explanation than evolution. There have been many different evolutionary theories of the origin of the solar system, beginning especially with the so-called "nebular hypothesis" of Kant and LaPlace. One could list the planetesimal hypothesis of Chamberlin, the tidal theory of Jeans, the dust-cloud theory of Whipple, and various others, but this would serve little purpose now, since all have been shown to have insuperable difficulties and no single theory is generally accepted today.

For example, Sir Harold Jeffreys, who is by any standard of measurement one of the world's outstanding geophysicists, after an extensive critique of the various theories, concludes:

> To sum up, I think that all suggested accounts of the origin of the Solar System are subject to serious objections. The conclusion in the present state of the subject would be that the system cannot exist. (Harold Jeffreys, 1970)

Sir Harold's evaluation was made, of course, before the results of most of the space explorations of the 1970's were available. The tremendous amounts of money budgeted for America's NASA program were defended mostly by the hope that it would lead to an understanding of the evolution of the earth and solar system, as well as of life on earth. As it has turned out, however, these questions have not been resolved at all, and now seem more confused than ever.

The manned voyages to the Moon, as well as the various

unmanned photographic missions to the various planets, have demonstrated nothing so clearly as the fact that all solar system bodies are vastly different from each other, and thus could hardly have been the products of any common evolutionary process. An official publication of NASA, written shortly before the first lander reached Mars, came to the following conclusion:

> It is important to be aware that there is no one theory for the origin and subsequent evolution of the Solar System that is generally accepted. All theories represent models which fit some of the facts observed today, but not all. (*Mars and Earth,* 1975a)

This conclusion has been strengthened by every subsequent discovery in the space program. More and more facts have been found which do not fit any of the standard theories. The tremendous variety of structures found in the planets and their moons is the most significant fact of all.

> There are striking differences among the five inner planets, and particularly among the Earth and the others. (*Mars and Earth,* 1975b)

As the space probes have penetrated further and further into space, more and more amazing have been the variations observed. Not only on Mars, but even more on Venus and Saturn and Jupiter, and still more so in their rings and many moons, the story has been one of continued surprise and variety.

The Earth and Moon have been found to be so different in physical composition that they could not possibly have had a common origin. The same is even more true of Saturn and its moons and Jupiter and its moons. Furthermore, each of the moons of each planet is drastically different from the others.

The net result of all these discoveries is that it has become essentially impossible to devise a unified evolutionary theory for the origin of the solar system. Every component of it seems to require an independent evolutionary history, and this is impossible even to conceive, let alone prove.

But all of it is beautifully consistent with the Creation Model! Just as does the universe as a whole, so the solar system exhibits a high degree of complexity, variety, and stability, with the only observed changes being those of decay and disintegration. The question of *why* there is such variety can only be answered philosophically, but the scientific *facts* support creation.

The Uniqueness of Life on Earth

The most distinctive feature of all is the increasingly strong evidence that life is unique to the earth. Before the implementation of the space program, it was widely believed that life would be found on Mars or Venus, or even on the Moon. In fact, the search for extraterrestrial life was widely publicized as probably the main justification for the expenditure of billions of dollars in space exploration. Furthermore, elaborate radio telescopes were constructed to monitor hoped-for radio messages from civilizations on distant stars or galaxies. A widely believed modern mythology has developed around the science fiction themes of "star trek," "chariots of the gods," "alien invaders," "star wars," and the like. The Cornell astronomer Carl Sagan has been sponsored in his humanistic speculations about extraterrestrial life to the extent of millions of dollars. Francis Crick and other have extensively promulgated their peculiar notions of "directed panspermia," the idea that "life-seeds" have been sown through space by civilizations in other worlds.

The naive readiness of both scientists and laymen to develop commitments to such unbased speculations is in stark contrast to their indignant rejection of the far more scientific concept of true creation. There is, to this point at least, not one iota of real scientific evidence for biological life anywhere in the universe except on earth.

The space program has at least shown there is no life anywhere else in the solar system. This fact is so fully accepted now as to require no documentation here. Many still hope, however, that evidence of life will be found elsewhere in the universe. After all, if life has evolved naturalistically on earth, it must have evolved in other parts of the universe, too, so the reasoning goes.

Nevertheless, there is no scientific evidence of it whatever. The radio telescopes have been such a complete exercise in futility that the whole program is currently scheduled for abandonment. There is no observational evidence even of any planets outside the solar system, let alone planets that could support life. A thorough study of the requisite conditions for life by astrophysicist William Pollard led him to the final conclusion:

> There is a deeply ingrained conviction in the great majority of mankind, to which the appeal of science fiction and fantasy bears witness, that the universe is so constituted that if an opportunity exists for hominids to evolve, that too will be actualized. Whatever may be the basis for such convictions, it clearly must be sought outside the domain of science. (William G. Pollard, 1979)

People may have philosophical or religious or moral reasons for wanting to believe in extraterrestrial life, but there is no *scientific* evidence for it. The earth, with its unique combination of type of sun, distance from sun, atmosphere, hydrosphere, lithosphere, and other ingredients, seems uniquely designed as a unique abode for life.

Even more surprisingly, evidence is accumulating that the entire universe is so constructed as to support life. Even though biological life exists only on Earth, so far as any scientific evidence is concerned, it would not even exist on Earth if the large-scale structure of the cosmos were significantly different. This is the conclusion of a growing school of thought among cosmologists who are now advocating what is known as "the anthropic principle." Although this remarkable concept depends to some degree on evolutionary cosmologies, it also builds on the fundamental constants of nature and the basic structure of matter, showing that if these were not almost exactly as they are, life could not exist in the cosmos.

At the least the anthropic principle suggests connection between the existence of man and aspects of physics that one might have thought would have little bearing on biology. In its strongest form the principle might reveal that the universe we live in is the only conceivable universe in which intelligent life could exist. (George Gale, 1981)

Whether or not the anthropic principle can really be proved, it surely does appear that the earth—in both its cosmic setting and its local situation—is uniquely designed for life. That this could merely be accidental is a conclusion that should not appeal to scientists.

Probability of Chance Origin of Life

Now that I have introduced the subject of the origin of life, as well as the origin of the universe, and since we will shortly be returning to the subject of the *age* of the universe and of life, it is well to point out that the complexity of life is so great that it could never have naturalistically evolved even *once* in the universe, let alone in many times and places. Even if the universe were indeed as much as 30 billion years old, as evolutionists have alleged, life even in its simplest form could never have evolved by *chance*. A few simple probability calculations will demonstrate this fact.

To investigate this situation, I shall assume that the known universe is 5 billion (5×10^9) light-years in radius (with a light-year equal to the distance light would travel in a year while moving at a speed of over 186,000 miles per second). Also let's assume that it is crammed with tiny particles of the size of an electron, the smallest known particle in existence. It has been estimated that 10^{80} such particles exist in the universe, but if there were no empty space, approximately 10^{130} particles conceivably could exist there. Every structure, every process, every system, every "event" in the universe must consist of these particles, in various combinations and interchanges.

If, to be extremely liberal, we assume that each particle can take part in 10^{20} (that is a hundred billion billion) events each second, and then allow 10^{20} seconds of cosmic history (this would correspond to 3,000 billion years, or 100 times the current maximum estimate of the age of the universe), then the greatest conceivable number of separate events that could ever take place in all of space and time would be

$$10^{130} \times 10^{20} \times 10^{20} = 10^{170} \text{ events.}$$

Now, in order for life to appear, one of these events (or some combination of them) must bring a number of these particles together in a system containing enough order (or stored information) to enable it to make a copy of itself. This system must be produced by chance, of course, since presumably no Creator is available to plan and direct the assemblage of all this information.

The problem is, however, that any living cell or any new organ to be added to an existing animal—even the simplest imaginable replicating system—would have to contain far more stored information than represented even by such a gigantic number as 10^{170}. A leading information scientist, Marcel E. Golay (1961), calculates the odds against such a system organizing itself randomly as 10^{450} to 1. Other studies (Frank B. Salisbury, 1971; Harold J. Morowitz, 1967; James E. Coppedge, 1973) have been made attempting to get a similar measure, but all calculate a much higher state of ordered information and improbability even than this.

If we take Golay's figure, giving the Evolution Model all possible benefit of the doubt, the odds against any accidental ordering of particles into a replicating system is at least 10^{450} to 1. This is so even if it is spread out over a span of time and a series of connected events. As a matter of fact, Golay calculated the figure on the assumption that it was accomplished by a series of 1,500 successive events, each with the generously high probability of ½ (note that $2^{1500} = 10^{450}$). The probability would be much lower if it had to be accomplished in a single chance event.

It is very generous, therefore, to conclude that the prob-

NUMBER OF
POSSIBLE EVENTS IN SPACE AND TIME

Available Time:
Assume 3 trillion years = 10^{20} seconds.

Available Space:
Assume 5 billion light-years radius.

Number of particles possible in universe = 10^{130} electrons.
Assume each particle can act in 10^{20} events/second

Therefore:
10^{130} (10^{20}) (10^{20}) = 10^{170} **events possible**

Figure 52. Maximum Number of Possible Events

ability of the simplest conceivable replicating system aris-
ing by chance just once in all the universe, in all time is:

$$\frac{10^{170}}{10^{450}} = \frac{1}{10^{280}}$$

These calculations are summarized in Figures 52, 53, and
54.

When the probability of occurrence of any event is
smaller than one out of the number of events that could
ever possibly occur—that is, as discussed above, less than
$1/10^{170}$—then the probability of its occurrence is considered by mathematicians to be zero. Consequently, it is
concluded that the chance origin of life is absolutely impossible. Life can only be explained by creation.

As noted by Dr. Parker in Chapter 1, Sir Fred Hoyle and
his colleague, the noted mathematician Wickramasinghe,
have recently become anti-evolutionists on the basis of
their own probability calculations, which convinced them
against their will that life could never have evolved by
chance anywhere in the universe.

It is hardly surprising, therefore, that biochemists have
found it impossible to synthesize living systems from
nonliving chemicals, or that space scientists are unable to
find evidence of extraterrestrial life. Life is not an accident, nor even something that can be fabricated by clever
men, using their extensive knowledge and sophisticated
equipment All the evidence supports the Creation Model
on this. Life must have been created!

The objection is sometimes posed that, even if the probability of a living system is 10^{-280}, every other specific combination of particles might also have a similar probability
of occurrence, so that one is just as likely as another. There
even may be other combinations than the one with which
we are familiar on earth that might turn out to be living.

Such a statement overlooks the fact that, in any group of
particles, there are many more meaningless combinations
than ordered combinations. For example, if a system has

four components connected linearly, only two (1-2-3-4, 4-3-2-1) of the 24 possible combinations possess really meaningful order. The ratio rapidly decreases as the number of components increases. The more complex and orderly a system is, the more unique it is among its possible competitors. This objection, therefore, misses the point. In the example cited above, only one combination would work. There would be 10^{280} that would not work.

Some might think that, even if the first living cell had to be created, further evolutionary advances could be brought about naturalistically. The complexity of each new subsystem to be added to the living system, however, is at least as complex as the first system. The improbabilities can only increase as the complexity increases. All of which is only another way of saying that, in the present order of things, the Second Law of Thermodynamics makes naturalistic evolution toward higher complexity impossible. No matter how old the earth and universe may be, there has not been enough time for evolution.

Is the Earth Really Old . . . or Just Tired?

Since the scientific evidence supports the Creation Model at every point where we can compare and contrast it with the Evolution Model, regardless of whether the earth is old or young, the question of the *date* of creation should be treated as a separate issue. It is an important scientific question in its own right and should be evaluated without reference to the need to provide time for evolution.

If the Creation Model is valid, then there is no real need to think the earth and the universe are much older than humankind and the beginning of human history. The hypothetical billions of years usually assumed are only necessary to accommodate evolution and the uniformitarian interpretation of the geologic column. The Creation Model can, therefore, take a serious look at the chronometric implications of *all* processes, not only the three or four processes that can be interpreted to yield ages old enough to allow for evolution.

In accordance with the Second Law of Thermodynamics, all systems are decaying. The decay rate for each

PRODUCTION OF
SIMPLEST LIVING SYSTEM BY CHANCE

Minimum requirement (Golay):
1500 successive events, each with ½ chance of success.

$$\text{Probability} = (1/2)^{1500} = (1/10)^{450}$$

That is, there is one chance out of $(10)^{450}$ that any series of 1500 successive chance events will generate a replicating system.

Figure 53. Probability of Chance Origin of Life

PROBABILITY OF CHANCE ORIGIN OF LIFE ANYWHERE ANYTIME IN UNIVERSE

$(10)^{170}$ = Number of possible events

$(10)^{167}$ = Number of possible sequences of 1500 events

$(10)^{-450}$ = Probability of any one such sequence producing life

Therefore, probability of
chance origin of life =

$$\frac{(10)^{167}}{(10)^{450}} = \frac{1}{(10)^{283}} \approx 0$$

(since number of possible events = **only** $(10)^{170}$)

Figure 54. Impossibility of Naturalistic Origin of Life

physical quantity varies, of course, with the particular process and with all the different factors that may affect the process. In general, a decay function tends to plot up as an exponential curve of some sort—falling off rapidly at first, then gradually slowing down as it approaches zero. At any point along the curve, if an external interruption (catastrophe) affects the process, the decay may speed up abnormally for a period, then settle back down to a normal decay rate.

In some decay functions, the half-life of the decaying quantity is constant. Radioactive minerals and certain other systems (though certainly not all systems) appear to decay in this fashion. Many follow a simple exponential decay. Some may even decay linearly, though these are rare.

In most cases (note Figure 55), the decaying quantity dissipates rapidly at first, slowing down later. It would usually be wrong to calculate a time duration on the assumption of linear dissipation with time, as this would almost invariably give too great an age. It is doubtful even that systems which are believed to decay with a uniform half-life have maintained even *that* quasi-uniform decay in the past.

If, for example, there has been some kind of traumatic environmental change in the past (catastrophe), then the parameters in its environment would have also accelerated its decay rate, again resulting in too large an "apparent age" of the system if calculated, on the assumption of uniformity, for the current process rate.

There are other effects which can discredit an age calculation also, such as the unknown initial conditions, unknown environmental factors which might affect the components of the system, etc. Radiometric systems are particularly vulnerable to such errors.

Every natural system changes with time and so, at least in principle, could be used to measure time. However, to do this, certain assumptions always have to be made about the system and the processes which are changing it. To illustrate these problems, let us consider a very simple system in which the quantities of its two components are

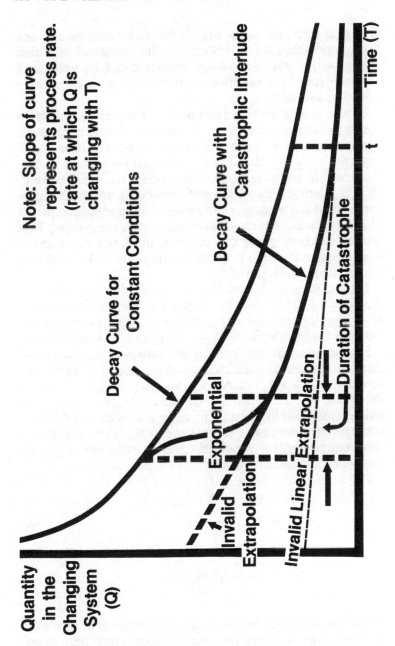

Figure 55. Uncertainties in Extrapolating Process Rates

changing with time, as in Figure 56. This could be any one of innumerable natural systems in the world, all of which change with time. Any such system could be used as a chronometer if the necessary information on it can be obtained or assumed.

In the simple system sketched in Figure 56, only two components are present, with reactions taking place such that component **A** is changing into component **B**, at a certain rate **r** at a certain time **t**. Although the system is confined within boundaries, no boundaries are impenetrable, so it is possible that increments are being added to either component from outside the system. Similarly, increments of either component may somehow escape the system. This process has been going on for some unknown time, and it is assumed that, when it started, components **A** and **B** had initial magnitudes A_0 and B_0.

If the quantities A_T and B_T are measured as they are now, the value of **T** (that is, the "apparent age" of the system, or at least the time since the changes began to occur in the system) can be calculated as shown in Fig. 57 Equation (1).

Examination of the equations, however, indicates the idealistic nature of such calculations. The only quantities actually measurable are A_T, B_T, and r_T (the process rate at the time **T**). Equation (1), therefore, contains five unknowns and is impossible to solve unless all five of these are arbitrarily assumed. One of them, **R**, can be calculated from equation (2) if function (3) is known, but the latter involves still other unknowns.

$$R = \frac{\int_0^T rdt}{T} \tag{2}$$

$$r = f(A_0, B_0, t, \text{----}) \tag{3}$$

In the above equations, **R** is the average process rate over the entire time **T**. Since the rate **r** changes with time, as expressed in the function defined in equation (3), this average

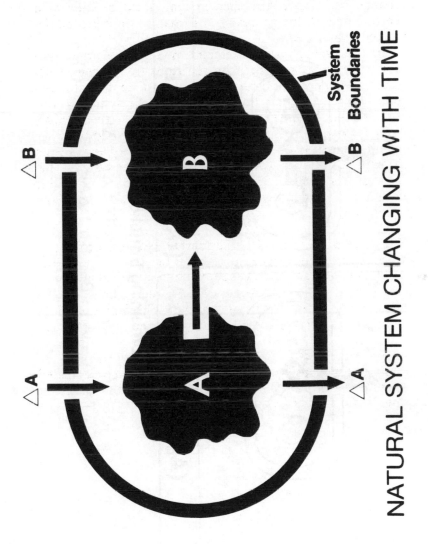

Figure 56. Natural System Changing With Time

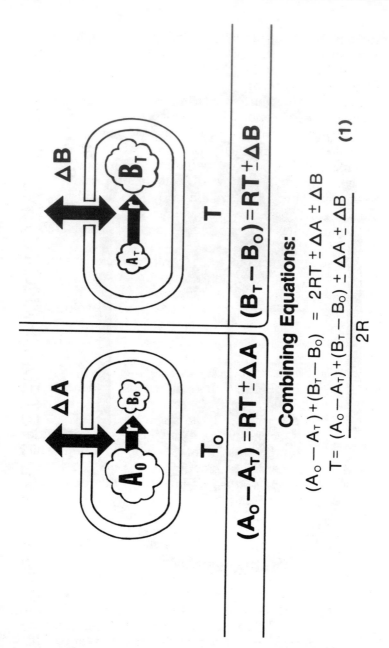

Combining Equations:

$$(A_0 - A_T) = RT \pm \Delta A \qquad (B_T - B_0) = RT \pm \Delta B$$

$$(A_0 - A_T) + (B_T - B_0) = 2RT \pm \Delta A \pm \Delta B$$

$$T = \frac{(A_0 - A_T) + (B_T - B_0) \pm \Delta A \pm \Delta B}{2R} \qquad (1)$$

Figure 57. Calculation of Apparent Age of Changing System

rate must be obtained by "integrating" it through the time T, as shown in the calculus notation of equation (2). Usually this will be impossible, since the functional relation is itself unknown.

The usual procedure in geochronometric calculations is to make the assumptions listed in Figure 58.

With these assumptions, it is now possible to make a calculation of apparent age from equation (1), replacing its five unknowns with the values assumed from equations (4) through (7). The result is the simple expression for T shown on Figure 58 as equation (8). This would be more complex, of course, if other assumptions are made. The implicit meanings of the assumptions are also tabulated on Figure 58.

With such unrealistic assumptions, one might just as well pick the age he wants in the first place, and then modify the assumptions until the apparent age agrees with his wishes. As a matter of fact, this is what evolutionists do, in effect, when they arbitrarily reject all chronometers and calculations which yield young ages for the earth or its different systems. There is nothing scientifically dishonest about this. Since all such calculations depend upon these arbitrary assumptions anyhow, it is logical for them to pick those which agree with their basic axiom of evolution. That is, this is scientifically honest if—but only if—they recognize and acknowledge that the entire calculation depends flatly on their arbitrary belief in evolution, which demands an immensity of time.

As a matter of fact, it is very interesting that even on the basis of the usual uniformitarian-evolutionary assumptions (as listed on Figure 58), there are far more chronometers that yield a young age for the earth than yield an old age. That is, if one analyzes any process of worldwide change (e.g., fall of extraterrestrial material on the earth, erosion of lands, influx of chemicals into the ocean, etc.) and then makes the standard evolutionary assumptions (initial boundary values of zero, uniformity of process rates, closed system), he will find that practically all such calculations yield a terrestrial age of far less than a billion years.

$$T = \frac{(A_O - A_T) + (B_T - B_O) + \Delta A + \Delta B}{2R} \quad (1)$$

(1) Assume $R =$ Constant ... i.e., Uniformitarianism   **(4)**

(2) Assume $\Delta A = \Delta B = O$ .... i.e., Isolated System   **(5)**

(3) Assume $B_O = O$ .... i.e., Initial Conditions   **(6)**

(4) Assume $A_O = A_T + B_T$ ...... i.e., Conservation   **(7)**

(Only Assumption **(4)** is valid!)

Then $T = B_T/R$ **(8)**

Figure 58. Necessary Assumptions in Apparent Age Calculation

For example, consider a little-known variation on "uranium dating." The different uranium/lead radiometric dating techniques are the most important of the handful of processes that seem to yield great ages for the earth. However, there is another uranium dating method that yields a much younger age. The ocean and its sediments have been accumulating uranium throughout their histories by the influx of dissolved uranium through river transport. According to a detailed recent study by Salman Bloch (1980):

> The ocean contains over 4 billion tons of dissolved uranium, ...

This amount corresponds to 3,640 trillion grams. Bloch then shows how a thorough calculation

> . . . gives 1.92×10^{10} gms per year as the total riverine influx of dissolved uranium.

This amount is 19.2 billion grams per year. Dividing the first number by the second gives about 189,000 years as the maximum age of the ocean, even with the very unlikely assumptions that the ocean contained no uranium when it was formed and the river influx was no greater in the past than at present (actually, all the world's rivers give abundant evidence of carrying much greater flows in the earlier years of their history). The true age would most likely be much smaller than this.

However, the old-earth proponent would undoubtedly counter by insisting that much of the dissolved uranium would probably be precipitated out in estuarine or oceanic sediments. Bloch, in fact, has carefully determined the effect of all such possibilities.

> A detailed mass-balance calculation for uranium has shown that only about 10% of the present-day river input of dissolved uranium can be removed by known sinks.

That is not all, however.

> Low and high-temperature alteration of basalts, organic-rich sediments and co-existing

phosphorites on continental margins, metal-liferous sediments, carbonate sediments, and sediments in anoxic basins deeper than 200 meters remove about three-fourths of the present-day riverine supply to the ocean.

Since these would seem to exhaust the possibilities, at least 15% of the annual riverine influx of uranium is still available to build up the ocean's uranium content. Making this allowance, the maximum possible age of the ocean, based on *this* type of uranium dating, becomes 189,000 ÷ 0.15, or 1,260,000 years.

Similar calculations can be made for all the other dissolved chemicals in the ocean. All will yield relatively small ages (at least in comparison to usual evolutionary estimates of the age of the ocean) but all will, of course, yield different ages. Again, however, even allowing for all realistically possible "sinks," sedimentation, recycling, etc., none will yield an age anywhere close to the billion-year ages required for evolution.

Although most evolutionists are firmly committed to belief in an old earth, there are a few who acknowledge that many global processes do seem to point to a young earth. For example, an excellent textbook by evolutionist William Stansfield (1977) cites at least ten different chronometers that could be reasonably interpreted as support for a young earth. Some of these are as follows:

1. Even at today's low rates of volcanism, "juvenile" water released from volcanoes would fill up all the oceans in far less time than the supposed 4½ billion-year-age of the earth.

2. The same is true for the amount of lava extruded on the continents from the same source.

3. The amount of meteorites accumulated in the strata and meteoritic dust in the crust, in relation to amounts reaching the earth at present, would indicate an age in thousands of years, not millions or billions.

4. The great pressures now existing in oil reservoirs could only have been sustained for a few thousand years.

5. The helium in the atmosphere could have accumulated at present rates in only a few thousand years.
6. The present worldwide buildup of radiocarbon in the atmosphere would have produced all the world's radiocarbon in several thousand years.

Stansfield also is refreshingly frank in recognizing the questionable assumptions in the standard radiometric dating methods. Noting the common occurrence of discordant ages obtained from different methods on the same rock system, and also noting that it is very common for isotope ratios used in dating igneous rocks to refer, not to the age of the rock, but to the ratios already existing in the magmas in the earth's mantle from which the rocks were formed, he says:

> It is obvious that radiometric methods may not be the reliable dating methods they are often claimed to be. Age estimates on a given geological stratum using different methods are often quite different (sometimes by hundreds of millions of years). There is no absolutely reliable long-term radiological clock." (William Stansfield, 1977b)

Since Stansfield is not a "young-earth creationist" but an "old-earth evolutionist," he is to be especially commended for recognizing that the age question is at least still open to discussion. Most evolutionists are completely closed-minded on this subject.

There are, as a matter of fact, scores of worldwide processes which give ages far too young to suit the standard Evolution Model. There are 68 types of such calculations listed in Table I, all of them independent of each other and all applying essentially to the entire earth, or one of its major components or to the solar system. All give ages far too young to accommodate the Evolution Model. All are based on the same types of calculations and assumptions used by evolutionists on the very few systems (uranium, potassium, rubidium) whose radioactive decay seems to indicate ages in the billions of years. As noted in items 25 and 26 in

Table I, even these methods (when based on real empirical evidence) yield young ages.

The most obvious characteristic of the values listed in the table is their extreme variability—all the way from 100 years to 500,000,000 years. This variability, of course, simply reflects the errors in the fundamental uniformitarian assumptions.

Nevertheless, all things considered, it seems that those ages on the low end of the spectrum are likely to be more accurate than those on the high end. This conclusion follows from the obvious fact that: (1) they are less likely to have been affected by initial concentrations or positions other than "zero;" (2) the assumption that the system was a "closed system" is more likely to be valid for a short time than for a long time; (3) the assumption that the process rate was constant is also more likely to be valid for a short time than for a long time.

Thus, it is concluded that the weight of all the scientific evidence favors the view that the earth is quite young, far too young for life and man to have arisen by an evolutionary process. The origin of all things by direct creation—already necessitated by many other scientific considerations—is therefore also indicated by chronometric data.

If space permitted, it would be instructive to examine in detail each of the 68 individual processes listed in the table, as well as the few processes (e.g., uranium-to-lead) which are so widely believed to prove an old earth. However, to do this adequately would require another complete book, as geochronometry is an intricate and technical subject. Most creationist scientists, including myself, are strongly convinced after examining all these data that the young-age calculations are on much stronger scientific footing than those few which yield old ages.

I should stress two important points again in closing, however:

(1) It will never be possible to *prove scientifically* whether the earth and universe are old or young. All calculations involving processes which antedate recorded

history must be based on assumptions which can never even be tested, let alone proved, scientifically.

(2) The basic scientific issue under discussion in this book is that of creation or evolution, not the question of young earth or old earth. These two questions are related to each other in certain ways, but they can be treated independently of each other. Dr. Parker and I have shown that, even if the earth and the universe were very old, the scientific evidence still favors creation over evolution.

TABLE I

Uniformitarian Estimates—Age of the Earth

(Unless otherwise indicated, based on standard assumptions of (1) zero initial "daughter" component; (2) closed system; (3) uniform rate. Reference numbers refer to documentation cited on pages immediately following this table.)

	Process	Indicated Age of Earth	Reference
1.	Decay of earth's magnetic field	10,000 years	1
2.	Influx of radiocarbon to the earth system	10,000 years	2
3.	Influx of meteoritic dust from space	too small to calculate	3
4.	Influx of juvenile water to oceans	340,000,000 years	3
5.	Influx of magma from mantle to form crust	500,000,000 years	3
6.	Growth of oldest living part of biosphere	5,000 years	3
7.	Origin of human civilizations	5,000 years	3
8.	Efflux of Helium-4 into the atmosphere	1,750 - 175,000 years	4
9.	Development of total human population	4,000 years	5
10.	Influx of sediment to the ocean via rivers	30,000,000 years	6
11.	Erosion of sediment from continents	14,000,000 years	6
12.	Leaching of sodium from continents	32,000,000 years	7
13.	Leaching of chlorine from continents	1,000,000 years	7
14.	Leaching of calcium from continents	12,000,000 years	7

	Process	Indicated Age of Earth	Reference
15.	Influx of carbonate to the ocean	100,000 years	7
16.	Influx of sulphate to the ocean	10,000,000 years	7
17.	Influx of chlorine to the ocean	164,000,000 years	7
18.	Influx of calcium to the ocean	1,000,000 years	7
19.	Influx of uranium to the ocean	1,250,000 years	8
20.	Efflux of oil from traps by fluid pressure	10,000 - 100,000 years	9
21.	Formation of radiogenic lead by neutron capture	too small to measure	9
22.	Formation of radiogenic strontium by neutron capture	too small to measure	9
23.	Decay of natural remanent paleomagnetism	100,000 years	9
24.	Decay of C-14 in pre-Cambrian wood	4,000 years	9
25.	Decay of uranium with initial "radiogenic" lead	too small to measure	10
26.	Decay of potassium with entrapped argon	too small to measure	10
27.	Formation of river deltas	5,000 years	11
28.	Submarine oil seepage into oceans	50,000,000 years	12
29.	Decay of natural plutonium	80,000,000 years	13
30.	Decay of lines of galaxies	10,000,000 years	14
31.	Expanding interstellar gas	60,000,000 years	15
32.	Decay of short-period comets	10,000 years	16
33.	Decay of long-period comets	1,000,000 years	17
34.	Influx of small particles to the sun	83,000 years	17
35.	Maximum life of meteor showers	5,000,000 years	17

Process	Indicated Age of Earth	Reference
36. Accumulation of dust on the moon	200,000 years	17
37. Instability of rings of Saturn	1,000,000 years	17
38. Escape of methane from Titan	20,000,000 years	17
39. Deceleration of earth by tidal friction	500,000,000 years	18
40. Cooling of the earth by heat efflux	24,000,000 years	18
41. Accumulation of calcareous ooze on sea floor	5,000,000 years	19
42. Influx of sodium to the ocean via rivers	260,000,000 years	20
43. Influx of nickel to the ocean via rivers	9,000 years	20
44. Influx of magnesium to the ocean via rivers	45,000,000 years	20
45. Influx of silicon to the ocean via rivers	8,000 years	20
46. Influx of potassium to the ocean via rivers	11,000,000 years	20
47. Influx of copper to the ocean via rivers	50,000 years	20
48. Influx of gold to the ocean via rivers	560,000 years	20
49. Influx of silver to the ocean via rivers	2,100,000 years	20
50. Influx of mercury to the ocean via rivers	42,000 years	20
51. Influx of lead to the ocean via rivers	2,000 years	20
52. Influx of tin to the ocean via rivers	100,000 years	20
53. Influx of aluminum to the ocean via rivers	100 years	20
54. Influx of lithium into ocean via rivers	20,000,000 years	20
55. Influx of titanium into ocean via rivers	160 years	20
56. Influx of chromium into ocean via rivers	350 years	20

Process	Indicated Age of Earth	Reference
57. Influx of manganese into ocean via rivers	1,400 years	20
58. Influx of iron into ocean via rivers	140 years	20
59. Influx of cobalt into ocean via rivers	18,000 years	20
60. Influx of zinc into ocean via rivers	180,000 years	20
61. Influx of rubidium into ocean via rivers	270,000 years	20
62. Influx of strontium into ocean via rivers	19,000,000 years	20
63. Influx of bismuth into ocean via rivers	45,000 years	20
64. Influx of thorium into ocean via rivers	350 years	20
65. Influx of antimony into ocean via rivers	350,000 years	20
66. Influx of tungsten into ocean via rivers	1,000 years	20
67. Influx of barium into ocean via rivers	84,000 years	20
68. Influx of molybdenum into ocean via rivers	500,000 years	20

Documentation Cited for TABLE I

1. Thomas G. Barnes, *Origin and Destiny of the Earth's Magnetic Field* (San Diego, Institute for Creation Research, 1973), p. 25.
2. Melvin A. Cook, "Do Radiological Clocks Need Repair?" *Creation Research Society Quarterly,* Vol. 5, October, 1968, p. 70.
3. Henry M. Morris, (Ed.,), *Scientific Creationism (Public Schools)* (San Diego, Institute for Creation Research, 1974), pp. 149-157, 185-196.
4. Melvin A. Cook, "Where is the Earth's Radiogenic Helium?" *Nature,* Vol. 179, January 26, 1957, p. 213.
5. Henry M. Morris, "Evolution and the Population Problem," *Impact Series No. 21,* Institute for Creation Research, November, 1974.
6. Stuart E. Nevins, "Evolution: The Ocean Says No." *Impact Series, ICR Acts and Facts,* Vol. 2, No. 8, October, 1973.
7. Dudley J. Whitney, *The Face of the Deep* (New York, Vantage Press, 1955).
8. Salman Bloch: "Some Factors Controlling the Concentration of Uranium in the World Ocean," *Geochimica et Cosmochimica Acta.* Vol. 44, 1980, pp. 373-377.
9. Melvin A. Cook, *Prehistory and Earth Models* (London, Max Parrish, 1966).
10. Harold S. Slusher, *Critique of Radiometric Dating* (San Diego, Institute for Creation Research, 1980).
11. Benjamin F. Allen, "The Geologic Age of the Mississippi River," *Creation Research Society Quarterly,* Vol. 9 (September, 1972), pp. 96-114.
12. R. D. Wilson, et al., "Natural Marine Oil Seepage," *Science* (Vol. 184), May 24, 1974, pp. 857-865.
13. "Natural Plutonium," *Chemical and Engineering News,* September 20, 1971.
14. Halton Arp, "Observational Paradoxes in Extragalactic Astronomy," *Science,* Vol. 174 (December 17, 1971), pp. 1189-1200.

15. V. A. Hughes and D. Routledge, "An Expanding Ring of Interstellar Gas with Center Close to the Sun," *Astronomical Journal,* Vol. 77, No. 3 (1972), pp. 210-214.
16. Harold S. Slusher, "Some Astronomical Evidences for a Youthful Solar System," *Creation Research Society Quarterly,* Vol. 8 (June, 1971), pp. 55-57.
17. Harold S. Slusher, *Age of the Cosmos* (San Diego, Institute for Creation Research, 1980), 76 pp.
18. Thomas G. Barnes, "Physics, A Challenge to Geologic Time," *Impact Series 16, ICR Acts and Facts,* Institute for Creation Research, July, 1974.
19. Maurice Ewing, J. I. Ewing, and M. Talwan, "Sediment Distribution in the Oceans—Mid-Atlantic Ridge," *Bulletin of the Geophysical Society of America,* Vol. 75 (January, 1964), pp. 17-36.
20. *Chemical Oceanography,* Ed. by J. P. Riley and G. Skirrow (New York, Academic Press, Vol. 1, 1965), p. 164. See also Harold Camping, "Let the Oceans Speak," *Creation Research Society Quarterly,* Vol. 11, (June, 1974), pp. 39-45.

Appendices

Appendix A

Questions and Criticisms

With the renewal of interest in creation that has taken place in recent years, there has also developed a well-orchestrated reaction against it, spearheaded by the evolutionist establishments in science, education, and the news media. These criticisms became especially strident with the passage in 1981 of "creation laws" in Arkansas and Louisiana.

Many of the criticisms being published against the creation movement are badly biased and distorted. Whether these false charges are based on sincere misunderstanding or deliberate misrepresentation is not for us to judge. In any case, we shall list the main criticisms merely as questions here in this section and try to set the record straight.

CREATION AND RELIGION

Question: "Since creationism is based on the Genesis creation story, why should it be included in public education?"

Answer: Scientific creationism is *not* based on Genesis or any other religious teaching. There is not a single quotation from the Bible in this entire book! Neither is any argument based on Biblical authority or doctrine. We have talked about genetics, paleontology, thermodynamics, geology, and other sciences, but not about theology or religion. Indeed, the scientific case for creation is based on our knowledge of DNA, mutations, fossils, thermodynamics, and other scientific terms and concepts which do not even appear in the Bible. Furthermore, we have tried to show that the scientific data explicitly support the Creation Model and contradict the Evolution Model.

Question: "But isn't this so-called scientific creationism simply a back-door method of getting Biblical creationism introduced?"
Answer: We could just as easily ask whether teaching evolution is a back-door method of introducing atheism. Scientific creationism and Biblical creationism can, in fact, be taught quite independently of each other. We ourselves are opposed to the teaching of Biblical creationism in public schools. Such instruction should require teachers to have a good knowledge of the Bible and a firm commitment to its authority, and these qualifications cannot be imposed on public school teachers. *Biblical* creationism, as well as other sectarian views of creation, should be taught in churches (as well as synagogues and mosques) but only *scientific* creationism in public schools. Both can well be taught in religious schools.

Question: "What is the difference between scientific creationism and Biblical creationism?"
Answer: The first is based solely on scientific evidence, of the sort outlined in this book; the second is based on Biblical teachings. The Genesis record includes the account of the six days of creation, the names of the first man and woman, the record of God's curse on the earth because of human sin, the story of Noah's ark, and other such events which could never be determined scientifically. Scientific evidence can point to the fact of a creation period, for example, but there is no way that the specific duration of that period could be determined scientifically. On the other hand, scientific creationism deals with such physical entities as fossils, whereas the Bible never refers to fossils at all. It is quite possible for scientific creationism to be discussed and evaluated without reference to Biblical creationism at all.

Question: "Why is it that only Protestant fundamentalists are concerned about creation?"

Answer: The doctrine of creation is of concern to people of a wide variety of religious views. Evolutionism is the basic premise of many religions, including Buddhism, Confucianism, Hinduism, Taoism, Liberal Protestantism, Modernist Catholicism, Reform Judaism, and others, not to mention humanism and atheism, so these all would naturally tend to oppose creationism. In view of these and other religious implications, it is absurd to claim that evolution is strictly scientific. On the other hand, creationism is also basic to a number of religions—not only all the denominations of conservative Protestantism, but also traditional Catholicism and Orthodox Judaism, as well as conservative Islam and other monotheistic religions. It is much broader in scope and importance than as a particular doctrine of Biblical fundamentalists. Indeed, it is offensive and discriminatory to these other creationists to hear constantly that creation is only of concern to certain Protestant conservatives.

Question: "But isn't the very fact that creationism requires a Creator proof that it is religious, rather than scientific?"
Answer: It must be remembered that there are only two basic models of origins, creation and evolution. Each model is essentially a complete world view, a philosophy of life and meaning, of origin and destiny. Neither can be either confirmed or falsified by the scientific method, since neither can be tested or observed experimentally, and therefore they must both be accepted on faith! Nevertheless, each is also a scientific model, since each seeks to explain within its framework all the real data of science and history. Creationism is at least as nonreligious as evolutionism. We have tried to show that the Creation Model fits the facts of true science better than the Evolution Model. It is true that creationism is a *theistic* model, but it is also true that evolutionism is an *atheistic* model (since it purports to explain everything without a creator). If *theism* is a religious faith, then so is *atheism*, since these are two fully comparable systems, each the opposite of the other.

Question: "Why can't evolution be regarded as the method of creation, instead of having two competing models of origins?"

Answer: It is important to define terms, especially on this issue. The belief that God used evolution to make man is properly called theistic *evolution,* not creation. Evolution purports to explain the origin of things by natural processes, creation by preternatural processes; and it is semantic confusion to try to equate the two. Theistic evolution says there is a God behind the natural processes which cause evolution; atheistic evolution says there is not. Both forms of evolution assume the same framework of evolutionary history and the same evolutionary mechanisms, so there is no scientific way to discriminate between the two, as there is between creationism and evolutionism. Theistic evolution must be judged on the basis of theological criteria, not scientific. The creation and evolution models, on the other hand, *can* be compared and evaluated on strictly scientific criteria, as we have tried to do in this book. Creationists maintain that evolution is a poor scientific model of origins, strictly on the basis of scientific criteria.

CREATIONIST QUALIFICATIONS

Question: "Why should such a small minority as the creationists expect to impose their beliefs on others?"

Answer: Creationists are not a small minority. A nationwide poll commissioned by the Associated Press and NBC News late in 1981 showed that over 86% of the people favored having creationism taught in the schools. Nevertheless, creationists only request *fair* treatment, not favored treatment, in the schools. The attitude of the liberal humanistic establishments in science and education, in trying to maintain an exclusive indoctrination in evolutionary humanism, seems incredibly intolerant and arrogant in a free country.

Question: "America's news media are apparently almost completely opposed to the creation movement; does not this fact refute the claim that a significant part of the population favors creation?''

Answer: Unfortunately, there is firm evidence that the leaders of the news media are completely out of touch with the opinions of the American people, even though they are supposed to be ''opinion makers.'' A recent article in *Public Opinion* magazine, for example, reported on detailed interviews with the 240 leading editors, reporters, columnists, TV anchormen, producers, correspondents, and film editors, the people judged to be the leaders of the media in deciding what news to report and how to report it. A strong indicator of the liberal bias of this group in America (as opposed to the leanings of the people they supposedly represent) is the fact that 81% of them voted for the liberal candidate in the presidential election recently, while the general populace overwhelmingly elected the conservative candidate. Only 8% of them regularly attend either church or synagogue, and over half have no religious affiliation whatever. With this kind of profile, it would be surprising to find even the smallest semblance of sympathy for creationism in the media. The creation movement and arguments are, as a result, almost always misrepresented and distorted, often viciously, in newspaper and magazine articles and in radio and television coverage.

Question: ''But why are all real scientists evolutionists?''
Answer: All real scientists are *not* evolutionists! There are thousands of bona fide scientists today who have become creationists, all of whom have post-graduate degrees, who are pursuing careers in science and who have records and credentials quite comparable to those of any other segment in the scientific professions. Most scientists are admittedly still evolutionists—especially those who control the scientific societies and journals—but the creationist minority is respectable and growing. There are creationist Ph.D.'s in every branch of pure and applied science today—biology, geology, physics, engineering, medicine, and all the rest—so it is obvious now that a man or woman can be well trained and experienced in any discipline of science and can understand the factual data of that science within the framework of the Creation Model. In fact, acceptance of

creation is known to be growing most rapidly today among people with scientific and technological training. This is all the more significant in light of the fact that practically all of these scientists were indoctrinated in evolutionism throughout their training. To become or remain creationists, they have had to study and think themselves through the evidences and arguments for both models, all on their own initiative, and usually against the opposition and ridicule of the majority of their scientific and educational colleagues. Most of them, like the two authors of this book, were themselves evolutionists throughout their college years and beyond, becoming creationists only as a result of later personal critical study and reevaluation.

Question: "Then why don't creationists publish in the standard scientific journals?"

Answer: Creationists *do* publish in the standard scientific journals, in their own respective scientific disciplines, and their publications' records compare well with any other comparable group. For example, the ten scientists on the staff of the Institute for Creation Research have published at least 150 research papers and 10 books in their own scientific fields—all in standard scientific journals or through secular book publishers—in addition to hundreds of creationist articles and about 50 books on creationism and related subjects. Whenever these articles or books have creationist implications, however, they must be "masked" in order to get them published in secular outlets. So far, at least, all frankly creationist articles or books are simply rejected out of hand by such publishers. For example, when the high school biology textbook produced by the scientists of the Creation Research Society was ready for publication in 1969, the 15 leading high school textbook publishers were contacted about possibly publishing the book. It was a comprehensive and well-organized book, written by a fully-qualified team of Ph.D. biologists and other scientists, and should have been financially profitable for any publisher. Nevertheless, not one of these publishers would even so much as look at the manuscript! They claimed their other books would be boycotted if they were to publish a creationist biology textbook, so it was necessary for the Society to have it published by a Christian book company. The book has now gone through two editions, with a new version scheduled shortly.

CREATIONIST MOTIVES AND ETHICS

Question: "Why do creationists make it appear that scientists are questioning evolution when they are really only questioning current beliefs about evolutionary mechanisms?"

Answer: This is an entirely unwarranted charge, usually made when creationists cite the writings of Stephen Gould or other modern evolutionary critics of neo-Darwinism. If those who make the charge would read or listen to the full context of what the creationists say, they would surely realize that no such misrepresentation was made or intended. Creationist scientists are all well aware that Gould and other modern advocates of "saltatory" evolution (as opposed to "gradualistic" evolution) are still evolutionists. This very fact has been made a key point of recent creationist writings and lectures. The fact is that the so-called "punctuationists" are now using exactly the same arguments against the neo-Darwinians that creationists have been using for years (e.g., the gaps in the fossil record), and these "revolutionary evolutionists" resent having this recognized. The latter still maintain their faith in evolution despite the complete lack of evidence for it. It does seem strange to creationists that evolutionists can be so confident about the "fact" of evolution and still remain so completely uncertain as to its mechanism. Evolution is claimed to be "scientific," and still going on, so it seems like it should be observable and measurable. Yet after 150 years of intense study of biological variations, evolutionists are still completely in the dark about the supposed mechanism of evolution. This fact surely is cause for beginning to doubt the validity of the very concept of evolution.

Question: "Isn't it unethical for creationists, in order to support their arguments, to quote evolutionists out of context?"

Answer: The often-repeated charge that creationists deliberately use partial quotes or out-of-context quotes from evolutionists is, at best, an attempt to confuse the issue. Creationists do, indeed, frequently quote from evolutionary literature, finding that the data and interpretations used by evolutionists often provide very effective arguments for creation. With only rare exceptions, however, creationists always are meticulously careful to quote accurately and in context. Evolutionists have apparently searched creationist writings looking for such exceptions and, out of the hundreds or thousands of quotes which have been used, have been able to find only two or three which they have been able to interpret as misleading. Even these, if carefully studied, in full light of their own contexts, will be found to be quite fair and accurate in their representation of the situation under discussion. On the other hand, evolutionists frequently quote creationist writings badly out of context. The most disconcerting practice of this sort, one that could hardly be anything but deliberate, is to quote a creationist exposition of a Biblical passage, in a book or article dealing with Biblical creationism, and then to criticize this as an example of the scientific creationism which creationists propose for the public schools. Another frequent example is that of citing creationist expositions of the Second Law of Thermodynamics and charging them with ignoring the "open system" question, when they are specifically dealing in context with that very question. In any case, evolutionists much more frequently and more flagrantly quote creationists out of context than creationists do evolutionists.

Question: "Do creation organizations and their leaders profit financially by promoting creationism?"

Answer: The Institute for Creation Research is a nonprofit organization, dependent primarily upon individual donations for its operation. Its staff scientists all work for smaller salaries than they could command in industry or public education, and they also turn over all honoraria at ICR meetings to ICR for its general operations. ICR is careful to maintain sound financial policies, with its books audited annually, and with expenditures always kept strictly within its income. Its fund-raising methods are always low-key and nonemotional. We cannot, of course, speak for other creationist organizations, except to say that we know of no individual or organization that has profited significantly in a financial way from promoting creationism. There may have been some who attempted to do so, but they soon found that this is no way to make money! The ICR is the largest creationist organization, but its annual expenditures are significantly less even than the budgets of most individual university science departments.

Question: "Why, then, does ICR lobby for the passage of creationist legislation which would require purchase of creationist books?"

Answer: Neither the Institute for Creation Research, the Creation-Life Publishers, nor the Creation Research Society is engaged in promoting, financing, or lobbying for creationist legislation. Neither do they file lawsuits or other political or legal actions aimed at compelling the teaching of creationism in public schools. This is a widely repeated charge, but it is completely false. The ICR constitution, in fact, precludes such activities. It is true that certain other creationist organizations do this, and ICR has been willing to provide assistance (when such assistance is requested and financed by such organizations) in the form of scientific and legal consultation, service as expert witnesses, etc. Such aid is made available for the purpose of trying to help keep such activities, if they take place at all, on a high scientific, academic, and constitutional level. Although individual creationists hold widely differing convictions on this particular subject, the two authors of this book believe that compelling unwilling teachers to teach creationism in the public schools is unwise and unnecessary. We much prefer the approach of education and persuasion to that of legislation and coercion. There is already no constitutional or legal impediment to teaching creation science along with evolution science in any state—regardless of widespread publicity to the contrary—except in Arkansas after a biased judicial decision following a poor state defense. It is simply a matter of persuading school boards and teachers that they ought to do so and then helping to provide materials to enable them to do so. Many are already doing this and no doubt many others will as time goes on, without any need for compelling laws or ordinances.

MISCELLANEOUS QUESTIONS

Question: "Why should creationists insist on teaching creationism in public schools when they do not teach evolutionism in their own churches and religious schools?"
Answer: This widely circulated criticism reveals a serious misunderstanding of the nature of public schools and other tax-supported institutions. These are supported by *both* groups of citizens—creationists and evolutionists—and therefore both basic scientific models of origins should be taught in them, as objectively as possible. If Christians want to have *only* creation taught, then they should establish private schools for that purpose. By the same token, if secularists or others want to have only evolution taught, they should establish private humanistic schools for *that* purpose. For evolutionists to insist that their evolutionary religion should be subsidized by the taxes of creationists is both arrogant and unconstitutional. The two-model approach—teaching both evolution and creation on a strictly scientific and objective basis—is the only approach in the public schools which is consistent with the constitution, with civil rights, religious neutralism, scientific objectivity, educational effectiveness, academic freedom, and general fairness.

Question: "Since creationism includes the creation of "apparent age," doesn't this imply the supposed Creator has deceived us?"
Answer: The concept of creation does, indeed, involve the creation of "apparent age"—or, better, the creation of

"functioning completeness." By its very essence, true creation involves processes no longer in operation. The products of these creative processes include the whole functioning universe. One may try to calculate an "apparent age" of any particular system in this functioning cosmos by use of some present (noncreative) process involved in that system, but at best this can only be as good as the assumption of the "initial conditions" which are used in the calculation (see the discussion of this subject in Chapter 7). The Creation Model quite reasonably implies that these initial conditions were produced in the system by the processes of creation and were of whatever nature and magnitude they needed to be for that system thenceforth to function optimally in the completed world as created. This concept is inherent in the very nature of creation. To say that there can be no creation of "functioning completeness" (or "apparent age," if you prefer) is the same as saying there can be no creation; this begs the whole question, of course, and is equivalent to defining away every option except atheism.

Question: "Since the creation/evolution question is actually involved in one way or another in every discipline, wouldn't it be impossibly expensive for schools to institute a real two-model approach?"
Answer: Creationists are sensitive to the costs of such changes, of course (they are taxpayers, too!), but there are reasonable ways in which they can be accomplished. All school districts order new textbooks every five years or so, anyway. If the appropriate textbook committees would simply specify the types of books desired, and make it clear they would not purchase any others, the publishing companies would quickly provide books to conform to these specifications. In the interim before the next adoption, workshops, supplemental materials, and other aids could be provided within existing budgets (which allow for this sort of thing anyway) to enable teachers to adapt their current textbooks and class instruction to a two-model approach. For teachers whose consciences recoil at teaching creationism, substitute teachers or teacher interchanges

could be scheduled for, say, three-week units on the creationist alternative in each course where the subject comes up. Enough creationist materials and teachers are already available, so that this interim period need not be either traumatic or costly. Such procedures are not unusual at all. School boards frequently mandate new curricula and provide for their implementation when they perceive a legitimate need, as in the need for health education, nondiscriminatory textbooks, etc. The study of origins is foundational in all disciplines and surely warrants openness and fairness in its classroom treatment.

Appendix B

Literature Cited

Adler, Jerry and John Carey. "Is Man a Subtle Accident?" *Newsweek*, Nov. 3, 1980.

Ager, Derek V. *The Nature of the Geographical Record.* New York: John Wiley Publ., 1981, pp. 54, 106-107, etc.

----------. "The Nature of the Fossil Record." *Proceedings of the Geological Association* 87(2):131-159, 1976.

----------. *The Nature of the Stratigraphical Record.* New York, John Wiley and Sons, 1973a, p. 20.

----------. *The Nature of the Stratigraphical Record.* New York, John Wiley and Sons, 1973b, p. 100.

Alfven, Hannes, and Asoka Mendis. "Interpretation of Observed Cosmic Microwave Background Radiation." *Nature*, Vol. 266, April 21, 1977, p. 698.

Allegro, John M. "Divine Discontent." *American Atheist*, Vol. 28, September 1986, p. 30.

Asimov, Isaac. Interview by Paul Kurtz. "An Interview with Isaac Asimov on Science and the Bible." *Free Inquiry*, Vol. 2, Spring 1982, p. 9.

----------, "The Voyage of Charles Darwin." *TV Guide*. Jan. 26, 1980.

----------, and Duane Gish. "The Genesis War." *Science Digest*, October 1981.

----------. "Can Decreasing Entropy Exist in the Universe?" *Science Digest*, May, 1973, p. 76.

Austin, Steven A. *Depositional Environment of the Kentucky No. 12 Coal Bed Middle Pennsylvanian of Western Kentucky, With Special Reference to the Origin of Coal Lithotypes.* Diss. Pennsylvania State University (University

Microfilms Int'l), Ann Arbor, MI, 1979, 390 pp., Order No. 8005972.

Ayala, Francisco. "Nothing in Biology Makes Sense except in the Light of Evolution: Theodosius Dobzhansky, 1900-75." *Journal of Heredity*, Vol. 68, No. 3, 1977, p. 9.

----------. "The Mechanisms of Evolution." *Scientific American* (and *Sci. Am.* book, Evolution), September 1978.

----------, and James W. Valentine. *Evolving: The Theory and Processes of Organic Evolution*. Menlo Park: Benjamin-Cummings Pub. Co., 1979.

Beadle, George W. "The Ancestry of Corn." *Scientific American*, January 1980.

Beardsley, Tim. *Nature*. 1986, 322:677.

Bethell, Tom. "Agnostic Evolutionists." *Harper's*, February 1985, p. 61. This was Bethell's report on interviews with a number of leading evolutionists.

Bliss, Richard B. *A Comparison of Two Approaches to the Teaching of Origins of Living Things to High School Biology Students in Racine, Wisconsin*. Diss. University of Sarasota, (ERIC Ed 152 568), 1979. See also, R. B. Bliss. "A Comparison of Students Studying the Origin of Life from a Two-Model Approach vs. Those Studying from a Single-Model Approach." *Acts and Facts*, Impact No. 60, June, 1978.

----------. *The Strange Case of the Woodpecker*. San Diego: CLP Video, 1985.

----------, and Gary E. Parker. *Origin of Life*. El Cajon: CLP Publishers, Two Models Creation/Evolution Series, 1984.

----------, Gary E. Parker, and Duane T. Gish. *Fossils: Key to the Present*. El Cajon: CLP Publishers, Two Models Creation/Evolution Series, 1980.

Bloch, Salman. "Some Factors Controlling the Concentration of Uranium in the World Ocean." *Geochimica et Cosmochimica Acta*, Vol. 44, 1980, pp. 373-377.

Bretz, Harlan. As quoted in "GSA Medals and Awards." *GSA (Geological Society of America) News and Information*, March 1980.

Capra, Fritjof. "The Dance of Life." *Science Digest*, Vol. 90 (April 1982), p. 33.

Chadwick, Arthur V. "Megabreccias: Evidence for Catastrophism." *Origins*, 1978, 5139-46. See also other articles in *Origins* for geologic evidences for creation and catastrophe.

Chang, K. Hong. "Unconformity-Bounded Stratigraphic Units." *Bulletin*. Geological Society of America, Vol. 86 (November 1975a), p. 1544.

----------. "Unconformity-Bounded Stratigraphic Units." *Bulletin*. Geological Society of America, Vol. 86 (November 1975b), p. 1545.

----------. "Rethinking Stratigraphy." *Geotimes*, Vol. 26 (March 1981), p. 23.

Cherfas, Jeremy. "The Difficulties of Darwinism." *New Scientist*, Vol. 102 (May 17, 1984), p. 29. Cherfas was reporting on special lectures by Dr. Gould at Cambridge University.

Cook, F. A., L. D. Brown, and J. E. Oliver. "The Southern Appalachians and the Growth of Continents." *Scientific American*, Vol. 243 (October 1980), p. 161.

Corner, E. J. H. *Evolution in Contemporary Botanical Thought*. Ed. by A. M. MacLeod and L. S. Cobly. Chicago: Quandrangle Books, 1961, p. 61.

"Cosmological Anomaly: A Trip You Can't Miss." *Science News*, Vol. 116 (December 22/29, 1979b), p. 421.

"Cosmological Stretch Marks." *Science News*, Vol. 119 (May 1981), p. 254.

Crick, Francis. "The Seeds of Life." *Discover*, October 1981.

Darwin, Charles. *The Origin of Species*. New York: Washington Square Press, 1859; rpt. 1963.

Davies, Paul C. W. "Universe in Reverse: Can Time Run Backwards?" *Second Look*, September, 1979, p. 27.

Davy, John. "Once Upon A Time." *Observer-Review*, London: Aug. 16, 1981.

de Beer, Sir Gavin. *Homology, an Unsolved Problem*.

London: Oxford University Press, 1971, p. 15.

de Chardin, Teilhard, as cited in Francisco Ayala, "Nothing in Biology Makes Sense Except in the Light of Evolution: Theodosius Dobzhansky, 1900-75." *Journal of Heredity*, Vol. 68, No. 3 (1977), p. 3.

Denton, Michael. *Evolution: A Theory in Crisis*. London: Burnett Books, 1985a, p. 289. Denton is an Australian researcher in molecular genetics.

----------. *Evolution: A Theory in Crisis*. London: Burnett Books, 1985b, 368 pp.

Dickerson, Richard E. "Chemical Evolution and the Origin of Life." *Scientific American* (and *Sci. Am.* book, *Evolution*), September 1978.

----------, and Irving Geis. *The Structure and Action of Proteins*. New York: Harper and Row, 1969.

Dingle, Herbert. "Science and Modern Cosmology." *Science*, Vol. 120 (October 1, 1954), p. 515.

Dobzhansky, Theodosius. "Changing Man." *Science*, Vol. 155 (January 27, 1967), p. 409.

----------, F. Ayala, L. Stebbins, and J. Valentine. *Evolution*. San Francisco: W. H. Freeman & Co., 1977.

----------. *Genetics and the Origin of Species*. 2nd Ed. New York: Columbia University Press, 1951, p. 4.

Dott, Robert H. "Episodic View Now Replacing Catastrophism." *Geotimes*, November 1982, p. 16.

Dunbar, C. O. *Historical Geology*. 2nd Ed. New York: John Wiley and Sons, Inc., 1960, p. 47.

Durant, Will. "Historian Will Durant: We Are in the Last Stage of Pagan Period." *El Cajon Daily Californian*, 8 Apr. 1980 (By Rogers Worthington of *The Chicago Tribune*).

Eldredge, Niles. *Time Frames: The Rethinking of Darwinian Evolution and the Theory of Punctuated Equilibria*. New York: Simon and Schuster, 1985a, p. 33. Eldredge was citing the book by Harvard taxonomist, Ernst Mayr, *Systematics and the Origin of Species*, 1942.

----------. *Time Frames*. New York: Simon and Schuster, 1985b, p. 52.

----------, as quoted by George Alexander. "Alternate

Theory of Evolution Considered: Lack of Fossil 'Missing Link' Evidence Causes Change in Thought." *Los Angeles Times*, 19 Nov. 1978.

----------, as quoted in the *Sunday Mail*. Brisbane, Australia, 14 Sept. 1986.

Felsenstein, Joe. "Evolution." a book review. *American Scientist*, Mar/Apr. 1978, pp. 225-226.

Futuyma, D. J. *Science on Trial*. New York: Pantheon Books, 1983, p. 197. This book is one of at least 50 anti-creationist books published in recent years, indicating the alarm of the evolutionary establishment at the revival of scientific creationism.

Gale, George. "The Anthropic Principle." *Scientific American*, Vol. 245 (December 1981), p. 154.

Gartner, Stefan, and James P. McGuirk. "Terminal Cretaceous Extinction: Scenario for a Catastrophe." *Science*, Dec. 14, 1979.

Gish, Duane T. *Evolution: The Challenge of the Fossil Record*. El Cajon: CLP Publishers, 1986.

----------, and Stephen Gould. *Discover*. May and July, 1981. An exchange of letters to the editor on creation/evolution.

Gliedman, John. "Miracle Mutations." *Science Digest*, Feb. 1982.

Gould, Stephen Jay, "The Ediacaran Experiment." *Natural History*, Vol. 93 (February 1984), p. 23. Dr. Gould is arguably the nation's most prominent evolutionist, as Professor of Geology at Harvard University.

----------. "Dr. Down's Syndrome." *Natural History*, Vol. 89 (April 1980), p. 144.

----------. "Evolution's Erratic Pace." *Natural History*, Vol. 86 (May 1977), p. 14.

----------. A review of "Darwin's 'Big Book'." *Science*, May 23, 1975, pp. 824-826.

----------. "Evolution's Erratic Pace." *Natural History*, May, 1977a.

----------. "The Return of Hopeful Monsters." *Natural History*, June/July, 1977b.

----------, and Niles Eldredge. "Punctuated Equilibria: the Tempo and Mode of Evolution Reconsidered."

Paleobiology, June/July, 1977c.

----------. "The Great Scablands Debate." *Natural History*, Aug/Sept. 1978. Also published Sept. 28, 1978 in *New Scientist* as "When the Unorthodox Prevails."

----------. "Of Turtles, Vets, Elephants, and Castles." *New Scientist*, Jan. 11, 1979a.

----------. "Smith Woodward's Folly." *New Scientist*, Apr. 5, 1979b.

----------. "A Quahog is a Quahog." *Natural History*, Aug/Sept. 1979c. Also published Aug. 2, 1979, in *New Scientist* as "Species Are Not Specious."

----------. "Is a New and General Theory of Evolution Emerging?" *Paleobiology*, Winter, 1980a.

----------. "In the Midst of Life...." *Natural History*, Feb. 1980b.

----------. "Dr. Down's Syndrome." *Natural History*, Apr. 1980c.

----------. "Hopeful Monsters." *Natural History*, Oct. 1980d.

----------. "Quaggas, Coiled Oysters, and Flimsy Facts." *Natural History*, Sept. 1981a.

----------. "The Brain Appraisers." *Science Digest*, Sept. 1981b.

----------. "A Visit to Dayton." *Natural History*, Oct. 1981c.

----------, and Niles Eldredge. "Punctuated Equilibria: the Tempo and Mode of Evolution Reconsidered." *Paleobiology*, Vol. 3 (Spring, 1977), pp. 145, 146.

----------. "Catastrophes and Steady-State Earth." *Natural History*, February 1975, pp. 16, 17.

Grasse', Pierre' Paul. *Evolution of Living Organisms*. New York: Academic Press, 1977a.

----------. *Evolution of Living Organisms*. New York: Academic Press, 1977, p. 4.

Greco, Frank A. "On the Second Law of Thermodynamics." *American Laboratory*, October 1982, p. 88.

Halstead, L. B. "Museum of Errors." *Nature*, Vol. 288 (November 20, 1980), p. 208.

Hardin, Garrett. *39 Steps to Biology*. A *Scientific American* book. San Francisco: W. H. Freeman & Co., 1968.

Harris, C. Leon. "An Axiomatic Interpretation of the Neo-

Darwinian Theory of Evolution." *Perspectives in Biology and Medicine*, Winter, 1975, p. 179.

Harris, Sydney. "Second Law of Thermodynamics." *San Francisco Examiner*, 27 Jan. 1984. Nationally syndicated Column.

Hedberg, H. D. "The Stratigraphic Panorama." *Bulletin of the Geological Society of America*, Vol. 72 (April 1961), p. 499.

Henig, Robin M. "Evolution Called a 'Religion,' Creationism Defended as a 'Science'." *BioScience*, Sept. 1979.

Hilts, Philip. "Science [sic] Loses One to Creationism." *The Washington Post*, 15 Oct. 1981.

Hooper, Judith. "Perfect Timing." *New Age Journal*, Vol. 11 (December 1985), p. 18.

Hoyle, Sir Fred. "The Big Bang in Astronomy." *New Scientist*, Vol. 92 (November 19, 1981), p. 527.

----------, and Chandra Wickramasinghe. As quoted in "There *Must* Be a God." *Daily Express*, Aug. 14, 1981; and "Hoyle on Evolution." *Nature*, Nov. 12, 1981, p. 105.

Huxley, Julian, "A New World Vision." *The Humanist*, Vol. 39 (March/April 1979), p. 35. This paper was kept "in-house" by UNESCO for about 30 years, before *The Humanist* was allowed to publish it.

Jeffreys, Harold. *The Earth: Its Origin, History, and Physical Constitution*. Cambridge, England: University Press, 1970, p. 359.

Johanson, Donald C. and T. D. White. "On the Status of *Australopithecus afarensis*." Science, Mar. 7, 1980.

----------, and Maitland Edey. "Lucy: The Beginnings of Humankind." *Reader's Digest*, Sept. 1981.

Ipcar, Dahlov. *The Wonderful Egg*. Garden City, New York: Doubleday, 1958.

Kemp, Tom. "A Fresh Look at the Fossil Record." *New Scientist*, Vol. 108 (December 5, 1985a), p. 67. Dr. Kemp is Curator of the University Museum at Oxford University.

----------. "A Fresh Look at the Fossil Record." *New Scientist*, Vol. 108 (December 5, 1985b), p. 67.

Kern, Edward and Donna Haupt. "Battle of the Bones." *Life*, Jan. 1982.

Kitts, David B. "Paleontology and Evolutionary Theory." *Evolution*, Vol. 28 (September 1974a), p. 466.

----------. "Paleontology and Evolutionary Theory." *Evolution*, Vol. 28 (September 1974b), p. 467.

----------. "Search for the Holy Transformation." *Paleobiology*, Vol. 5 (Summer 1979), pp. 353, 354.

Lagerkvist, Ulf. "Codon Misreading: A Restriction Operative in the Evolution of the Genetic Code." *American Scientist*, Mar/Apr. 1980.

Land, Michael. "Nature as an Optical Engineer." *New Scientist*, Oct. 4, 1979.

Layzer, David. "The Arrow of Time." *Scientific American*, Vol. 233 (December 1975), p. 60.

Leakey, Mary D. "Footprints in the Ashes of Time." *National Geographic*, Apr. 1979.

----------. "Happy Trail for Three Hominids." *Science News*, Feb. 9, 1980, p. 87.

Lee, Robert E. "Radiocarbon, Ages in Error." *Anthropological Journal of Canada*, Vol. 19, No. 3 (1981), p. 9.

Leslie, John. *Ex Nihilo Technical Journal*. Volume 1 (1984).

Lester, Lane, and Ray Bohlin. *The Natural Limits to Biological Change*. Grand Rapids: Zondervan, 1984.

Lewin, Roger. "A Downward Slope to Greater Diversity." *Science*, Vol. 217 (September 24, 1982), p. 1239.

----------. "Evolutionary Theory Under Fire." *Science*, Nov. 21, 1980.

----------. "A Response to Creationism Evolves." *Science*, Nov. 6, 1981.

Lewontin, Richard C. "Adaptation." *Scientific American* (and *Sci. Am.* book, *Evolution*), Sept. 1978.

----------. "Opinion—Evolution/Creation Debate: A Time for Truth." *Bioscience*, Sept. 1981.

Lipson, H. S. "A Physicist Looks at Evolution." *Physics Bulletin*, May, 1980, p. 138.

Mars and Earth. Washington, D.C.: U.S. Government Printing Office, NF-61, August 1975a, p. 1.

Mars and Earth. Washington, D.C.: U.S. Government Printing Office, NF-61, August 1975b, p. 2.

Marsden, George M. "Creation versus Evolution: No Middle Way." *Nature.* Vol. 305 (October 13, 1983), p. 572.

Matthews, L. Harrison. "Introduction." *The Origin of Species,* by Charles Darwin. London: J. M. Dent and Sons, Ltd., 1971, p. x.

Mayr, Ernst. "Evolution." *Scientific American* (and *Sci. Am.* book *Evolution*), Sept. 1978.

Moorhead, Paul S., and Martin M. Kaplan. *Mathematical Challenges to the Neo-Darwinian Interpretation of Evolution.* Wistar Symposium No. 5. Philadelphia: Wistar Institute Press, 1967.

Nevins, Stuart E. "Origin of Coal." *Acts and Facts,* "Impact" Series No. 41, El Cajon: Institute for Creation Research, Nov. 1976.

Newell, Norman D. "Crises in the History of Life." *Scientific American,* Feb. 1963.

Novick, Richard. "Plasmids." *Scientific American,* December 1980.

O'Connor, Rod. Fundamentals of Chemistry. 2nd Ed. New York: Harper and Row, 1977, p. 888.

Oparin, A. I. *The Origin of Life.* 2nd Ed. New York: Dover Publishers, 1965.

O'Rourke, J. E. "Pragmatism versus Materialism in Stratigraphy." *American Journal of Science,* Vol. 276 (January 1976), p. 51.

Osborn, Henry. "The Evolution of Human Races." Jan/Feb. 1926. Rpt. *Natural History,* Apr. 1980.

Ostrom, John H. "Bird Flight: How Did It Begin?" *American Scientist,* Jan/Feb. 1979.

Oxnard, Charles E. "Human Fossils: New View of Old Bones." *American Biology Teacher,* May 1979.

Parker, Gary E. "The Origin of Life on Earth." *Creation Science Research Quarterly,* Sept. 1970.

----------, W. Ann Reynolds, and Rex Reynolds. *DNA: The Key to Life.* Rev. ed. Programmed Biology Series. Chicago: Educational Methods, Inc., 1977a.

----------, W. Ann Reynolds, and Rex Reynolds. *Heredity.*

Rev. ed. Programmed Biology Series. Chicago: Educational Methods, Inc., 1977b.

Patrusky, Ben. "Why is the Cosmos 'Lumpy'?" *Science 81*, June 1981, p. 96.

Patterson, Colin. "Cladistics." BBC Interview. 4 March 1982. Dr. Patterson is Senior Paleontologist at the British Museum of Natural History.

----------. Address at American Museum of Natural History, New York. 5 Nov. 1981.

Pollard, William G. "The Prevalence of Earthlike Planets." *American Scientist*, Vol. 67 (November/December, 1979), p. 659.

Prigogine, Ilya, Gregoire Nicolis, and Agnes Babloyants. "Thermodynamics of Evolution." *Physics Today*, Vol. 25 (November 1972), p. 23.

----------. "Can Thermodynamics Explain Biological Order?" *Impact of Science on Society*, Vol. XXIII, No. 3 (1973), p. 169.

Puzzle of the Ancient Wing. Prod. Thomas Kelly. Canadian Broadcasting Corp, "Man Alive" Series, 1981.

Raup, David M. "Probability Models in Evolutionary Biology." *American Scientist*, Vol. 166 (January/February 1977), p. 57.

----------. "Conflicts Between Darwin and Paleontology." *Field Museum of Natural History Bulletin.* Jan. 1979.

----------. "The Revolution in Evolution." *World Book Science Year 1980.*

----------. "Evolution and the Fossil Record." *Science*, Vol. 213 (July 17, 1981), p. 289.

Renfrew, Colin. *Before Civilization.* New York: Alfred Knopf, 1973, p. 25.

Ridley, Mark. "Who Doubts Evolution?" *New Scientist*, Vol. 90 (June 25, 1981), p. 831. Dr. Ridley is Professor of Zoology at Oxford University.

----------. "Who Doubts Evolution?" *New Scientist*, Vol. 90 (June 25, 1981), p. 831.

Richardson, Don. *Eternity in Their Hearts.* Ventura, Calif.: Regal, 1981, 176 pp.

Rifkin, Jeremy. *Algeny.* New York: Viking Press, 1983a, p. 188.

----------. *Algeny.* New York: Viking Press, 1983b, p. 195.

----------. *Algeny.* New York: Viking Press, 1983c, p. 244.

----------. *Algeny.* New York: Viking Press, 1983d, p. 255.

----------. *Entropy: A New World View.* New York: Viking Press, 1980a, p. 6.

----------. *Entropy: A New World View.* New York: Viking Press, 1980b, p. 55.

Ross, John. Letter. *Chemical and Engineering News.* July 7, 1980, 40. Ross was at Harvard University.

Russell, Dale. "The Mass Extinctions of the Late Mesozoic." *Scientific American,* Jan. 1982.

Sagan, Carl. "A Gift for Vividness." As quoted in *Time,* Oct. 20, 1980, p. 68.

Scadding, S. R. "Do 'Vestigial Organs' Provide Evidence for Evolution?" *Evolutionary Theory,* Vol. 5 (May 1981), p. 173.

Schindewolf, O. H. "Comments on Some Stratigraphic Terms." *American Journal of Science,* Vol. 255 (June 1957), p. 394.

Shea, James H. "Twelve Fallacies of Uniformitarianism." *Geology,* Vol. 10 (September 1982), p. 457.

Simons, Elwyn. "Just A Nasty Little Thing." As quoted in *Time,* Feb. 18, 1980.

Simpson, George Gaylord. *The Major Features of Evolution.* New York: Columbia University Press, 1953, p. 360.

Smith, Charles J. "Problems with Entropy in Biology." *Biosystems,* Vol. I (1975), p. 259.

Sommerfeld, Arnold. *Thermodynamics and Statistical Mechanics.* New York: Academic Press, 1956, p. 155.

Stanley, Steven M. *Macroevolution: Pattern and Process.* San Francisco: W. M. Freeman and Co., 1979a, p. 39.

----------. "Macroevolution and the Fossil Record." *Evolution,* Vol. 36, No. 3 (1982), p. 460.

----------. "Darwin Done Over." *The Sciences,* October 1981.

----------. *Macroevolution: Pattern and Process.* San Francisco: W. M. Freeman & Co., 1979b, p. 159.

----------. *Macroevolution: Pattern and Process.* San Francisco: W. M. Freeman & Co., 1979c, p. 145.

Stansfield, William D. *The Science of Evolution*. New York: Macmillan, 1977a, p. 84.

----------. *The Science of Evolution*. New York, MacMillan, 1977b, pp. 80-84.

Szent-Gyorgyi, Albert. "Drive in Living Matter to Perfect Itself." *Synthesis* 1(1), 1977.

Thaxton, Charles, Walter Bradley, and Roger Olsen. *The Mystery of Life's Origin: Reassessing Current Theories*. New York: Philosophical Library, 1984.

"Thin View of Appalachian Formation." *Science News*, Vol. 115 (June 2, 1979a), 374.

Thomsen, Dietrick V. "Cosmology Against the Grain." *Science News*, Vol. 114 (August 26, 1978), p. 138.

Thomson, Keith S. "The Meanings of Evolution." *American Scientist*, Vol. 70 (September/October 1982), p. 529.

U. S. Geological Survey. *The Channeled Scablands of Eastern Washington—The Geologic Story of the Spokane Flood*, 1976.

Valentine, James W. "The Evolution of Multicellular Plants and Animals." *Scientific American* (and *Sci. Am.* book, *Evolution*), Sept. 1978.

----------, and Cathryn A. Campbell. "Genetic Regulation and the Fossil Record." *American Scientist*, Vol. 63 (Nov/Dec. 1975), p. 673.

Van Wylen, Gordon J., and Richard E. Sonntag. *Fundamentals of Classical Thermodynamics*. 2nd Ed. New York: John Wiley and Sons, 1973, p. 248.

Von Engeln, O. D., and K. E. Caster. *Geology*. New York: McGraw-Hill, 1952, p. 417.

Wald, George, as reported in "A Knowing Universe Seeking to Be Known," by Dietrick E. Thomsen. *Science News*, Vol. 123 (February 19, 1983), p. 124.

Washburn, Sherwood L. "The Evolution of Man." *Scientific American* (and *Sci. Am.* book, *Evolution*), Sept. 1978.

Weier, T. E., C. R. Stocking, and M. G. Barbour. *Botany*. 5th ed. New York: John Wiley and Sons, 1974.

Weisz, Paul B. *The Science of Biology*. 3rd ed. New York: McGraw-Hill Book Co., 1967, pp. 9 and 229.

West, Ronald R. "Paleontology and Uniformitarianism."
     Compass, Vol. 45 (May 1968), p. 216.
Wicken, Jeffrey S. "The Generation of Complexity in
     Evolution: A Thermodynamic and Information-
     Theoretical Discussion." *Journal of Theoretical
     Biology*, Vol. 77 (April 1979), p. 349.
Wieland, Carl. "A Tale of Two Fleas." *Ex Nihilo*, Journal
     of the Creation Science Association of Australia, July
     1979.
Wilder-Smith, A. E. *The Natural Sciences Know Nothing
     of Evolution*. El Cajon: CLP Publishers, 1981.
Willemin, J. H., P. L. Guth, and K. V. Hodges. "High
     Fluid Pressure, Isothermal Surfaces, and the Initiation
     of Nappe Movement." *Geology*, Vol. 8 (September
     1980), p. 406.
Zihlman, Adrienne, and Jerold Lowenstein. "False Start
     of the Human Parade." *Natural History*, Aug/Sept.
     1979.
Zwemer, Samuel. *Origin of Religion*. New York: Loizeaux
     Bros., 1945, 256 pp.

Index of Subjects

D